This Hallowed Ground: Guides to Civil War Battlefields

SERIES EDITORS

Brooks D. Simpson
Arizona State University

Mark Grimsley
The Ohio State University

Steven E. Woodworth
Texas Christian University

GETTYSBURG

A BATTLEFIELD GUIDE

BY MARK GRIMSLEY AND

BROOKS D. SIMPSON

Cartography by Christopher L. Brest

and Marcia McLean

•

University of Nebraska Press

Lincoln and London

Library of Congress Cataloging in Publication Data
Grimsley, Mark.
Gettysburg: a battlefield guide / Mark Grimsley and
Brooks D. Simpson: Cartography by Christopher L.
Brest and Marcia McLean.
p. cm. – (This hallowed ground: guides to Civil
War battlefields. Includes bibliographical refer-
ences. ISBN 0-8032-7077-1 (pbk.: alk. paper)
1. Gettysburg National Military Park (Pa.) – Guide-
books. 2. Gettysburg (Pa.), Battle of, 1863. I. Simpson,
Brooks D. II. Title. III. Series: This hallowed ground.
E475.56G75 1999 917.48'42—dc21 99-12067 CIP

Contents

Acknowledgments

In preparing this guide, we received assistance from friends and colleagues who share our interest in battlefield interpretation and Gettysburg itself. Carol Reardon offered good advice at an early stage; several anonymous readers reviewed the manuscript for the University of Nebraska Press; and our series coeditor, Steven E. Woodworth, gave it a field test and came up with several good suggestions. Among those people who walked the battlefield with us, Wayne Motts and Bill Odom contributed various insights and listened to our assessments. Others, including Michael Burlingame, Anne Berlin, and numerous Army and Marine Corps officers who were part of several battlefield walks, served as a helpful audience. Members of the Gettysburg Discussion Group answered our queries on several topics; so did Tom Desjardin and Tim Smith, each of whom gave generously of their expertise. Thomas Goss checked mileage during one field test; Jean Berlin assisted in refining descriptions and directions; John Peterson helped cool us off after long days on the battlefield with a few beers at the Farnsworth House Tavern.

Christopher L. Brest prepared the excellent maps that accompany the text. We would also like to extend our appreciation to Ron McLean of The Ohio State University for his extensive cartographical assistance. Finally, we want to acknowledge the patience and sacrifice of Elaine M. Grimsley, who weathered not one but three serious basement floods while her husband was off traipsing the fields of Gettysburg.

For both authors of this guide, Gettysburg is a special place. Even after our many visits, we recall what happened there with a sense of awe. In preparing this guide, we have sought to help visitors gain a better grasp of the hows and whys of the fighting. But we also hope that their explorations of Gettysburg will deepen their emotional understanding of a tragic, transcendent moment in American history.

The illustrations reproduced in this book first appeared in *Battles and Leaders of the Civil War*, ed. Robert Underwood Johnson and Clarence Clough Buel, 4 vols. (New York: Century Co., 1887–88). The volume and page number from which each illustration was taken are indicated at the end of each caption.

For Ed Bearss . . . who makes battlefields come alive

Raid upon a Union baggage train by Stuart's cavalry. From a wartime sketch. 2:501

Uniform of the 146th New York Regiment. 3:315

Introduction

The battle of Gettysburg has captured the imagination of Americans as has no other battle in the American Civil War. Its dramatic narrative and human interest stories have the stuff of prize-winning novels and epic movies; it helped inspire Abraham Lincoln to deliver one of the most memorable addresses in the English language. Historians might question whether it indeed deserves to be labeled "the turning point of the war" or the Confederacy's "high-water mark," but these debates do not detract from the fascination many Americans have for this battle.

Not surprisingly, more people visit Gettysburg than any other Civil War battlefield. They drive out to McPherson's Ridge, where the opening skirmish evolved into a battle on July 1; walk along the slopes of Little Round Top, site of a heroic struggle on July 2; and view the Union position on Cemetery Ridge, where a final Confederate assault on July 3 failed to break the Federal lines. Devil's Den, the Wheatfield, the Peach Orchard, Cemetery Hill—even lesser-known Barlow's Knoll and Culp's Hill—remain embedded in memory, as does the formative impact of terrain on the battle. It was because of the nature of the ground that Union commanders chose to make their stand south of the small Pennsylvania town; it was because of the sanguinary nature of the contest that Lincoln later christened it as "this hallowed ground."

It is to see that ground that people come to Gettysburg; this guide represents an effort to help them understand what they see. It seeks to fill a niche between the overviews of the battle available in pamphlets and handouts and the rather detailed treatment of battle terrain and action offered in several volumes, exemplified by the series of U.S. Army War College guides. It is designed for people who are willing to invest a day in examining the battlefield with some care in order to understand how the battle unfolded and why it turned out as it did. Descriptions and maps outline the appearance of the terrain in 1863, the positions of the contending forces, and the action in various areas on the field. Although the guide is not an exhaustive treatment of the three days of combat, it explores the major (and some of the not-so-major) engagements that made up the battle of Gettysburg. Finally, although users of the guide might benefit from examining it before visiting the battlefield, such preparation is not essential: one can pick up the guide, drive out to the battlefield, and begin a tour immediately.

The main tour can be completed in approximately six hours: two hours for July 1, three hours for July 2, and one hour for Cemetery Ridge on July 3. Also included are a rather more detailed treatment of the struggle in the Wheatfield, a walking tour of the Confederates' July 3 assault on Cemetery Ridge, and excursions to the two cavalry battlefields. Short summaries of the campaign and of each day's operations help to establish context. At the end of the guide are abbreviated Orders of Battle listing the units present on the battlefield, a discussion of tactics and weaponry, and a bibliography for further reading.

Union cavalryman — *The Water Call.* 3:441

How to Use This Guide

This book is divided into 20 main stops, proceeding from one part of the battlefield to another in chronological order. That is, the tour follows the battle as it progressed, from the morning of July 1 through the afternoon of July 3. Most stops require about 10 to 15 minutes to complete. A few, such as Little Round Top and the High Water Mark of Pickett's Charge, take a bit longer. It takes about six hours to complete the entire tour. Only a few stops require people to walk more than 50 yards from their cars; those that do give optional directions for those whose mobility is limited.

Most of the main stops are divided into two or more substops. Substops seldom ask you to do any additional walking or driving around. They are simply designed to develop the action at each point in a clear, organized fashion, and there are as many substops as required to do the job. In the guidebook, each substop has a section of text "married" to a map. This enables you to visualize the troop dispositions and movements at each stop without having to flip around the guide looking for maps.

The stops and substops follow a standard format: **Directions, Orientation, What Happened, Analysis, and/or Vignette.**

The **Directions** tell you how to get from one stop to the next (and sometimes from one substop to another). They not only give you driving instructions, but they also ask you, once you have reached a given stop, to walk to a precise spot on the battlefield. When driving, keep an eye on your odometer; many distances are given to the nearest tenth of a mile. The directions often suggest points of interest en route from one stop to another. We have found that it works best to give the directions to a given stop first and then to mention the points of interest. These are always introduced by the italicized words *en route.*

Once you've reached a stop, the **Orientation** section describes the terrain around you so that you can quickly pick out the key landmarks and get your bearings.

What Happened is the heart of each stop. It explains the action succinctly but without becoming simplistic, and whenever possible it explains how the terrain affected the fighting.

Some stops have a section called **Analysis**, which explains why a particular decision was made, why a given attack met with success or failure, and so on. The purpose is to give you additional insight into the battle.

Other stops have a section called **Vignette**, designed to give you an additional emotional understanding of the battle by offering a short eyewitness account or by telling a particularly vivid anecdote.

Although the basic tour can be completed in about six hours, you can also take **Excursions** to places of special interest. These excursion tours follow the same format as the basic tour.

A few conventions are used in the guidebook to help keep confusion to a minimum. Names and unit designations are used as sparingly as possible and still convey a solid understanding of the battle. Names of Confederate leaders and units are in italics. Confederate corps are spelled out (e.g., *Third Corps*); those of Union corps are indicated by roman numerals (e.g., III Corps). The full name and rank of each individual is usually given only the first time he is mentioned.

Directions are particularly important in a guidebook, but they can often be confusing. We have therefore tried to make them as foolproof as possible. At each stop, you are asked to face toward a specific, easily identifiable landmark, often a battlefield monument. From that point, you may be asked to look to your left or right. To make this as precise as possible, we may sometimes ask you to look to your left front, far left, left rear, and so on, according to the system shown below:

straight ahead

left front   *right front*

left   *right*

left rear   *right rear*

behind/directly to the rear

Often, after the relative directions (left, right, etc.), we add the ordinal directions (north, south, etc.) in parentheses. The maps can also help you get your bearings.

The many monuments at Gettysburg are also an excellent tool for understanding the battlefield. Every Union regiment has a monument that was placed at the key point where it fought, usually its main line of defense. The monument itself usually occupies the center of the position. Most monuments have flank markers that show the right and left limits of the regiment's position. The guidebook uses monuments and flank markers to help you orient yourself.

Although this guidebook is intended primarily for use on the battlefield, it also contains information helpful for further study of the battle. An introductory section at the beginning of the book describes the action that preceded the battle; a similar section at the end tells what happened after the battle ended. The stops for each day are preceded by overviews that outline the day's main developments. Appen-

dixes at the end of the book give the organization of each
army (Orders of Battle). Suggestions for further reading are
in the back.

We hope you enjoy your battlefield tour of Gettysburg.

Mark Grimsley,
Brooks D. Simpson, &
Steven E. Woodworth
SERIES EDITORS

Buford's cavalry opposing the Confederate advance upon Gettysburg. 3:255

Gettysburg

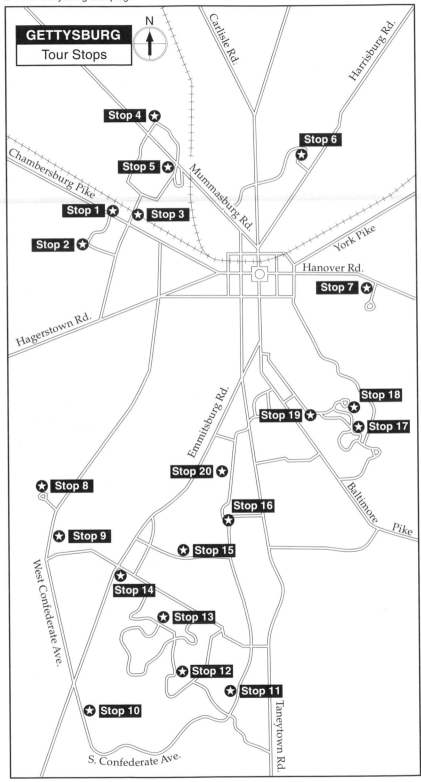

GETTYSBURG
Tour Stops

N

Carlisle Rd.

Harrisburg Rd.

Stop 4 ★

Stop 6 ★

Chambersburg Pike

Stop 5 ★

Mummasburg Rd.

Stop 1 ★   ★ Stop 3

Stop 2 ★

York Pike

Hanover Rd.

Stop 7 ★

Hagerstown Rd.

Stop 18 ★

Emmitsburg Rd.

Stop 19 ★

★ Stop 17

Stop 20 ★

Baltimore

★ Stop 8

Pike

★ Stop 9

Stop 16 ★

★ Stop 15

West Confederate Ave.

★ Stop 14

★ Stop 13

★ Stop 12

★ Stop 11

★ Stop 10

Taneytown Rd.

S. Confederate Ave.

The Gettysburg Campaign: May – June 1863

During the first week of May 1863, Gen. Robert E. *Lee's Army of Northern Virginia,* for the second time in six months, turned back an effort by the Army of the Potomac to crack the defensive perimeter south of the Rapidan and Rappahannock Rivers in central Virginia. The triumph at Chancellorsville, however, proved far more costly than had *Lee's* previous victory at Fredericksburg. Not only had the Confederate commander lost some 12,000 men – over 20 percent of his strength – but he had also lost one of his most able lieutenants, Thomas J. "Stonewall" *Jackson,* who died on May 10 of wounds received during the battle. Nevertheless, *Lee* and *Jackson* had succeeded in frustrating the daring design of the commander of the Union's Army of the Potomac, Maj. Gen. Joseph Hooker, despite being outnumbered by more than a two-to-one margin.

In the aftermath of victory, *Lee* pondered his next move. Although still greatly outnumbered, he had little taste for remaining on the defensive and awaiting his foe's next move. Unless he took the initiative, the Army of the Potomac and other Union forces in the east would rebuild and refit themselves at their leisure before renewing offensive operations. Moreover, he was worried by news that some of the authorities at Richmond (as well as one of his own generals, Lt. Gen. James Longstreet) were entertaining the idea of detaching part of *Lee's* army for service west of the Appalachian Mountains. These circumstances, plus *Lee's* own penchant for offensive operations, led him to propose an invasion of the North for the late spring and summer of 1863. The opportunity was there: a Confederate offensive, coming on the heels of Chancellorsville just as the Union army bade farewell to those volunteers who had signed up in 1861 to serve two years, might catch the enemy weakened in both body and spirit.

What did *Lee* hope to achieve? The presence of a Confederate army north of the Potomac might well increase opposition to the war in the North; with this in mind *Lee* advised Confederate president Jefferson *Davis* not to discourage any talk of peace negotiations, regardless of whether their avowed purpose was reunion or the recognition of Confederate independence. Moreover, a movement north would take the war out of Virginia, allowing farmers to grow their crops while offering the Confederates an opportunity to forage in the North. Although *Lee* gave lip service to the possibility that Confederate successes might force Maj. Gen. Ulysses S. Grant to abandon the siege of Vicksburg, Mississippi, in truth that played no part in his decision: "If anything can be done in that quarter," he pointed out, "it will be over by that time, as the climate in June will force the enemy to retire."[1]

Thus *Lee* justified his invasion as a way to take the war out of Virginia, gather supplies for his command, and demoralize Northern public opinion. Nevertheless, if the opportunity presented itself, he hoped to deal the Army of the Potomac yet another defeat; if he could catch a part of it at a disadvantage, he told one of his generals, he planned to "crush it, follow up the success, drive one corps back and another, and by successive repulses and surprises before they can concentrate, create a panic and virtually destroy the army."[2]

The army that marched northward in June looked different from the one that had defeated Hooker at Chancellorsville. The return of *Longstreet* and two of his divisions from southeast Virginia and *Jackson's* death compelled *Lee* to reorganize his army into three corps, each with three infantry divisions headed respectively by *Longstreet*, Lt. Gen. Richard S. *Ewell*, and Lt. Gen. Ambrose P. *Hill*. Maj. Gen. James Ewell Brown "Jeb" *Stuart* remained in command of the cavalry. *Lee* was pleased with this arrangement. He understood how important skilled military leadership was to the success of his plans. "I agree with you in believing that our army would be invincible if it could be properly organized and led," he told Maj. Gen. John Bell *Hood*, one of *Longstreet's* division commanders. "There never were such men in an army before. They will go anywhere and do anything if properly led. But there is the difficulty–proper commanders. Where can they be obtained?"[3]

His army thus reorganized, *Lee* prepared to move north during the first half of June. Hooker, suspicious, made noises about crossing the Rappahannock at Fredericksburg, but a flurry of activity came to naught. A Federal cavalry reconnaissance in force against *Lee's* right, however, brought results when it collided with *Stuart's* troopers at Brandy Station on June 9. The resulting battle may have humiliated *Stuart's* pride–the previous day he had held a grand review to show off his command to *Lee*–but it did not deter *Lee* from implementing his plan. The next day he ordered *Ewell's* corps to the Shenandoah Valley; on June 15 it drove away the Union garrison at Winchester, opening up the valley for the remainder of the *Army of Northern Virginia*. Learning that Hooker's army had withdrawn from its camps north of the Rappahannock, *Lee* set his men in motion toward the Potomac River.

Hooker was not surprised by *Lee's* move, but Lincoln vetoed his counterproposal to threaten Richmond. "I think Lee's army, and not Richmond, is your true objective point," observed the president.[4] In response, Hooker shifted his army back to Centreville to keep it between *Lee* and Washington, preferring not to act on Lincoln's hint that he strike at *Lee's* army on the march. The president issued a call for 100,000 militia for six months to counter the invasion; he also tried to smooth over the rather rough relations between Hooker and General in Chief Henry Halleck. Meanwhile, Hooker did what he could to discover *Lee's* intentions, but the Confederates blocked Union efforts to penetrate several gaps along the Blue Ridge to probe for information. Thus shielded, *Lee* continued to move north. Ordering *Ewell* to advance toward the Susquehanna River near the state capital at Harrisburg, he supervised the other two corps as they made they way across the Potomac. By June 26 the main body of *Lee's* army was north of the river. Hooker did not follow; *Lee's* men began to forage in earnest.

Much of the foraging had to be done by infantrymen, for on June 22 *Lee* had authorized *Stuart* to take three brigades of cavalry and swing east to shield the Confederate right and gather supplies; the next day, in response to the cavalryman's request, he gave him the discretion to "pass around their army" if it could be done "without hinderance." [5] Seeing in these words a chance to remove the tarnish of Brandy Station and garner new laurels, *Stuart* embarked on what promised to be yet another of his famed rides around the Army of the Potomac. This time, however, it proved to be a difficult task. As the Union army shifted north and east across the Potomac, *Stuart* also had to shift eastward, away from the main Confederate army; moreover, his insistence on retaining the 125 wagons he captured at Rockville, Maryland, on June 28, slowed his progress. His absence impaired *Lee's* ability to gather information on the location of Union forces. The Confederate commander failed to employ the cavalry brigades that remained with the army to handle reconnaissance duties; what was missing were not horsemen but *Stuart* and his ability to deploy them.

Nevertheless, *Stuart's* absence was at first not critical, for Hooker's response to *Lee's* northward advance was at best deliberate and at worst marked by confusion. He contemplated striking westward to cut *Ewell* off; it was not until June 25 that he realized that *Lee's* entire army was heading north of the Potomac. During the next two days he shifted his command north into Maryland and established headquarters at Frederick. Meanwhile, Lincoln and Halleck worried that he was not up to the task of confronting the foe on the battlefield. Telegrams from army headquarters revealed Hooker to be indecisive, nervous, and eager to shift responsibility from his shoulders. One of Hooker's staff officers believed that he was once again losing his nerve: "He knows that Lee is his master & is afraid to meet him in fair battle." Despite initial statements of support for the general in the aftermath of Chancellorsville, Lincoln had considered replacing him for some time. Upon reading the telegraphic exchanges between Halleck and Hooker over questions of who would control various garrisons, especially at Harpers Ferry, climaxing in Hooker's threat to resign his command, the president decided to act. On June 27 he directed Hooker to turn over command of the Army of the Potomac to Maj. Gen. George G. Meade; the transfer was effected early on the morning of June 28. If the timing of the change in command was inopportune, the choice was a good one. Meade had performed solidly as a division and corps commander; if his men did not adore him, his peers respected him. When he heard the news, *Lee* reportedly remarked, "General Meade will commit no blunder in my front, and if I make one he will make haste to take advantage of it."[6]

On the morning Meade took command, the Army of the Potomac was concentrating at Frederick. *Lee's* three infantry corps were spread across Pennsylvania in a semicircle from Chambersburg in the west to Carlisle, York, and the banks of the Susquehanna to the east. It was not until later that day that *Lee* learned that the Army of the Potomac was definitely north of its namesake; that information came not from *Stuart* but from one of *Longstreet's* spies. Much has been made of *Lee's* surprise at learning this information, but he had long expected Hooker to follow him north; however, *Stuart* was still in Maryland. *Lee* began to concentrate his command, ordering *Ewell*, whose command was approaching the Susquehanna, to use the convergence of the road network at Gettysburg. *Hill* marched east from Chambersburg, reaching Cashtown, less than ten miles northwest of Gettysburg, on June 30, with *Longstreet's* corps to follow. In the meantime, Meade moved his army northward toward Taneytown, Maryland, with plans to establish a defensive line along Pipe Creek, which ran south of the town. His cavalry shielded his advance and searched for the Confederates; close behind Brig. Gen. John Buford's two brigades at Gettysburg in the evening of June 30 was the advance of the Army of the Potomac, consisting of the I, III, and XI Corps under the direction of Maj. Gen. John F. Reynolds, commander of the I Corps.

Thus, as June drew to a close, both armies were maneuvering for position in south-central Pennsylvania and western Maryland. Both commanders anticipated fighting a major battle during the first week of July; neither was prepared for what would happen on July 1.

Notes

1. Lee to James A. Seddon, May 10, 1863, in Clifford, Dowdey and Louis H. Manarin, eds., *The Wartime Papers of R. E. Lee* (Boston: Little, Brown, 1961), 482.

2. Emory M. Thomas, *Robert E. Lee: A Biography* (New York: Norton, 1995), 293.

3. Lee to Hood, May 21, 1863, in Dowdey and Manarin, eds., *Wartime Papers of Lee*, 490.

4. Lincoln to Hooker, June 10, 1863, in Roy P. Basler, ed., *The Collected Works of Abraham Lincoln*, 9 vols. (New Brunswick: Rutgers University Press, 1953–55), 6:257.

5. Lee to Stuart, June 23, 1863, in Dowdey and Manarin, eds., *Wartime Papers of Lee*, 526.

6. Edwin B. Coddington, *The Gettysburg Campaign: A Study in Command*, (New York: Scribners, 1968), 84; Thomas, *Lee*, 293.

Charge of Alexander's artillery. 3:357

Assault of Brockenbrough's
Confederate brigade (Heth's
division) upon the stone barn
of the McPherson Farm. 3:278

Overview of the First Day, July 1

Early on the morning of July 1, Confederate skirmishers in advance of Maj. Gen. Henry *Heth's* division, marching east along Chambersburg Pike, encountered Union cavalry pickets several miles west of Gettysburg. *Heth* had expected some resistance but believed that only militia barred his way to Gettysburg, where (he later claimed) he hoped to seize shoes. *Third Corps* commander A. P. *Hill*, however, advised army commander Robert E. *Lee* that Union cavalry was in the area; *Lee* did not object to *Hill's* plan of advance for July 1.

Upon hearing of *Heth's* approach, Union cavalry general John Buford ordered one of his brigades to deploy on Herr Ridge; under pressure they slowly withdrew to McPherson's Ridge (stop 1a and 1b). This delaying action bought time for John Reynolds to hurry his I Corps to McPherson's Farm; orders went out notifying XI Corps commander Maj. Gen. Oliver O. Howard of the impending battle. By 10:00 A.M. the first Union infantry was arriving on the field astride Chambersburg Pike; before long the two armies were engaged in a fierce engagement (stops 1c, 1d, 2a, and 3). Behind *Heth* two more Confederate divisions started marching toward Gettysburg; of equal importance was the anticipated arrival of Richard S. *Ewell's Second Corps*, which would come from the north. Unless Howard's XI Corps arrived in time, the I Corps might well share the fate of its commander, who was killed as he rushed his men into position at Herbst Woods.

As noon came the first sign of *Ewell's* command, in the form of Maj. Gen. Robert E. *Rodes's* division, deploying along Oak Hill (stop 4a); however, poor leadership and the lay of the land thwarted his first attack on the I Corps right (stops 5a and 5b). Howard ordered two of his divisions to take up position north of Gettysburg, while a third remained due south of town at Cemetery Hill (stop 5c). When division commander Brig. Gen. Francis C. Barlow advanced his line northward toward a knoll, however, he rendered it vulnerable to an attack from *Ewell's* second division, led by Maj. Gen. Jubal *Early* (stop 6). As the XI Corps gave way, renewed Confederate attacks on the I Corps finally forced the Union left to give way (stops 2b and 2c). Union soldiers retreated in some disorder through the town before reforming south of it along Cemetery Hill; eventually they also took positions from Culp's Hill to Cemetery Ridge. *Ewell*, exercising the discretion allowed him by *Lee*, decided not to launch an attack on the Union position before night fell (stop 7a); *Lee*, however, determined to follow up on his initial triumph the next day (stop 7b). Meade, acting on the advice of his subordinates, decided to hold his ground and await *Lee's* next move.

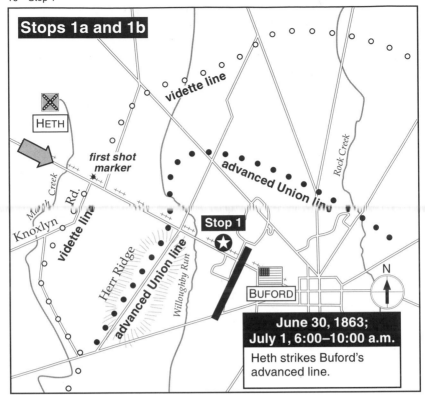

Stops 1a and 1b

vidette line

HETH

first shot marker

advanced Union line

Rock Creek

Marsh Creek

Knoxlyn Rd.

vidette line

Herr Ridge

advanced Union line

Willoughby Run

Stop 1

BUFORD

N

June 30, 1863; July 1, 6:00–10:00 a.m.

Heth strikes Buford's advanced line.

STOP 1   McPherson's Ridge   June 30–July 1, 6:00–10:45 A.M.

Directions   From the Visitor Center, *turn right* (north) onto STEINWEHR
AVENUE (which soon becomes BALTIMORE STREET), *proceed* 0.8
mile to WEST MIDDLE STREET (PA 116). *Turn left* (west) and *continue* 1.2 miles to REYNOLDS AVENUE (not to be confused with
Reynolds Street, a residential street en route). *Turn right* at
REYNOLDS AVENUE and *proceed* to the intersection of REYNOLDS
AVENUE and CHAMBERSBURG PIKE (U.S. 30). *Turn left* and *continue* 0.2 mile to STONE AVENUE. (You will see a National Park
Service guide/information building just beyond the intersection.) *Turn left* and drive about 25 yards to a parking lot on the
right. Leave your vehicle, walk back to the intersection of
STONE AVENUE and CHAMBERSBURG PIKE, and cross the road.
High-speed traffic is on the pike, so use care. (If traffic is too
heavy, you may view stop 1 from the two artillery pieces on
the Stone Avenue side of the pike.)

En route, as you cross the open fields along Reynolds Avenue,
notice the regimental monuments that line the roadway. Although the morning action occurred at the stops toward
which you are heading, by midafternoon the fighting had extended into this area.

STOP 1a   June 30

"You'll Have to Fight Like the Devil"

Directions   Go to the large equestrian statue of Gen. John F. Reynolds
and face west, the same direction Reynolds is facing.

Orientation   You are standing on McPherson's Ridge, a key piece of terrain
on the battle's first day. Straight ahead is the valley of
Willoughby Run and, beyond it, Herr Ridge. Moving counter-
clockwise, the woodland 90 degrees to the left (south) is
known as Herbst Woods (often erroneously called McPherson
Woods). The McPherson Barn is visible about 30 yards to the
southeast. To your right (north) is Oak Hill (easily distinguished by the Eternal Peace Light Memorial at its crest). A
line of vegetation, about 50 yards distant as you look toward
Oak Hill, marks the edge of a railroad cut that figured prominently in the fighting here.

What Happened   Brig. Gen. John Buford's cavalry division arrived in Gettysburg around 11 A.M. on June 30. Buford's duty was to screen
the left wing of the Union Army of the Potomac, consisting of the I, III, and XI Corps. The I and XI Corps, still about

12 miles south, had orders to march to Gettysburg. In the meantime, Buford's instructions were to "hold Gettysburg at all hazards until supports arrive."

Soon after his arrival, reports from scouts and local civilians convinced Buford that heavy concentrations of Confederate infantry were north and west of the town. Closest was the division of Maj. Gen. Henry *Heth*, at Cashtown about 6 miles to the west. *Heth* made a tentative foray against Buford's outposts on the afternoon of June 30; Buford predicted that next morning the Rebels would return in force. "You'll have to fight like the devil to hold your own until support arrives," he told a subordinate. "The enemy know the importance of this position and will strain every nerve to secure it."

The importance of Gettysburg derived from the web of 11 highways that converged on the town from all points of the compass. The best defensive ground in the area was Cemetery Hill and Culp's Hill immediately south of the town, but Buford understood that his thin cavalry division (about 2,750 men) could not hold those hills for long against a determined infantry attack. Instead he opted to conduct a flexible defense along the ridges west of Gettysburg. Using one of his two brigades, Buford established a line of videttes on Whisler (now called Knoxlyn) Ridge near Marsh Creek to provide early warning. Once under attack, these troopers would fall back to join a more extensive line of cavalry on Herr Ridge. The troopers would fight a delaying action as long as possible, then withdraw to McPherson's Ridge—Buford's main line of defense—and if necessary Seminary Ridge. (Buford's second brigade initially deployed in support of the first but later redeployed to the north, to guard against a possible Confederate advance from Carlisle.)

Analysis

Buford's eye for ground and his battle arrangements are often and justly praised. But equally important was his ability to sift intelligence and create an accurate picture of enemy dispositions. His report to cavalry chief Maj. Gen. Alfred Pleasonton on the evening of June 30 is filled with detailed, correct information about the deployment of the entire Confederate army—this at a time when Pleasonton erroneously believed that Robert E. *Lee* and much of *Lee's* army was most likely at Berlin, Pennsylvania, fully 40 miles from *Lee's* real location at Chambersburg.

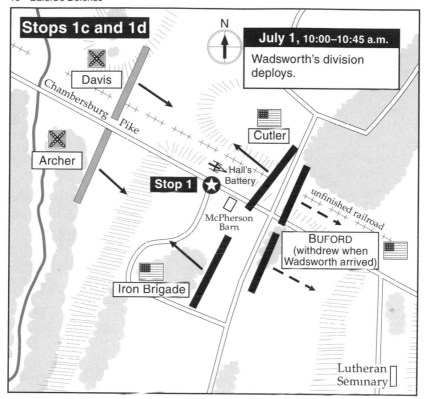

Stops 1c and 1d

N

July 1, 10:00–10:45 a.m.
Wadsworth's division deploys.

Davis

Chambersburg Pike

Archer

Cutler

Hall's Battery

Stop 1

McPherson Barn

unfinished railroad

BUFORD
(withdrew when Wadsworth arrived)

Iron Brigade

Lutheran Seminary

STOP 1b

July 1, 6:00–10:00 A.M.

Buford's Defense

Directions

Remain in place.

What Happened

Heth got his division under way at 5 A.M. He deployed several hundred soldiers in a loose skirmish line as his column approached Marsh Creek. Striking Buford's line of videttes on Whisler's Ridge, the skirmishers pushed slowly toward Buford's advanced cavalry line on Herr Ridge. It took until 9:30 A.M. for the Confederates to capture this second ridge; at that point *Heth* deployed his two lead brigades into line, a maneuver that required about 30 minutes to accomplish. Meanwhile, the Union troopers fell back to Buford's main position on McPherson's Ridge, where you now stand.

Buford's cavalry fought dismounted using breech-loading Sharps carbines. Although these were single-shot carbines (not repeaters like the seven-shot Spencers), they could still be loaded and fired more rapidly than the muzzle-loading rifled muskets carried by the infantry, thus generating considerable firepower. They were supported by a six-gun battery under Lt. John H. Calef (represented by the two cannon on the south side of Chambersburg Pike).

A lieutenant in the 8th Illinois Cavalry described the fighting: "I could see the enemy skirmish line . . . reaching from left to right . . . for a distance of a mile and a half. . . . Dismounting my entire company and sending the horses to the rear [I] called in the pickets, and formed the first line of twenty men including myself. . . . The enemy advanced slowly and cautiously. Our first position [on Whisler's Ridge] proved to be well taken. Scattering my men to the right and left at intervals of thirty feet and behind posts and rail fences . . . I directed them to throw their carbines sights up for 800 yards. . . . We gave the enemy the benefit of long range practice. . . . The firing was rapid from our carbines, and induced the belief of four times the number actually present."

If you would like to explore the terrain of Buford's morning action in more detail, turn to the brief Buford's Defense Excursion following stop 1d.

STOP 1c

10:00 A.M.

Reynolds Arrives

Directions

Remain in place.

What Happened

Late on June 30, Buford sent a report to I Corps commander Maj. Gen. John F. Reynolds informing him that he expected to be attacked in the morning. Reynolds therefore made sure to get his troops on the road early. After breaking camp at Greenmount, Pennsylvania (about 5 miles south of Gettysburg), at 7 A.M., by 10 A.M. the lead division of the I Corps was nearing Gettysburg via the Emmitsburg Road. The crash of gunfire was clearly audible, and Reynolds rode forward to examine the situation and consult with Buford. He found the cavalry general in the cupola of the Lutheran Theological Seminary.

"What's the matter, John?" Reynolds called up.

"The devil's to pay," Buford replied. Clambering down from the cupola, he took Reynolds to a vantage point on McPherson's Ridge – probably the same spot you now occupy. Reynolds approved Buford's dispositions and rode back to hurry his infantry forward, then scribbled messages to the army's commander, George G. Meade, and Oliver O. Howard of the XI Corps. He told Meade the Confederates were advancing in force but that he would hold them off as long as possible and if necessary would barricade the town. His message to Howard was simple: come as fast as you can.

STOP 1d

10:45 A.M.

The Union Infantry Deploys

Directions

Remain in place.

What Happened

The leading brigade of Union infantry arrived about 30 minutes later, marching cross-country to save time. By then, two brigades from *Heth's* division had nearly reached McPherson Ridge: Brig. Gen. James J. *Archer's* brigade was attacking south of Chambersburg Pike to your left front, with Brig. Gen. Joseph R. *Davis's* brigade north of it. Buford's dismounted cavalrymen were starting to give way under the pressure, and Buford had already ordered Calef's battery of horse artillery to withdraw.

Reynolds now ordered the 2nd Maine Battery, under Capt. James A. Hall, to take position immediately in front of you to protect the infantry while it deployed. As soon as the artillerists could unlimber, they began firing at a Confederate battery 1,300 yards away atop Herr Ridge. The fire effectively suppressed the enemy cannon while the infantry moved into position.

Brig. Gen. Lysander Cutler's brigade was the first to form into line. Two of its regiments deployed south of the pike; the other three advanced to the far side of the railroad cut and took position there. *Davis's* brigade confronted them almost as soon as they got into line. A short time later, Brig. Gen. Solomon Meredith's "Iron Brigade" advanced into Herbst Woods from Seminary Ridge to your left rear. Just as it did, a bullet struck General Reynolds in the head, killing him instantly. Command of the I Corps fell to Maj. Gen. Abner Doubleday.

Analysis

Although Buford deserves much credit for a well-planned and well-executed delaying action, *Heth* greatly misgauged the situation confronting him; he deployed too few troops to overcome the Union resistance quickly. At first he used only part of one brigade (*Archer's*) to attack Buford's cavalry, which he initially mistook for local militia. He made better progress once *Davis's* brigade got into action, only to find that the arriving Union infantry blocked him once again. Still, *Heth* persisted in head-on attacks against an enemy whose strength and dispositions he only dimly understood.

Buford's Defense Excursion

This short excursion—as little as 10 minutes, depending on traffic—takes you to the ground west of Gettysburg where Buford's cavalry conducted its flexible holding action.

Directions

Return to your vehicle. As you pull out of the parking lot, *Turn right.* STONE AVENUE becomes MEREDITH AVENUE as it bends to the east. *Proceed* to the T intersection of MEREDITH AVENUE and REYNOLDS AVENUE. When you reach the intersection of REYNOLDS AVENUE and CHAMBERSBURG PIKE (U.S. 30), reset your odometer.

Turn left and *proceed* 1.6 miles to KNOXLYN ROAD. *Turn left* again, and when you have gone a short distance, *reverse course.* When you are about 20 yards short of the intersection with Chambersburg Pike, pull over to the right shoulder of the road.

STOP A

7:30 A.M.

The First Shot

Directions

Look across Chambersburg Pike and locate a 5-foot rectangular stone marker on the embankment. You need not leave your vehicle.

Orientation

You are looking at the "first shot" marker erected by veterans of the 8th Illinois Cavalry. It is about three-quarters of a mile east of where Marsh Creek crosses Chambersburg Pike. On the evening of June 30 and early morning of July 1, this was the location of the 8th Illinois's vidette post no. 1.

What Happened

Inscribed on all four sides, the marker reads, "First shot at Gettysburg, July 1, 1863, 7:30 A.M."—"Fired by Captain M. E. Jones with Sergeant Shafer's carbine, Co. E, Eighth Regiment Illinois Cavalry"—"Erected by Captain Jones, Lieutenant Riddler, and Sergeant Shafer"—"Erected 1886."

Pickets deployed here saw the head of *Heth's* column approaching at about 7:00 A.M. They sent for their sergeant, Levi S. Shafer, who came up to see for himself. A short time later he was joined by the picket commander, Lt. Marcellus E. Jones (the marker erroneously identifies him as a captain). He asked to borrow Shafer's carbine, leveled it on a nearby rail fence, and at about 7:30 A.M. squeezed off the alleged first shot of the battle. It was aimed at a mounted Confederate some half mile distant and is unlikely to have hit its mark.

Not surprisingly, there are numerous other claimants for the honor of having fired the first shot at Gettysburg. Indeed, there are reports of a firefight north of Gettysburg along the Carlisle Road at dawn. But the 8th Illinois indisputably inaugurated the main action of the day.

STOP B   7:30–11:00 A.M.

Herr's Tavern

Directions   *Proceed* to the intersection and *turn right. Continue* 1 mile to Herr's Tavern, a large, distinctive brick building with a parking lot in front. Pull into the parking lot. Drive or walk to a point from which you have a good view of the fields to the east (i.e., the same direction in which you were traveling a moment ago).

Orientation   From this point, you can see the battlefield from *Heth's* perspective. Oak Hill, surmounted by the Eternal Peace Light Memorial, is to your left about 2,000 yards. Straight down Chambersburg Pike at the top of the next ridge are the statues of Buford and Reynolds, distant about 1,100 yards.

What Happened   Buford's cavalry occupied this ridge as its forward line of defense (see stop 1b) until about 9:30 A.M., when *Heth's* advancing infantry ejected them. But they had bought valuable time for the I Corps to march to the field. Two other circumstances are worth mentioning in regard to the opening action. *Heth,* although he anticipated an encounter with hostile forces on July 1, formed his line of march with his artillery battalion in the lead; indeed, artillery shelled this position early on. And those historians who portray Reynolds as anxious for battle overlook the fact that the I Corps did not commence marching that day until after 8 A.M. Had he moved earlier, Buford's troopers would not have had to hold their ground so long, and the infantry battle might well have commenced in earnest in this area.

This concludes the Buford's Defense Excursion. If you came here from stop 1b and would like to continue the basic tour, *pull out* onto CHAMBERSBURG PIKE, *continue* 0.6 mile to STONE AVENUE, and read the directions for stop 1c.

STOP 2   Herbst Woods   10:45–11:45 A.M.

Directions   Return to your car. *Exit the parking lot, turn right,* and *drive* 0.2 mile along STONE AVENUE to the pinkish granite marker to the *26th North Carolina.* Pull over into the unimproved turnout just short of the marker.

En route, notice how the ground in the Herbst Woods area bulges westward (i.e., to your right) a bit. Troops posted on that ground could enfilade Confederate infantry attacking along Chambersburg Pike. You will also see a statue commemorating John Burns, a 70-year-old Gettysburg man who took his rifle and joined the Union defense. Although captured by Confederates during the first day's fighting, he was released and became instantly famous for his doughty exploit. He is buried in Evergreen Cemetery adjacent to National Cemetery on Baltimore Pike.

The Lutheran Seminary. From a wartime photograph. 3:268

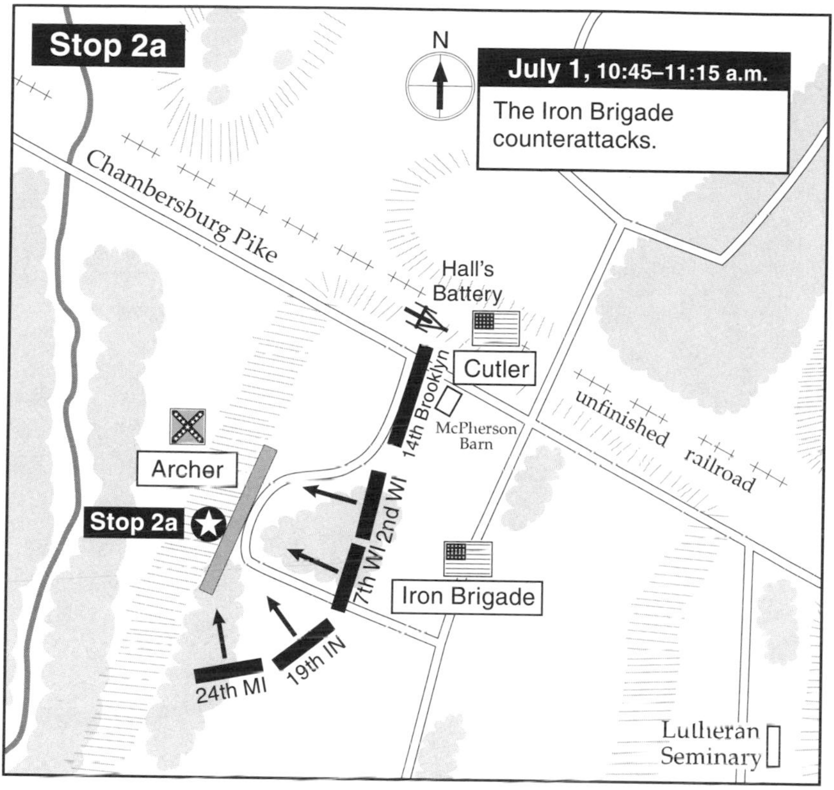

Stop 2a

N

July 1, 10:45–11:15 a.m.

The Iron Brigade counterattacks.

Chambersburg Pike

Hall's Battery

Cutler

14th Brooklyn

McPherson Barn

Archer

Stop 2a

7th WI 2nd WI

unfinished   railroad

Iron Brigade

24th MI

19th IN

Lutheran Seminary

| STOP 2a | 10:45–11:15 A.M. |

The Iron Brigade Holds

Directions

Stand behind the *26th North Carolina* marker and face west (downhill).

Orientation

About 50 yards down the dirt path in front of you is Willoughby Run. *Archer's* attacking Confederates came from that direction. The Iron Brigade arrived from the woods behind you. Note the downhill slope of the terrain. If you have time, the short walk to Willoughby Run will give you a better appreciation of the ground. (Note: the *26th North Carolina* was *not* involved in the morning action. The marker commemorates its participation in the afternoon phase of the battle.)

What Happened

The Iron Brigade reached this vicinity just as *Archer's* brigade was advancing up from the valley of Willoughby Run. The initial clash occurred in the center of the woods about 100 yards behind you. The two forces were only about 50 yards apart when the Confederates fired the first volley. As they advanced, the left regiments of the Iron Brigade overlapped

Archer's right flank, so that soon the Confederates faced Union troops on two sides. *Archer's* brigade attempted to withdraw back across Willoughby Run, but its organization fell apart and pursuing Union troops captured hundreds of prisoners. Although the initial clash in Herbst Woods lasted less than an hour, it wrecked *Archer's* brigade and cost the Iron Brigade heavily as well. Hardest hit was the 2nd Wisconsin, which fought on the ground where you stand. The regiment suffered 112 men killed or wounded, a loss rate of 36 percent.

Vignette

The Confederate prisoners included *Archer* himself–the first general in *Lee's* army to suffer such a fate. Exhausted by heat and fatigue, he was bodily seized by a private in the 2nd Wisconsin and taken to the rear. There he encountered Abner Doubleday, who recognized *Archer* from their days together at West Point. Doubleday extended his hand and boomed pleasantly, "Good morning, Archer! How are you? I am glad to see you!" *Archer* brusquely refused the handshake, saying, "Well, I am not glad to see you, by a damned sight, Doubleday."

STOP 2b

11:45 A.M.–3:30 P.M.

The Afternoon Fight

Directions

Remain in place.

What Happened

The repulse of *Archer's* brigade in this area, coupled with a similar disaster to *Davis's* brigade at the railroad cut to the north (stop 3), gave Doubleday sufficient breathing room to create a strong defensive line on McPherson's Ridge that grew even stronger as additional infantry and artillery arrived. *Heth* withdrew his two battered lead brigades to Herr Ridge and began organizing a new attack that would bring two remaining brigades into action. In the meantime additional Confederate forces arrived from the direction of Carlisle (stop 4) and struck the northern end of Doubeday's line (stop 5).

Not until 2:30 P.M. did *Heth* resume his advance, this time using the brigades of Col. John M. *Brockenbrough* and Brig. Gen. James J. *Pettigrew*–over 3,500 men. "They marched along quietly and with confidence, but swiftly," wrote a Union colonel. "I watched them . . . and am confident that when they advanced they outflanked us at least half a mile on our left. . . . There was not a shadow of a chance of our holding this ridge." Nevertheless, the Federals tried. Nowhere was the

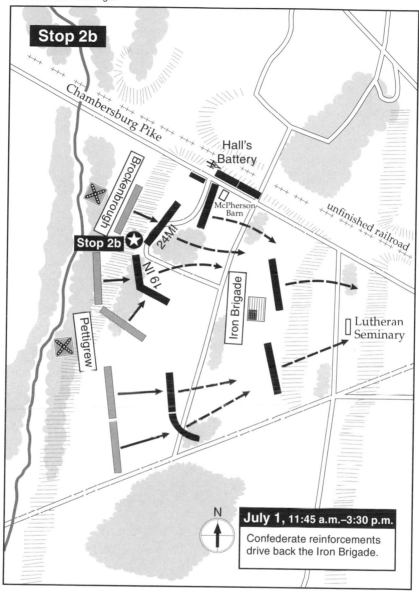

Stop 2b

Chambersburg Pike

Hall's Battery

Brockenbrough

Stop 2b ⭐

McPherson Barn

24 MI

19 IN

unfinished railroad

Pettigrew

Iron Brigade

Lutheran Seminary

N

July 1, 11:45 a.m.–3:30 p.m.

Confederate reinforcements drive back the Iron Brigade.

fighting more severe than in this area, where the *11th* and *26th North Carolina Regiments* traded volleys with the 24th Michigan and 19th Indiana Regiments at a range of 40 yards or less. Initially deployed on the ground where you stand, the 24th Michigan presently withdrew to a second line a few dozen yards to the east (behind you). There it made a determined stand until around 3:30 P.M., when the Confederate pressure became overwhelming and the regiment joined the rest of the Iron Brigade in a general withdrawal from McPherson's Ridge.

Vignette

The casualties on this part of the field were some of the very worst of the battle. The *26th North Carolina* lost 549 out of about 800 men, the *11th North Carolina* 250 out of 550. Many Union regiments lost over two-thirds of their numbers. The 24th Michigan lost 363 men, including 99 killed or mortally wounded. General *Heth* would report that the 24th's dead marked the location of the unit's second line "with the accuracy of a line at a dress parade."

STOP 2c

2:45–4:45 P.M.   [This is an optional stop.]

The Attack on the Seminary

Directions

Return to your vehicle. STONE AVENUE soon becomes MEREDITH AVENUE, but it is the same road. *Travel east* along MEREDITH AVENUE; pull over just before the T intersection with REYNOLDS AVENUE. You may choose to leave your vehicle. Face east toward the Lutheran Seminary.

Orientation

Immediately in front of you, across Reynolds Avenue, is a statue of Abner Doubleday, who succeeded Reynolds as commander of the I Corps on July 1; behind you to your left, in Herbst Woods, a small obelisk mounted on an earth mound marks where Reynolds fell dead. As you look at the seminary, you will note on the left a church spire; on the right, atop the main seminary building, is the green-roofed cupola used by Buford on the morning of July 1. Chambersburg Pike borders the seminary to the left (north), while Fairfield Road runs just to the right (south) of it.

What Happened

Col. Chapman Biddle's brigade of the I Corps deployed along Reynolds Avenue from where you stand south to the Fairfield Road at midday; from where you stand north to Chambersburg Pike the brigades of Meredith and Col. Roy Stone held an advanced position in the area of Herbst Woods and the McPherson Farm. This salient would become vulnerable should the Confederates break through to either the north (left) or south (right). At approximately 3:00 P.M. *Heth* ordered two fresh brigades forward; they succeeded in flanking the Iron Brigade on its left (south) and in driving off Biddle's line; rumor had it that Biddle's division commander was intoxicated. At the same time a renewed Confederate assault north of Chambersburg Pike drove back Stone's brigade.

Several intermixed Union brigades conducted a fighting withdrawal across the fields due west of the seminary before establishing a final line of battle just west of the seminary itself, where they took advantage of some makeshift fortifi-

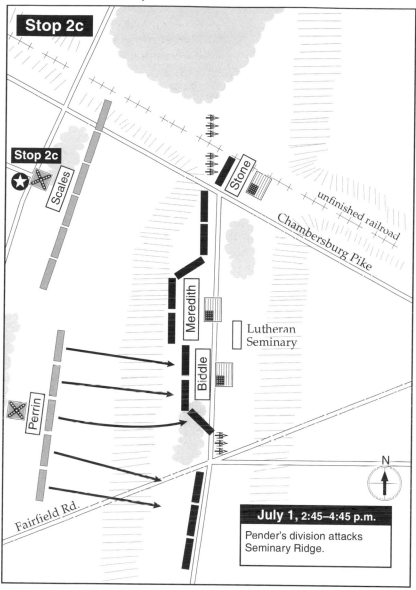

Stop 2c

Stop 2c

Scales

Stone

unfinished railroad

Chambersburg Pike

Meredith

Lutheran
Seminary

Biddle

Perrin

N

Fairfield Rd.

July 1, 2:45–4:45 p.m.

Pender's division attacks
Seminary Ridge.

cations erected earlier that day. It fell to Maj. Gen. William
Dorsey *Pender's* division to crack this position. He deployed
three brigades in line from Chambersburg Pike southward
across Fairfield Road; you are standing between the brigades
of Brig. Gen. A. M. *Scales* (to your left) and Col. Abner *Perrin*
(to your right), while Brig. Gen. James H. *Lane* deployed his
brigade south of Fairfield Road. At about 4:00 P.M. *Pender's*
men advanced. To your left *Scales's* assault came under a hail
of cannon fire from Union batteries posted astride Chambersburg Pike: "After a few moments of the belching of the

artillery," noted one officer of the 2nd Wisconsin, "the blinding smoke shut out the sun and obstructed the view." *Scales* fell wounded at the bottom of the swale; his regiments were shattered, as all but one field officer (colonel, lieutenant colonel, and major) were hit. To the right, south of Fairfield Road, *Lane's* men came under fire from Union cavalrymen posted behind a stone wall; some observers claimed that his men began to form in a square formation to repel a possible cavalry charge, although this point is much disputed.

It was thus left to *Perrin's* South Carolinians to take the Union position; *Perrin* ordered them to hold their fire as they advanced. They came under heavy Union fire before *Perrin* noticed that the breastworks ended just south of the seminary. His center regiments forced the gap in the Union line between that point and Fairfield Road. At approximately 4:30 P.M., Doubleday, his line untenable, gave the order to withdraw. Some units obeyed the order with precipitate haste; others followed at a more measured pace, periodically turning to fire a volley at the pursuing Confederates. Shortly thereafter Robert E. *Lee* rode up to the northern edge of the seminary along Chambersburg Pike, established his headquarters, and began to contemplate what to do next.

Analysis

It was only a matter of time before Doubleday would have had to abandon his position along Reynolds Avenue north toward Herbst Woods and McPherson Farm; while his advanced line may have bought him some time, it did so at high cost and rendered it less likely that he could hold on to Seminary Ridge. Although the seminary offered little cover, it possessed excellent fields of fire westward; better management might have enabled Doubleday to hold the Confederates in check for some time.

At the conclusion of this optional stop, return to your vehicle. *Turn left* onto REYNOLDS AVENUE, *cross* CHAMBERSBURG PIKE, and park your vehicle before the bridge spanning the railroad cut.

Major General Abner Doubleday. 3:277

STOP 3   The Railroad Cut   10:30–11:30 A.M.

Directions   Return to your car and *continue* south on STONE AVENUE,
                          which loops almost at once to the east, and becomes MERE-
                          DITH AVENUE. *Drive* to the T intersection with REYNOLDS AVE-
                          NUE and *turn left*. *Proceed* to the intersection with the CHAM-
                          BERSBURG PIKE (U.S. 30), *cross*, and park at the turnout just
                          before the bridge.

                          En route you will have a good view of the Lutheran Semi-
                          nary, dead ahead as you reach the intersection of Meredith
                          and Reynolds Avenues. Just after you make the turn you will
                          see a stone monument on a dirt mound to the left, marking
                          the spot where General Reynolds was killed. The monuments
                          and cannon you will pass along Stone Avenue trace the
                          Union line as it extended north from the Iron Brigade's posi-
                          tion in Herbst Woods.

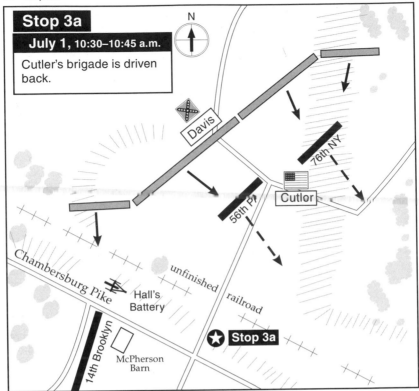

Stop 3a

July 1, 10:30–10:45 a.m.

Cutler's brigade is driven back.

N

Davis

76th NY

Cutlor

56th Pk

Chambersburg Pike

unfinished   railroad

Hall's Battery

14th Brooklyn

McPherson Barn

★ Stop 3a

STOP 3a   10:30–10:45 A.M.

Cutler's Brigade Goes into Action

Directions   Exit your car and, without leaving the turnout, face west.

Orientation   You should have little trouble regaining your bearings. The
                      position you now occupy is on East McPherson Ridge about
                      150 yards from stop 1 – the Reynolds and Buford statues are
                      plainly visible to your front. The McPherson Barn is also vis-
                      ible as you look to the left; beyond it is Herbst Woods. The
                      nearby bridge spans a railroad cut. Today the Western Mary-
                      land Railroad runs through it; at the time of the battle no
                      tracks had yet been laid.
                         To the left of the bridge and at the far edge of the railroad
                      cut, you will see a grove of trees on a slight rise about 200
                      yards away. From your present position the terrain around
                      the grove seems nearly level; in fact it slopes significantly to
                      the west, so that from a Confederate perspective the grove
                      appears to occupy the crest of a hill.
                         You will need to reorient yourself chronologically as well:
                      the action at this stop took place concurrently with the Iron

Brigade's clash with *Archer's* brigade, several hours before the action discussed at stop 2b.

What Happened

As discussed at stop 1d, Hall's 2nd Maine Battery took position astride Chambersburg Pike. Its fire covered Maj. Gen. James Wadsworth's division as it deployed. While the Iron Brigade deployed into Herbst Woods, a second brigade under Lysander Cutler took up a position in this area. Two of Cutler's regiments (76th New York and 56th Pennsylvania) deployed behind you, in the valley between Seminary Ridge and East McPherson's Ridge. Thus shielded from Confederate artillery fire they advanced in line of battle toward West McPherson's Ridge in front of you. Two others (14th Brooklyn and 95th New York) covered the area between Herbst Woods and Chambersburg Pike. A fifth regiment, the 147th New York, initially received no orders. Its colonel prudently placed his men near the McPherson Barn, where the crest of West McPherson's Ridge offered some protection from Rebel shells.

These maneuvers were not yet complete when Confederate infantry suddenly appeared where the railroad cut crosses West McPherson's Ridge in front of you. Captain Hall ordered four of his six guns to open fire on these troops with double canister, which forced them back into the cover of the railroad bed. Simultaneously, two Confederate regiments confronted the 56th Pennsylvania and 76th New York from a wheatfield beyond the railroad cut, about 400 yards to your right (due north). A tremendous firefight quickly ensued in which the two Union regiments were outflanked and forced back to Seminary Ridge.

Analysis

Because the first day's battle at Gettysburg was a "meeting engagement," both sides were obliged to deploy their forces hurriedly in a highly dynamic situation in which information about enemy strength and dispositions was limited. As a result, it was not uncommon for troops to march straight into heavy resistance or to have their flanks turned by enemy units whose lines overlapped their own by sheer chance. In the initial clash at Herbst Woods, *Archer's* brigade was the victim of such a misfortune. Here, the 56th Pennsylvania and 76th New York suffered the same fate.

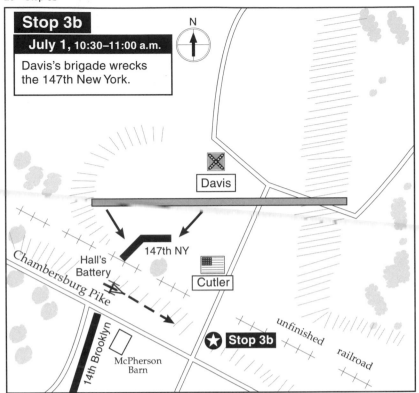

Stop 3b

July 1, 10:30–11:00 a.m.

Davis's brigade wrecks
the 147th New York.

N

Davis

147th NY

Hall's
Battery

Chambersburg Pike

Cutler

14th Brooklyn

McPherson
Barn

★ Stop 3b

unfinished

railroad

STOP 3b   10:30–11:00 A.M.

The Ordeal of the 147th New York

Directions

Remain in place, but face directly toward the grove of trees identified in stop 3a.

What Happened

Barely five minutes after the 147th New York halted near the McPherson Barn, it was ordered to take position near this grove of trees to protect Hall's battery. Although from this point the regiment was barely 100 yards from the 56th Pennsylvania, the colonel of the latter unit never saw the 147th deploy: a rail fence heavily covered with vegetation blocked his vision. As a result, when the 56th Pennsylvania and 76th New York were forced to retreat, no effort was made to maintain contact with the 147th New York, which was now isolated and exposed. Its predicament became even more dire when Hall's battery withdrew from its position on West McPherson's Ridge.

The full strength of *Davis's* Confederate brigade now bore down on the 147th, which changed front slightly to face threats from the west and north. Rebel efforts to strike the

regiment from the west had to cross low-lying ground dominated by the Union troops, so the weight of the Confederate
attack gradually shifted to the north, where the terrain was
more nearly level. Soon two Confederate regiments climbed
over the rail fence on the 147th's right flank and opened a
blistering fire. Seeing that the 147th was about to be cut off
entirely, General Wadsworth sent his adjutant to order its retreat. Some of the Union infantrymen retreated across the
fields north of the railroad cut; others withdrew directly
south into the cut itself, where many fell into the hands of
Confederate troops who materialized on either side of the
bank.

The 147th went into battle with 380 men. In just 30 minutes of fighting, it lost 76 men killed, 144 wounded, and between 60 and 70 captured: a loss rate of 76 percent.

Vignette   As the 147th began its retreat, a badly wounded private, Edwin Aylesworth, begged Lt. J. Volney Pierce not to leave him
behind. Pierce and a sergeant tried to take the man with
them, but his weight and the severity of his injuries made
him difficult to carry; they reluctantly set him down. "Don't
leave me boys," Aylesworth cried out. He died soon afterward. The incident haunted Pierce the rest of his life. In 1888
he wrote that Aylesworth's plea "has rung in my ears and
lived in my memory these five and twenty years."

Union dead at Gettysburg. From a photograph. 3:275

Stop 3c

July 1, 11:00–11:30 a.m.

An inspired Union counter-attack stops Davis cold.

N

Chambersburg Pike

14th Brooklyn

95th NY

Davis

Stop 3c

McPherson Barn

6th WI

6th WI (1 co.)

unfinished railroad

STOP 3c   11:00–11:30 A.M.

Encounter in the Railroad Cut

Directions   Walk down to your right toward the railroad cut in the vicin-
                      ity of the 95th New York Monument (identified by the big red
                      ball on top) and face toward Chambersburg Pike (south).

What Happened   *Davis's* Confederate brigade had now mauled three-fifths of
                      Cutler's brigade and was squarely on the Union right flank,
                      in position to roll up the entire Union position on McPher-
                      son's Ridge. Wadsworth's division had only one regiment in
                      reserve–the 6th Wisconsin–and its colonel, Rufus Dawes,
                      now received instructions to "move your regiment at once to
                      the right and go like hell." The regiment moved in column
                      formation until it reached Chambersburg Pike, then de-
                      ployed in line of battle behind a rail fence, facing north.
                      Davis's brigade was already advancing across the ground in
                      front of you. Colonel Dawes instructed the 6th Wisconsin to
                      "fire by files"–a tactic by which the soldiers discharged their

rifles, two by two, in an orderly progression from one end of the line to the other. This steady barrage forced the Confederates back to the protection of the railroad cut, where you now stand.

Unaware of the existence of the cut, Dawes believed the Rebels must be retreating. At this time the 95th New York appeared on his left; beyond it the 14th Brooklyn also swung into line facing north. Previously both units had been threatened by *Archer's* advance into Herbst Woods, but the Iron Brigade's victory in that sector had ended that danger. On their own initiative, the colonels of the two regiments changed front to address the new threat from *Davis*. Dawes went to a major in the 95th and told him, "We must charge." "Charge it is," the major replied, and the 95th New York and 6th Wisconsin swept forward. The colonel of the 14th Brooklyn followed suit, and soon three fresh Union regiments were bearing down upon *Davis's* victorious but battered and disorganized Confederates.

Dawes had no idea of the railroad cut's existence until his regiment closed with the enemy, but it soon became obvious that the cut was too deep to afford the enemy much advantage and was instead a trap that blocked their quick retreat. As the Confederates milled about in the cut, some aware that the enemy was almost upon them but many oblivious to the threat, the 6th Wisconsin reached the lip of the cut and aimed their weapons into the packed Southerners. Simultaneously, the adjutant of the 6th led 20 men into the eastern end of the cut (to your left) where the ground is level. They were now in position to fire straight down the length of the cut. Dawes demanded the surrender of the Confederates in the cut. Although many Rebels were able to escape via the western end of the cut, more than 200 were taken prisoner. The prompt Union counterattack restored the McPherson's Ridge position, enabling the Federals to continue resistance for another four hours.

Analysis   The action at the railroad cut shows small unit leadership at its best. After the initial decision to commit the 6th Wisconsin, no general officer influenced the Union dispositions. Cutler, the brigade commander, was on Seminary Ridge reforming the 56th Pennsylvania and 76th New York. Wadsworth, the division commander, and Doubleday, the acting corps commander, were similarly engaged elsewhere. The colonels of the 14th Brooklyn and 95th New York displayed good awareness of the overall situation and excellent initiative in their independent decisions to confront *Davis's*

Confederate brigade. Colonel Dawes of the 6th Wisconsin seems to have been the driving force behind the decision to charge, a maneuver hastily coordinated with the neighboring 95th New York and carried out with determination and élan.

Confederate prisoners. From a wartime photograph. 2:156

July 1, 10:30 a.m.–1:00 p.m.

Rodes's division deploys for action.

STOP 4   Oak Hill   10:30 A.M.–1:00 P.M.

Directions   Return to your vehicle. *Drive north* across the bridge span-
                     ning the railroad cut to the T intersection; *turn left* (west)
                     onto BUFORD AVENUE. *Follow this road* as it swings to the right
                     and crosses MUMMASBURG ROAD (and becomes NORTH CON-
                     FEDERATE AVENUE). Park in the parking lot in front of the Eter-
                     nal Light Peace Memorial–approximately 1 mile driving
                     distance from the bridge. Leaving your car, walk up to the

monument, then turn to the right and make your way to the first of two cannon marking the position of *Fry's* battery of *Carter's* battalion.

En route you will first traverse the area in which *Davis's* brigade advanced and overran the 147th New York in the fields just north of the area between the middle and western railroad cuts (south of Buford Avenue before it bears to the right). As you drive northward on Buford Avenue, you will see a series of monuments marking the right flank of Buford's division–these units actually deployed north of Gettysburg, where they fended off a Confederate advance for several hours.

STOP 4a   10:30 A.M.–1:00 P.M.

Rodes Joins the Fray

Directions   Look back southward toward the bridge spanning the railroad cut.

Orientation   You are standing on Oak Hill, just north of the right flank of the Union I Corps. Once you locate the bridge spanning the railroad cut, you should look to the right and be able to locate (left to right) the McPherson Barn, Chambersburg Pike, the Reynolds Monument, and finally the guide headquarters house in the distance. To the left of the bridge is a wooded lot, then a low stone wall, and finally several lines of trees that continue northward to your immediate left. The stone wall marks Oak Ridge. It is important to note that the tree line just due north (left) of the stone wall was not nearly as thick in July 1863. If you look through the opening in the trees where Mummasburg Road slices through the trees on Oak Ridge, you may be able to see the walls of the McLean Barn.

Readers wanting to gain some idea of the dimensions of the battlefield from north to south should look at the tops of the trees in the far distance just to the left of the railroad bridge. The observation tower in the distance marks the area where James *Longstreet* launched his assault on the Union left on July 2.

What Happened   After the Union counterattack secured control of the railroad cut and the Iron Brigade punished *Archer's* men, the fighting died down as both sides brought up reinforcements. *Third Corps* commander Ambrose P. *Hill* came upon *Heth's* battered brigades. It was *Hill's* first opportunity to exercise corps command, but illness hampered his efforts to respond to the situation before him. Nevertheless, he ordered up William D. *Pender's* division and prepared to renew the attack, this time under the supervision of army commander Robert E. *Lee,* who arrived on the field early in the afternoon. Of equal importance was *Hill's* earlier decision to notify *Second Corps* commander Richard S. *Ewell* of his decision to march toward Gettysburg. Upon receiving *Hill's* message between 8:00 and 9:00 A.M., *Ewell* turned his divisions toward the crossroads town, keeping in mind *Lee's* directive not to bring on a general engagement if he encountered the enemy in force.

Robert E. *Rodes's* division, some 8,000 strong, was marching south along Middletown Road (now PA 34) toward Gettysburg when the men heard the sound of the morning's battle. Noting the woods to your rear, *Rodes* decided to take advantage of the cover it and the ridge afforded his command: "I found that by keeping along the wooded ridge . . . I could strike the force of the enemy . . . upon the flank, and that, besides moving under cover, whenever we struck the enemy we could engage him with the advantage in ground." With this in mind, *Rodes* aligned his five brigades in the woods and moved south to attack, deploying his artillery on this hill. At 1:00 P.M. two of his batteries opened fire. Cutler's brigade took cover in the railroad cut and the wooded area to the northeast (just left of the bridge from where you stand); Union cannon boomed in reply, bringing Oak Hill under fire.

Meanwhile, the Union position received reinforcements. The I Corps, now under Doubleday, strengthened its position west of the seminary. Two brigades of Brig. Gen. Thomas A. Rowley's division (minus a brigade of Vermonters destined to play a critical role later in the battle) formed in line on either side of the Iron Brigade, extending the I Corps's flank southward along what is now Reynolds Avenue to Fairfield Road (PA 116 — the route you took to get to stop 1). Brig. Gen. Henry Baxter's brigade of Brig. Gen. John C. Robinson's division moved to a position along the eastern slope of Oak Ridge just south of Mummasburg Road. At the same time, the XI Corps, under the command of Oliver O. Howard, arrived at Gettysburg. Leaving one division on a hill south of the town, Howard directed his other two divisions to relieve Col. Thomas C. Devin's cavalry and establish a line of defense north of Gettysburg — although he lacked sufficient manpower to link up with Robinson's division, leaving a gap some 600 feet across. As the ranking Union officer, Howard assumed overall command of the Federal forces on the field, leaving division commander Maj. Gen. Carl Schurz in charge of the XI Corps.

The arrival of these Union reinforcements complicated *Rodes's* plan, although it also offered him new opportunities. He detached Brig. Gen. George *Doles's* Georgia brigade to keep an eye on the XI Corps, posting it east of Oak Ridge, confident that before long *Ewell's* other divisions would appear from the north. Col. Edward A. *O'Neal's* brigade of Alabamians formed astride the ridge, while Brig. Gen. Alfred *Iverson's* four regiments of North Carolinians took their position just south of where you are now standing, in the vicinity of a small clump of trees due south of the Eternal Peace Light Memorial that marks the spot of the Forney Farm. To their (and your) right Brig. Gen. Junius *Daniel* positioned his brigade composed of Tar Heels, while the fifth brigade, under Brig. Gen. Stephen *Ramseur*, remained in reserve. *O'Neal* and *Iverson* were to move forward together, while *Daniel* followed on *Iverson's* right. The attack column would come crashing down on the railroad cut; *Rodes* made minimal adjustment to meet Baxter's brigade along Oak Ridge, in part because the Federals used the cover of a stone wall and a reverse slope to help conceal themselves. Apparently he thought they were part of Cutler's brigade, rashly exposing themselves to an assault; surely he did not fully appreciate how Baxter's presence would alter his plans. Although he had plenty of artillery in the area, he trained his guns on the Union forces in the area of the railroad cut and Chambersburg Pike, rather than turning them on Baxter.

STOP 4b   **Arms and Ammunition: Artillery**

Directions   Turn right, walk across the front of the Eternal Peace Light Memorial, and locate the plaque for W. P. Carter's Battery, just west of the memorial. Stand behind the right-most of the two cannon, facing the same direction as the barrel.

Orientation   The cannon faces generally toward Buford Avenue (fringed by battle monuments), which runs southward toward the hill occupied by the 147th New York. The McPherson Barn is clearly visible about 1,600 yards to your left front. The bridge over the railroad cut is also visible farther to the left at a somewhat lesser distance. The town of Gettysburg lies about a mile beyond the trees just across the parking lot. If you look carefully to the far right, where Chambersburg Pike (U.S. 30) climbs over Herr Ridge, you will be able to discern Herr Tavern, about 2,000 yards distant.

Analysis

This vantage point furnishes a good opportunity to discuss the principal weapons employed at Gettysburg. The artillery piece in front of you is a 12-pounder Napoleon, a smoothbore cannon that was highly versatile and had a maximum effective range of about 1,500 yards–far enough to strike the bridge over the railroad cut. At such distances the Napoleon could use solid shot, spherical case, or shell. At ranges of under 350 yards the projectile of choice was canister–essentially a can containing 27 cast-iron shot, which converted the cannon into a gigantic sawed-off shotgun.

Two varieties of rifled cannon were common at Gettysburg: the 10-pounder Parrott, easily identified by the cast-iron band around its breech, and the 3-inch ordnance rifle. Both weapons had a maximum effective range of about 2,500 yards–easily enough to strike Herr Tavern. Although rifled cannon could fire farther than the smoothbore, its chief advantage was its greater accuracy. In situations that did not require accuracy, the smoothbore–more versatile and with a higher rate of fire–was perhaps the better weapon.

Practically all Civil War cannon were muzzle-loaders: ordnance specialists had only recently created the technology for an effective breech-loading cannon (the opening at the breech tended to seal imperfectly, permitting gas from the burning gunpowder to escape). An exception were the two 12-pounder Whitworths used by the Confederates at Gettysburg. Donated by an Englishman sympathetic to the South, these British-made cannon were not only breech-loaders but had a maximum range of nearly 6 miles. Two Whitworths are on display immediately behind you. The 6-mile statistic is a bit misleading, however: at ranges beyond 3,000 yards the Whitworth had little accuracy or effect.

STOP 4c   **Arms and Ammunition: Muskets and Carbines**

Directions   Remain in place.

Analysis

By far the majority of Civil War wounds were inflicted by small arms fire. A variety of shoulder arms were used at Gettysburg, but they divide basically into two types: muskets, which were carried by the infantry; and carbines, which were shorter weapons favored by the cavalry.

Most muskets were rifled, which gave them a maximum effective range of about 350 yards: roughly the distance from the ground you occupy to the second regimental monument (9th New York Cavalry) beyond Mummasburg Road. Civil War units, however, commonly deliberately held their fire until the enemy had closed to 200 yards or less (the distance to the first regimental marker is slightly under 200 yards). And a few units were still armed with smoothbore muskets, which had a maximum effective range of less than 150 yards.

Regardless of type, Civil War small arms generally used a soft lead conical bullet called the minié ball. A bit over half an inch in diameter (the most common calibers were .577, .58, and .69), minié balls traveled at rather low velocities and tended to flatten on impact, splintering bones, ripping flesh, and in general inflicting wounds that would be difficult to treat even today.

More detailed information on Civil War weaponry can be found in appendix A.

Hall's battery on the first day, resisting the Confederate advance on the Chambersburg Road. 3:290

STOP 5   Oak Ridge   1:00–3:00 P.M.

Directions   Return to your car. *Exit* the parking lot to the left and *continue*
                          your drive east along NORTH CONFEDERATE AVENUE, which
                          again crosses MUMMASBURG ROAD. This is a busy intersection,
                          and drivers on Mummasburg Road may not always see cross-
                          ing vehicles in time, so cross with care. You will now find
                          yourself on DOUBLEDAY AVENUE. Pull over into the parking lot
                          below the observation tower, exit your vehicle, and walk
                          back to a regimental monument resembling a tree trunk,
                          marking the position of the 90th Pennsylvania Infantry. Face
                          north toward the intersection you just crossed.

                          En route you may be able to gain a better look at the
                          McLean Barn to your left. It helps to locate the ground where
                          O'Neal's men advanced.

Orientation   You are on the eastern slope of Oak Ridge. Ahead of you to
                          your left is Oak Hill; over to your right is the area where the
                          XI Corps deployed on the afternoon of July 1. Locate the
                          McLean Farm across Mummasburg Road in a somewhat
                          wooded area to your right; to the right of that, more than
                          halfway down the slope, you should be able to see a thin tree
                          line running from north to south where it meets Mummas-
                          burg Road near a railroad crossing.

                          It is important to note two characteristics of the terrain in
                          this area. First, the woods directly to the west of the park-
                          ing lot were not nearly as thick in July 1863 as they are now.
                          The low stone wall that runs along the shoulder of Double-
                          day Avenue was most likely displaced when the avenue was
                          constructed on the crest of the ridge, which in turn lowered
                          the ridge's height. It is probably more accurate to say that the
                          stone wall once topped the ridge crest, much as it does to the
                          north of the Mummasburg Road intersection in front of you.

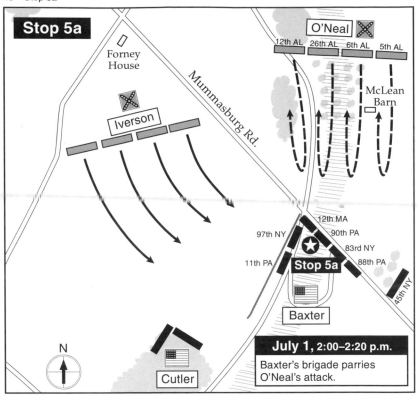

Stop 5a

Forney House

O'Neal ✕

12th AL 26th AL 6th AL 5th AL

Mummasburg Rd.

Iverson ✕

McLean Barn

12th MA

97th NY   90th PA

83rd NY

11th PA   88th PA

Stop 5a ★

45th NY

Baxter

N

July 1, 2:00–2:20 p.m.

Baxter's brigade parries O'Neal's attack.

Cutler

STOP 5a   2:00–2:20 P.M.

Baxter Checks *O'Neal*

Directions   Remain in place, facing north.

What Happened   Baxter deployed the six regiments of his brigade on the extreme right of the I Corps. Noting the presence of *Rodes's* division, Baxter decided to position four of his regiments–the
12th Massachusetts, 90th Pennsylvania, 83rd New York, and
88th Pennsylvania (from left to right)–along a fence bordering the south side of Mummasburg Road.

The Confederate advance proved abortive. *O'Neal* used only
three regiments (the *6th, 12th*, and *26th Alabama*) in his assault; *Rodes* had detached a fourth (the *5th Alabama*) to fill the
gap between the attack column and *Doles's* brigade to the
east, while a fifth (the *3rd Alabama*) remained in the woods
where *Rodes* had placed it during the artillery exchange.
O'Neal apparently believed that it was no longer his to control. Instead of shifting to the left (east) to strike the flank of
the Union position, *O'Neal's* men, some 1,000 strong, ran head

first into Baxter's line. As one Pennsylvanian recalled, "With a sharp crack of the muskets a fleecy cloud of smoke rolled down the front of the brigade and the Minie balls zipped and buzzed with a merry chorus toward the Southern line, which halted, and after a brief contest, retired to the shelter of the woods." Offering some additional assistance was the 45th New York, positioned on the extreme left of the XI Corps. Its commander ordered his men up to the tree line just east of McLean Farm, where they fired into the Confederate left flank. It did not help that *O'Neal* had chosen this moment to remain in the rear with the *5th Alabama*, thus forfeiting control of his brigade. *Rodes's* plans were already falling victim to poor execution and changed circumstances.

Before you leave, locate the flank markers of the 90th Pennsylvania. They are shaped like tree stumps; if you draw a line connecting them to the main regimental monument, you will have an idea of where the apex of the battle line was located (although the markers themselves mark the position of the regiment subsequent to *O'Neal's* attack). Then look just southeast of the intersection of Mummasburg Road and Doubleday Avenue. There a small marker designates the site of the stand of the 16th Maine on the afternoon of July 1, when a second Confederate attack from the north against Brig. Gen. Gabriel Paul's brigade (which had relieved Baxter) cracked the right of the I Corps. Reference will be made to this point during the discussion of combat at Barlow's Knoll (stop 6).

Major General R. E. Rodes, c.s.a.
From a photograph. 2:580

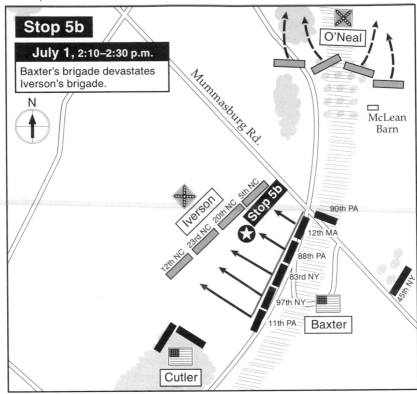

STOP 5b   2:10–2:30 P.M.

Iverson's Assault

Directions   Cross Doubleday Avenue, turn left, and walk south along the shoulder opposite the parking lot. Ahead of you is a statue of I Corps division commander John C. Robinson. Across Doubleday Avenue from the statue is a monument to the 88th Pennsylvania. Take the path to your right through the woods and into a clearing leading to a small marker. Face northwest toward the Eternal Light Peace Memorial (to your right).

What Happened   Once *O'Neal's* brigade fell back, Baxter's men were free to concentrate on *Iverson's* advance. Several regiments wheeled westward, while others shifted their position in response to the enemy advance, stretching the Union line southward along the ridge to the woods to your left. The stone wall along what is now Doubleday Avenue proved a sufficient if impromptu fortification for their protection; so did the fact that they occupied the eastern slope of the ridge, while *Iverson* would advance along the west slope, unaware of what might be in the vicinity of the ridge. *Iverson's* four regiments advanced across Mummasburg Road and through a field of wheat before entering the meadow where you stand. No skirmishers felt out the enemy position; *Iverson* did not accompany his men. Before long the men shifted from marching due south to southeast, as if they were wheeling to the left. "Our alignment soon became false," one Tar Heel later complained. "There seems to have been utter ignorance of the force crouching behind the stone wall." The Federals along the wall watched and waited, rifles loaded and cocked, as the Confederates marched forth in perfect parade order. "When we were in point blank range," a Rebel later remembered, "the dense line of the enemy rose from its protected lair and poured into us a withering fire." At the same time, Cutler's men, located in the woods to the south behind you, opened fire. Those North Carolinians who survived the rifle fire huddled in the swale just to your left in an effort to shield themselves; before long they tied handkerchiefs to their guns and began to wave them as a sign of surrender. Members of the 88th Pennsylvania ran forward and gobbled up hundreds of prisoners and several flags—the act memorialized by the marker (although members of several other regiments also captured Confederate colors). Baxter tried to press his advantage, but heavy Confederate gunfire from Oak Hill put an end to thoughts of a counterattack. Nevertheless, *Iverson's* brigade was shattered. "Deep and long must the desolate homes and orphan children of North Carolina rue the rashness of that hour," one survivor later lamented.

Vignette

Later in the day, after the Confederates managed to drive the I Corps back through Gettysburg, a Confederate artilleryman passed through this area. He counted "seventy-nine (79) North Carolinians laying dead in a straight line.... Three had fallen to the front; the rest had fallen backward; yet the feet of all these dead men were in a perfectly straight line." Nearly half of the attackers were killed or wounded, while at least 322 were captured—a total casualty count of at least two-thirds of the entire brigade. The area literally ran red with blood, according to several observers. Eventually, those who fell here were buried in the swale to your left: the area gained the name of the "Iverson Pits," with a reputation for being haunted.

Analysis

O'Neal and *Iverson* simply did not prove equal to the task of combat leadership on July 1. Neither general advanced with his men. *O'Neal* hit Baxter's regiments head-on instead of on the flank; *Iverson*, upon seeing the white handkerchiefs waving in the air, reported to *Rodes* that one of his regiments had "gone over to the enemy"—a remark he would later regret. *Rodes* must also bear some of the responsibility for what happened, for he chose *O'Neal* and *Iverson* to spearhead his assault. He appeared unaware of the precise position and strength of Baxter's command, and he blundered in detaching the *5th Alabama* from *O'Neal*. Baxter conducted his defense ably and took advantage of enemy errors to drive off an attack on a potentially vulnerable position.

STOP 5c   1:00–3:00 P.M.

The XI Corps Deploys

Directions

Retrace your steps to Doubleday Avenue, then cross it. You may choose to view the terrain from the observation tower or in front of the parking lot. In either case, face east toward the valley north of the town of Gettysburg.

Orientation

In front of you is the ground that two divisions of the XI Corps defended on the afternoon of July 1. As you look due east across Mummasburg Road, you will see a car dealership adjacent to a north-south road–Carlisle Road (PA 34). Beyond that, slightly to the left, you will notice a small hill where a park road does a hairpin turn by a small grove of trees. That is Barlow Knoll (then known as Blocher's Knoll). To your right, at the base of Oak Ridge, just south of Mummasburg Road, is Gettysburg College. Several campus buildings stood at the time of the battle to house the students and faculty of what was known in 1863 as Pennsylvania College; most of the playing field plainly visible to you belonged to area farmers. Locate a tower on campus made of red brick topped with a charcoal cone. To the left of that tower is Culp's Hill: you may be able to make out the observation tower on it. To the right of the college tower is Cemetery Hill, marked by a light green water tower. The town of Gettysburg lies beyond the college to the southeast.

What Happened

On the morning of July 1, Buford sent Devin's cavalry brigade north of Gettysburg to watch for Confederate infantry advancing from the north (to your left). They made contact with the advance elements of *Ewell's* corps. Armed with this information, Howard, who had previously intended simply to extend the I Corps's line northward along Oak Ridge, deployed two divisions at right angles to Robinson's position. They were in position by 2:00 P.M., just before *Rodes* commenced his attack. On Howard's left Brig. Gen. Alexander

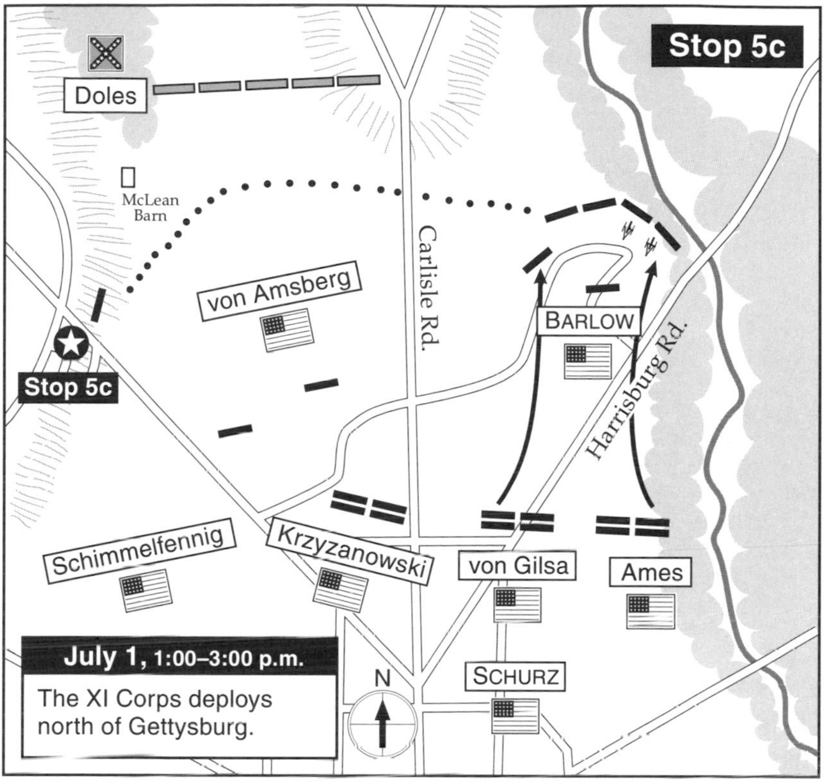

Stop 5c

Doles

McLean
Barn

von Amsberg

Carlisle Rd.

BARLOW

Harrisburg Rd.

Stop 5c

Schimmelfennig

Krzyzanowski

von Gilsa

Ames

SCHURZ

July 1, 1:00–3:00 p.m.

The XI Corps deploys
north of Gettysburg.

N

Schimmelfennig, who had just assumed command of Carl
Schurz's division (Schurz had taken over Howard's XI Corps;
Howard had replaced Reynolds as commander of the left
wing of the Union army), strung out three regiments of skirmishers in a semicircle running from the tree line to the east
of the McLean Farm to the Carlisle Road to the north (left) of
where the car dealership now stands. He placed two other
regiments and his artillery along the line marked by the park
road called Howard Avenue, between Mummasburg Road
and Carlisle Road; a second brigade remained in reserve
south of this line along Carlisle Road, along the northern
fringe of present-day Gettysburg. To the north of Carlisle
Road Francis C. Barlow initially deployed his division along a
road leading to an almshouse off of Harrisburg Road.

Analysis   Although Howard was aware of Ewell's approach, he did not
explicitly call for reinforcements from the III Corps until
1:30 P.M.; 90 minutes later he made the same request of the
XII Corps. III Corps commander Maj. Gen. Daniel E. Sickles,
confronted with conflicting orders from Meade that called
on him to stay in place at Emmitsburg, Maryland, eventually
ordered two-thirds of his command forward, but his men

would not arrive for some time. XII Corps chief Maj. Gen. Henry W. Slocum remained at Two Taverns, some five miles southeast of Gettysburg, within sound of the battle, and displayed a lack of aggressiveness that even some of his men found questionable. This meant that the I and XI Corps were basically on their own for the rest of the day. Moreover, although the I Corps found itself in possession of some useful defensive terrain, the XI Corps did not have such luck. The ridges in this area run north and south, but the two divisions of the XI Corps had to deploy from east to west, in an area where the road network from the north converged as it approached Gettysburg. *Ewell's* men were making their way south along those roads, the XI Corps would eventually find itself outnumbered and outflanked, not so much by Confederate generalship as by the design of the road network. As *Doles's* brigade came into view, however, Barlow looked for better ground on which to anchor his division and thus advanced from the almshouse line to the knoll that now bears his name.

Pennsylvania College, Gettysburg. From a photograph. 3:267

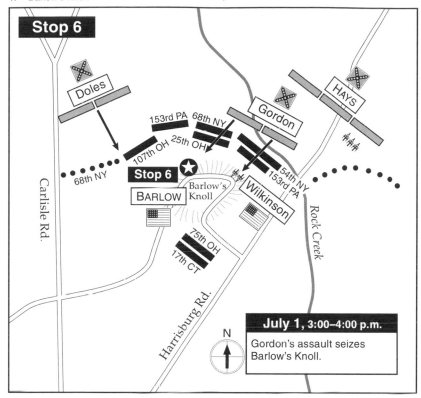

STOP 6

Barlow's Knoll 3:00–4:00 P.M.

Directions

Return to your vehicle. Exit the parking lot and take the short winding road (ROBINSON AVENUE) to MUMMASBURG ROAD. *Turn right. Cross* the railroad tracks (not present at the time of the battle) and *turn left* onto HOWARD AVENUE. *Cross* CARLISLE ROAD and *continue* to Barlow's Knoll, just over 1.2 miles from the Oak Ridge parking lot. Pull to the side of the road, park your car, and walk to the base of the bronze statue of a bareheaded Union officer with field glasses in his left hand–Francis Barlow. At the base of the statue, face west, looking back across toward Oak Ridge.

Orientation

As you face west, the town of Gettysburg is due left of you; Oak Ridge and Oak Hill are straight ahead, as is Carlisle Road in the middle distance.

What Happened

You will notice that Barlow is facing westward (as is the bugler atop the monument to the right, which marks the stand of the 153rd Pennsylvania). The only enemy unit in their view was *Doles's* brigade of Georgians on the eastern slope of Oak Ridge and perhaps members of *O'Neal's* brigade. Had that been the only enemy force in the vicinity, Barlow's decision to seize the knoll and face his command westward would have made sense.

Communications among Union commanders must have been seriously flawed, however. Buford had warned Howard of *Ewell's* advance from the north; in turn, Howard had warned Schurz, temporarily in command of the XI Corps, of the imminent threat to the Union right. Barlow's dispositions, detailed below, suggest that he was not totally unaware of *Early's* approach, although they also imply that he gave that information insufficient attention.

Directions   Turn to your right (north), cross Howard Avenue, and walk to the left of the artillery battery at the bend in the road. Face roughly northeast in the direction the cannon points.

What Happened   On the morning of July 1, Devin's brigade shifted north of Gettysburg to patrol the roads leading to town. Skirmishers engaged the Confederate advance that afternoon along Heidlersburg Road (now Harrisburg Road [Business U.S. 15], which you can see if you look eastward to your right), as Jubal *Early's* division made its way toward Gettysburg. Later in the day Devin pulled back; his efforts to shield Barlow's right were negated when his men came under friendly artillery fire from Cemetery Hill, driving them away. Although Barlow detached several companies of the 17th Connecticut to serve as skirmishers along Heidlersburg Road north of Rock Creek, they arrived too late to give him adequate advance notice. Thus the first time Barlow would know of *Early's* arrival for certain was when he came under attack.

The nature of the terrain to the north of the knoll also aided the Confederates. Woods stretched from just north of the knoll to Rock Creek, effectively shielding *Early's* column from observation from the knoll. As a result, *Early* unlimbered his artillery just north of the creek, from where they could pour a devastating flank fire into Union ranks. At the same time, a brigade of 1,200 Georgians under the command of Brig. Gen. John B. *Gordon* made their way across Rock Creek and used the woods to conceal their advance. Barlow, fixated on *Doles's* brigade as it crossed Carlisle Road and made its way forward, never knew what hit him. After a sharp firefight, *Gordon's* men finally overran the knoll. "We had a hard time moving them," recalled one Georgia private. A counterattack failed; Barlow fell, wounded; the XI Corps began to break. A valiant effort to establish a second line of defense in the fields north of town proved abortive when *Early's* other brigades, moving east of Heidlersburg Road, outflanked it.

It did not take long for the Union position along Oak Ridge to crumble as the three remaining brigades of *Rodes's* division pushed back both Schurz's and Robinson's divisions. Recall the marker on Oak Ridge locating the stand of the 16th Maine. Ordered to defend the apex of the Union line, it suffered tremendous losses as it bought time for other units to withdraw. Elsewhere the news was no better for Federal forces; to the south Rowley's division gave way, forcing the Iron Brigade to abandon McPherson's Woods. After establishing a temporary line along Seminary Ridge, the I Corps began to withdraw under pressure from Confederate attackers. After some seven hours of fighting, the Confederates had won the field.

Vignette

Many accounts of Gettysburg (including a marker in this area and an exhibit at the Cyclorama Center) record that *Gordon* came upon the wounded Barlow, offered him water, and promised to convey his dying thoughts to his wife. Barlow survived: according to the story, the two men, each believing the other had been killed in combat, encountered each other years later in the halls of Congress.

It makes a good story, drawn entirely from *Gordon's* imaginative mind, but it is not accurate. Barlow never mentioned encountering *Gordon*; other details, especially *Gordon's* description of how Barlow's wife, Arabella, a nurse with the U.S. Sanitary Commission, made her way to her husband's side, do not mesh with other accounts. In light of the postwar political prominence of both Barlow and *Gordon*, it stretches credulity to think that each man thought the other dead.

More compelling is the story associated with Lt. Bayard Wilkinson, who commanded the battery of Union artillery (Battery G, 4th U.S.) represented by the four cannon on the knoll. Wilkinson was only 19 years old when he took his men into action on July 1. Mounted, he came under fire from the Confederate cannon north of Rock Creek. One shell nearly tore off his right leg. He took out a pocket knife and amputated what remained of the limb. That night he died at the almshouse south of Barlow's Knoll moments after passing a canteen to another wounded soldier. Wilkinson's father, Samuel, was a reporter for the *New York Times*; when he heard of his son's death, he remarked that his battery "should never have been sent" to the knoll.

Analysis

Barlow's decision to post his right flank on this knoll is a good example of the need to evaluate the usefulness of terrain in the context of the larger situation. It might seem logical to want to seize high ground whenever possible, but in this case Barlow's initiative proved a mistake. His advance caused Schurz to realign his entire position so the two divisions could maintain contact. They thus came under artillery fire from the cannon stationed just north of Rock Creek. Although Union cavalry previously had reported *Early's* approach, Barlow did not take that information into account; in turn, *Gordon* used the woods north of the knoll to shield his advance from view, enabling him to approach the knoll without coming under fire. In later years, Barlow would defend his decision, argue that *Gordon* did not outflank him, and blame his soldiers for giving way–a most damaging charge, as the brigade posted on this knoll, under the command of Col. Leopold von Gilsa, had crumbled under the impact of Stonewall *Jackson's* flank attack at Chancellorsville on May 2. In light of the Georgia private's observation that the Federals conducted an orderly retreat and that they were "harder to drive than we had ever known them before," Barlow's charge rings false, failing to conceal his own responsibility for what happened that afternoon. In truth, the converging columns of *Early's* division with its superior numbers meant that sooner or later the XI Corps would have to retreat south.

Lieutenant Bayard Wilkeson holding his battery (G, 4th U.S. Artillery) to its work in an exposed position. 3:280

STOP 7   Benner's Hill   July 1–2

Directions   Return to your car. *Continue* on HOWARD AVENUE to the inter-
                      section with HARRISBURG ROAD (Business U.S. 15) and *turn
                      right.* Nearly 0.5 mile down the road, Harrisburg Road swings
                      to the right and becomes LINCOLN STREET. Immediately af-
                      ter this point, *turn left* onto STRATTON STREET. *Proceed* four
                      blocks to YORK STREET (PA 116) and *turn left.* (York Street soon
                      becomes HANOVER ROAD, but continue straight on.) *Drive*
                      0.9 mile to the turnoff for BENNER'S HILL and *turn right.* A
                      National Park Service sign will alert you to the turnoff, but
                      be sharp: the road to Benner's Hill comes up quickly, and
                      there is high-speed traffic on Hanover Road. Once you have
                      made the turn, *drive* to a point between the first two cannon
                      markers (Rockbridge Artillery and Chesapeake Artillery) and
                      pull over.

                      En route you may wish to take a short side trip to COSTER
                      AVENUE. Two blocks south of LINCOLN STREET on STRATTON
                      STREET, *turn left* and park your vehicle. In July 1863 this area
                      lay at the northern edge of Gettysburg and was the site of a
                      large brickyard. A Union brigade under Coster fought a spir-
                      ited rear-guard action here against *Early's* advancing Confed-
                      erates. Over the years this part of the battlefield was nearly
                      swallowed by urban growth and largely forgotten; in 1988 a
                      mural commemorating the fighting here was unveiled.

Major General Francis C. Barlow.
From a photograph. 4:218

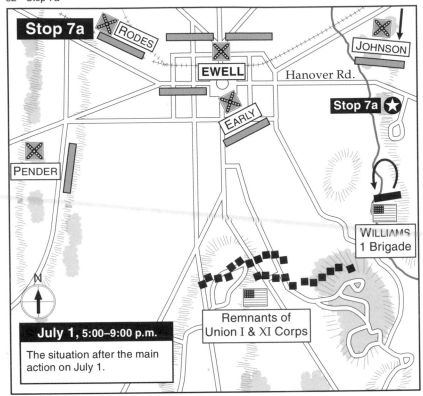

Stop 7a

RODES

JOHNSON

EWELL

Hanover Rd.

Stop 7a ★

EARLY

PENDER

WILLIAMS
1 Brigade

N

July 1, 5:00–9:00 p.m.

The situation after the main
action on July 1.

Remnants of
Union I & XI Corps

STOP 7a

July 1, 5:00–9:00 P.M.

A Lost Opportunity?

Directions

Exit your car and face in the same direction the cannon are
pointed (southwest).

Orientation

You are standing on Benner's Hill (100 feet above its base). To
your left front, and about 1,100 yards distant, is Culp's Hill
(140 feet). Culp's Hill is surmounted by a National Park Service observation tower, which will confirm its identification.
To the right, distant about 1 mile, is Cemetery Hill (60 to 80
feet above its base), distinguishable by the brick gatehouse to
Evergreen Cemetery and by the modern water tower just to
the right of the hill. The town of Gettysburg is visible still farther to the right. The cannon here did not play a role in the
first day's battle.

What Happened

Benner's Hill affords a good place to consider the situation at
the end of the first day. By 4:30 P.M. the Union lines north
and west of Gettysburg had collapsed and the Federals were
retreating through the town. Although this retreat was not a

panicked rout, the necessary movement through the narrow town streets resulted in much confusion and loss of unit cohesion. The town became a bottleneck in which hundreds of Northern troops fell captive to pursuing Confederates before they could make it to safety.

One of the greatest "might have beens" of Gettysburg centers on this stage of the battle. As the Union lines collapsed, *Lee*–then on Seminary Ridge just west of Gettysburg–debated the possibility of seizing the heights south of the town. The troops from *Hill's* corps and *Rodes's* division were "weakened and exhausted by a long and bloody struggle," *Lee* thought; if any Confederate troops were in condition to make such an assault, they belonged to *Ewell's* divisions under *Early* and Maj. Gen. Edward *Johnson*. *Lee* therefore sent a message to *Ewell* asking him to consider an attack on Cemetery Hill. The order was transmitted verbally and its exact wording remains in some dispute, but it seems fair to use *Lee's* words in his official report: "General Ewell was instructed to carry the hill occupied by the enemy [Cemetery Hill] if he found it practicable, but to avoid a general engagement until the arrival of the other divisions of the army which were ordered to hasten forward."

Ewell elected not to attack. In reaction to the *Second Corps* commander's hesitation, a former member of Stonewall *Jackson's* staff is supposed to have said, "Oh, for the presence and inspiration of Old Jack for just one hour!" Generations of Southern writers have endorsed this sentiment. To them, *Ewell's* choice betrayed a fatal timidity that may have cost the Confederacy its independence.

Analysis

Why did *Ewell* make this decision? When the order reached him, he was in the Gettysburg town square. Soon afterward he conferred there with *Early* and *Rodes*; accompanied by their staffs, the three generals rode south to the vicinity of Baltimore and High Streets, debating all the while the merits of renewing offensive action. From their advanced position, they could see that Federal troops occupied Cemetery Hill in some strength: indeed, they came under fire and had to retreat to the cover of a nearby alley. At about this time an officer on *Ewell's* staff, who had visited *Lee*, returned with word that although *Lee* had given permission for an attack, *Ewell* could count on little assistance from *Hill's* corps and none from *Longstreet's*.

Ewell believed an attack through the town against Cemetery Hill would be disastrous–the troops, channeled by the city streets, would present massed targets to the Union defenders. The assault would have to be made either southwest of the town, where there were no good positions for artillery support, or east of the town, which would require a considerable march by the attacking troops simply to reach their jump-off point. Further, he knew that *Rodes's* division had lost 30 percent of its strength in the fighting around Oak Ridge and that only two brigades from *Early's* division were near enough to attack immediately.

Although an attack on Cemetery Hill might be impractical, another possibility was to seize Culp's Hill. *Ewell* considered this option as well. His third division, under *Johnson*, reached Gettysburg about 6:00 P.M. and received orders to take the hill if it was found to be unoccupied. A staff officer sent to scout the hill believed (incorrectly) that it was. But in any event, darkness fell before *Johnson's* division could reach Culp's Hill. It went into bivouac for the night about 700 yards north of where you are standing.

An awkward position, a dearth of available troops, the unlikelihood of support from A. P. *Hill*, and the approach of night all contributed to *Ewell's* decision not to attack—a decision that seems to have been made more by default than anything else. In addition, *Ewell* had received vague reports of Union troops on York Pike to the northeast. Although no record survives, it is possible that he also heard of Union troops on Hanover Road. A Union brigade approached within 300 yards of Benner's Hill early in the evening, until reports of the retreat of the I and XI Corps led to its swift withdrawal.

Would an attack have succeeded? With the benefit of hindsight, we know that a Union brigade (from Brig. Gen. Adolph von Steinwehr's division of the XI Corps) had occupied Cemetery Hill all day. Unlike the Confederate attackers, it was fresh and unbloodied. Surviving units from the I and XI Corps were on the hill as well, and the Iron Brigade had occupied the western slope of Culp's Hill. The Federals enjoyed adequate artillery support, something the Confederates would not have had. The best answer, then, is that an evening attack would have ended in the same sort of bloody reversal as had befallen *Archer*, *Davis*, and *Iverson*.

STOP 7b	July 1, 5:00–9:00 P.M.

Lee Plans to Renew the Battle

Directions	Remain in place.
What Happened	Around 5 P.M. *Lee* was joined on Seminary Ridge by *Longstreet*, his *First Corps* commander and chief lieutenant. As *Longstreet*

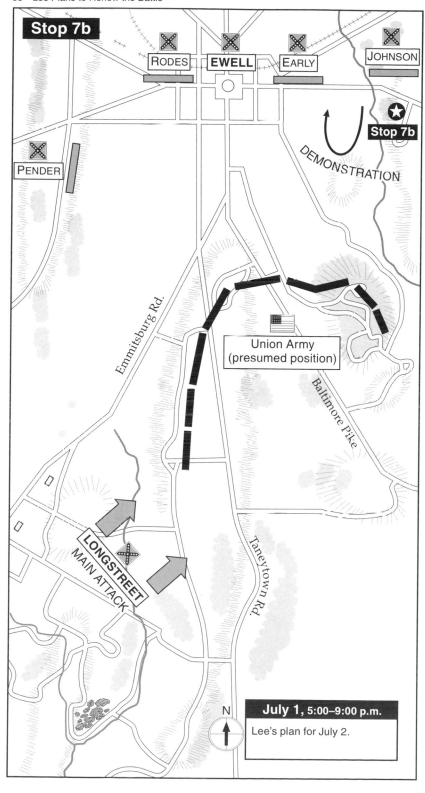

Stop 7b

RODES **EWELL** EARLY JOHNSON

★ Stop 7b

PENDER

DEMONSTRATION

Emmitsburg Rd.

Union Army
(presumed position)

Baltimore Pike

LONGSTREET
MAIN ATTACK

Taneytown Rd.

N

July 1, 5:00–9:00 p.m.

Lee's plan for July 2.

recalled the meeting, he examined the Union position on Cemetery Hill for five or ten minutes, then urged *Lee* not to attack the position directly. Instead, *Longstreet* argued, the Confederate army should try to get far around the Union left and lunge eastward so as to place itself between the Union army and Washington. That, in turn, might well force the Union army to attack the Confederates on favorable ground. *Lee*, however, rejected the idea. Pointing at Cemetery Hill, he said, "If the enemy is there tomorrow, we must attack him."

Analysis

In his report on Gettysburg, *Lee* made it seem as if he had no choice but to continue the offensive inadvertently begun on July 1. "It had not been intended to deliver a general battle so far from our base unless attacked, but coming unexpectedly upon the whole Federal army, to withdraw through the mountains with our extensive trains would have been difficult and dangerous. At the same time we were unable to await an attack, as the country was unfavorable for collecting supplies in the presence of the enemy, who would restrain our foraging parties by holding the mountain passes with local and other troops. A battle had, therefore, become in a measure unavoidable, and the success gained gave hope of a favorable issue."

But how best to renew the fighting? After discussing the situation with *Longstreet*, *Lee* next visited *Ewell* at *Second Corps* headquarters sometime after sunset. *Lee* asked whether the *Second Corps* could attack Cemetery Hill at daybreak. Division commander Jubal A. *Early* piped up and opined that such an attack would be highly problematic because of the steep slope of the hill. *Lee* then inquired about the possibility of withdrawing the *Second Corps* from its advanced position, since unless it was used as a springboard for attack the position simply attenuated the Confederate line with little compensating advantage. *Early* suggested that such a withdrawal would be bad for morale and would also require the abandonment of hundreds of wounded soldiers in the town of Gettysburg.

The discussion quickly turned to the possibility of attacking the Union left flank on Cemetery Ridge, as well as seizing two high hills (the Round Tops) that commanded the Union position from the south. Eventually this proposal crystallized into an assault made the next day by two divisions from *Longstreet's* corps, joined by a third division from A. P. *Hill's* corps (see stop 8).

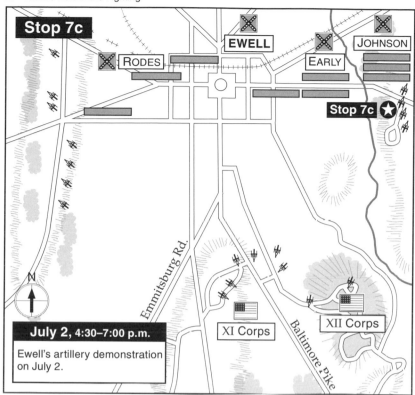

Stop 7c

EWELL

JOHNSON

RODES

EARLY

Stop 7c ★

N

July 2, 4:30–7:00 p.m.

Ewell's artillery demonstration
on July 2.

Emmitsburg Rd.

XI Corps

XII Corps

Baltimore Pike

STOP 7c   July 2, 4:30–7:00 P.M.

Ewell's Role in the Fighting

Directions   Remain in place.

What Happened   Lee's orders for July 2 called for *Longstreet* to make the main
attack. A. P. *Hill* would send one of his divisions in support
and use his other two divisions to threaten the enemy forces
in front of him and pin them in place. As soon as *Longstreet's*
attack got under way, *Ewell* was supposed to make a "demonstration" against the Union right at Cemetery and Culp's
Hills, "to be converted into a real attack if opportunity
should offer."

Although *Ewell* has sometimes been criticized for overly
passive conduct on July 2, in fact he did exactly as *Lee* ordered. A "demonstration" is, in effect, a mock attack not re-
quiring contact with the enemy. Although it can be made by
infantry, it need not be, and *Ewell* chose to make his demonstration with artillery. Since infantry attacks are usually preceded by an artillery bombardment, it was as good a way as
any to threaten the Federals on the Union right without risk

of significant casualties. Early on the morning of July 2, Confederate artillery batteries began arriving on Benner's Hill. By midafternoon, 24 guns and their crews occupied positions from north of Hanover Road to the end of the paved road you came in on. As soon as *Longstreet's* attack began, these cannon opened fire. Union artillery on Cemetery Hill replied at once, and soon, in the words of one Confederate artillerist, "Benner's Hill was simply a hell infernal" as solid shot ripped the ground and shells exploded overhead.

Vignette

A Federal lieutenant on East Cemetery Hill described the bombardment in a letter home: "One man had a piece of his head knocked off, all the flesh between his shoulder and neck taken away, and his right hand almost knocked off, he was still living when we left Gettysburg. He was a terrible sight when first struck, and when I had him carried to the rear, it almost turned my stomach, which is something that, as yet, has never been done. . . . I had one very narrow escape from a shell. One of the gunners, who saw the flash of one of the rebel guns, hallowed to me to 'look out, one's coming,' and I had just time to get behind a tree before the shell exploded within a foot of where I had been standing."

Lieutenant General
Richard S. Ewell, C.S.A.
From a photograph.
1:251

Overview of the Second Day, July 2

During the night of July 1 both armies began to concentrate their forces around Gettysburg. The Army of the Potomac held a line, often compared to a fishhook, that began at Culp's Hill (the barb), swung around Cemetery Hill to the northwest (the hook), then stretched south along Cemetery Ridge to Little Round Top. By midmorning on July 2, Henry W. Slocum's XII Corps held Culp's Hill; what remained of the XI Corps defended Cemetery Hill; Maj. Gen. Winfield Scott Hancock's II Corps deployed along Cemetery Ridge; Daniel E. Sickles's III Corps was responsible for the area from the southern end of that ridge to Little Round Top, which had first been occupied by a division of the XII Corps. The three divisions of the I Corps, now under Maj. Gen. John Newton, were distributed between Culp's Hill and Cemetery Ridge. The V Corps, commanded by Maj. Gen. George Sykes, remained in reserve; Maj. Gen. John Sedgwick's VI Corps would not arrive until midafternoon. Meade established his headquarters at a small farmhouse on Taneytown Road due south of Cemetery Hill.

Robert E. *Lee's Army of Northern Virginia* occupied a position roughly flanking the town of Gettysburg to the east and west. Richard S. *Ewell's Second Corps* held a line from Gettysburg east to Benner's Hill, thus threatening both Culp's Hill and Cemetery Hill; Ambrose P. *Hill's Third Corps* gathered west of town, while two divisions of James *Longstreet's First Corps* remained west of the seminary by Herr Ridge. Approaching the field was *Longstreet's* third division, under the command of Maj. Gen. George E. *Pickett*, as well as several other detached brigades and—at long last—Jeb *Stuart's* horsemen. *Lee* used the seminary as a vantage point from which to evaluate the Union position.

A Confederate reconnaissance of the Union position on south Cemetery Ridge and the Round Tops reported the latter uncovered and the former vulnerable to attack. Acting on this information, *Lee* decided to replicate his Chancellorsville plan of marching part of his army under cover to a point from which they could deliver a crushing assault on the Union flank. He assigned *Longstreet* to this task; *Longstreet* was to deploy his two divisions astride Emmitsburg Road and launch an attack *en échelon*, committing one brigade at a time in a sequence moving from right (east) to left (west). At the same time, *Ewell* was to threaten Culp's Hill to distract Meade (stop 7c). But *Longstreet's* divisions did not reach their positions along Warfield Ridge and Pitzer's Woods until midafternoon—which in later years sparked much controversy over who or what was responsible for such a seemingly long delay in deployment (stop 9).

Meanwhile, Daniel E. Sickles, learning of a brief engagement between Col. Hiram Berdan's sharpshooters and a Confederate force north of Pitzer's Woods (stop 8), decided to move his corps westward. In so doing, he replicated his previous halfhearted advance against the rear of Stonewall *Jackson's* flanking column at Chancellorsville: he was concerned lest *Lee* attempt the same sort of maneuver to strike at the III Corps. Although Berdan had in fact battled portions of *Hill's Third Corps*, Sickles had nevertheless arrived, however fortuitously, at a promising assessment of *Lee's* plans; his reaction to that conclusion proved far more debatable. By midafternoon, one of Sickles's divisions stretched north along Emmitsburg Road from a peach orchard; the other, with the aid of massed artillery, attempted to cover the sector from the orchard east to the foot of Little Round Top, leaving the hill itself unoccupied by combat forces. In later years, Sickles, speaking with the clarity afforded by hindsight, claimed that he had forced Meade to remain on the field by inviting an attack and that the position of his corps disrupted *Lee's* plans (stop 9, stop 14b vignette, stop 15a). The former assertion is fiction; the latter one is, in a sense, true, although *Lee's* plan was based on a misappraisal of the position of Union forces long before Sickles acted.

As *Longstreet's* divisions, after having to countermarch to avoid detection from a Union signal station on Little Round Top, reached their jumping-off point, they discovered that the Federals occupied the Peach Orchard (stop 9). This forced them to alter their alignment before attacking; at the same time, division commander John Bell *Hood* pushed for yet another change of plan in order to strike directly at Little Round Top (stop 10a). *Longstreet*, aware that *Lee*, who had rejected earlier alternatives, was growing impatient, rejected the proposal and ordered the attack to commence (stop 10b). What followed did not correspond to any battle plan laid out by either army commander. Two of *Hood's* brigades (under Brig. Gen. Evander M. *Law* and Brig. Gen. Jerome B. *Robertson*) swept all the way across the western slope of Big Round Top; only the timely reaction of several Union officers and two brigades saved Little Round Top (stop 11). A third brigade (Brig. Gen. Henry L. *Benning*) joined with several of *Robertson's* regiments to crack the left end of the III Corps at Devil's Den and Houck's Ridge (stop 12), while a fourth (Brig. Gen. George T. *Anderson*) advanced with two of Maj. Gen. Lafayette *McLaws's* brigades to attack the Wheatfield, which changed hands several times in fierce and confused fighting (stop 13 and Wheatfield Excursion). *McLaws's* remaining two brigades overran the apex of Sickles's line at the Peach Orchard (stop 14) and pursued the defeated Federals past the Trostle Farm (stop 15). Sickles's redeployment shattered his corps; his men paid the price for his alleged genius.

Meade and his subordinates responded to *Longstreet's* assault by shifting the V Corps and parts of the II Corps to Little Round Top and the Wheatfield, thereby denuding South Cemetery Ridge of troops and rendering it vulnerable to *McLaws's* breakthrough. Hancock assembled forces to plug the gap (stop 16a) as dusk came. To the north, along Cemetery Ridge, an assault by parts of Maj. Gen. Richard H. *Anderson's* division of the *Third Corps* fell short of piercing the Union center along Cemetery Ridge (stop 16b). In detaching parts of the XII Corps to shore up the Union left, however, Meade had weakened his right along Culp's Hill; late in the afternoon *Ewell* set his men in motion, capturing part of the vacated Union line (stops 17a and 17b) but failing to drive the Federals off the hill (stop 18). An attack against Cemetery Hill also ultimately failed (stop 19). By night Meade had solidified his position; the arrival of the VI Corps gave him a powerful reserve. Nevertheless, it had been a bloody day – the most costly of the battle – and the Army of the Potomac had barely held on in several cases. Although the implementation of *Lee's* plan had failed to achieve what the Confederate commander had desired, his army had delivered several punishing blows. Meade would stay in place; *Lee* planned to attack again the next day.

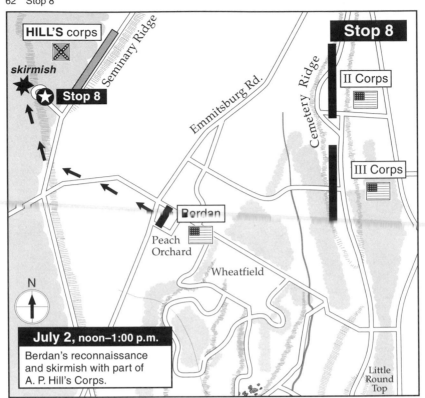

STOP 8

Berdan's Loop   noon – 1:00 P.M.

Directions

Return to your vehicle and reset your trip odometer. Leaving Benner's Hill, *turn left* onto HANOVER STREET. Be careful: this intersection has several blind spots. *Drive west* just over a half mile, *turn left* onto SOUTH FOURTH STREET, then *right* onto EAST MIDDLE STREET. To your left is Culp's Hill. *Drive* through town until you reach WEST CONFEDERATE AVENUE (1.75 miles). *Turn left.* About a half mile after you pass the Virginia Monument you will see a road to your right (3.5 miles) – the Berdan Loop. *Turn right*, follow the road to the loop at the end, then pull over. You need not exit your vehicle.

En route you will encounter three Confederate headquarters sites. Almost immediately after turning onto Hanover Street you will spot a cannon barrel that marks the spot of *Ewell's* headquarters. As you drive south along West Confederate Avenue you will pass a marker noting the location of *Third Corps* commander A. P. *Hill's* headquarters (2.6 miles) and the Virginia Monument (2.9 miles) topped by a statue of Robert E. *Lee* – where *Lee* established temporary headquarters on July 3. *Lee* had formally established headquarters in the vicinity of the junction of Chambersburg Pike and Seminary Avenue late in the afternoon of July 1.

What Happened At about noon on July 2, Maj. Gen. Daniel Sickles, in charge of the III Corps, authorized a reconnaissance of the woods west of Emmitsburg Road. Col. Hiram Berdan led four companies of sharpshooters and the 3rd Maine– some 300 men in all–forward to the area south of here, then swept north through these woods. Here they encountered Confederates from *Hill's* corps. After a sharp, short firefight, Berdan withdrew. When reports of the skirmish reached Sickles, the general decided to redeploy his corps westward from Cemetery Ridge.

General Lee's headquarters on the Chambersburg Pike. From a wartime photograph. 3:270

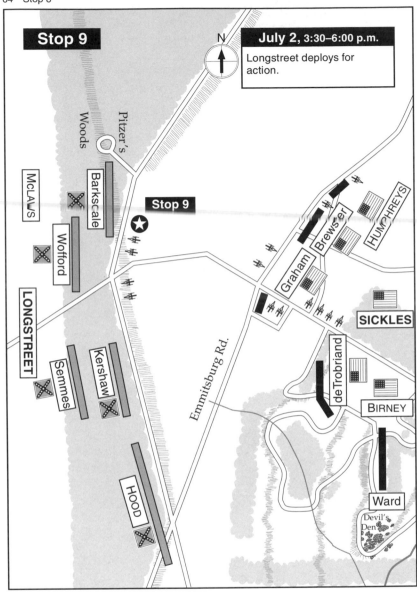

Stop 9

N

July 2, 3:30–6:00 p.m.
Longstreet deploys for action.

Woods

Pitzer's

McLAWS

Barkscale

Stop 9

Wofford

HUMPHREYS

Brewster

Graham

LONGSTREET

Semmes

Kershaw

Emmitsburg Rd.

SICKLES

de Trobriand

BIRNEY

HOOD

Ward

Devil's
Den

STOP 9   Pitzer's Woods   3:30–6:00 P.M.

Directions

Return to WEST CONFEDERATE AVENUE, *turn right*, and *continue* driving south. Pull off to the shoulder just short of 4 miles on your odometer. Exit your vehicle and cross the street. Ahead of you are two state monuments: Louisiana (left) and Mississippi (right). Walk to the benches in front of the Louisiana Monument and face east.

Orientation

You are just east of Pitzer's Woods, where Lafayette *McLaws's* division of James *Longstreet's First Corps* formed on the afternoon of July 2. Locate the Cyclorama Center to your left, distinguished by the large white cylinder that houses the famed painting by Paul Philippoteaux. It marks the center of the Union position. To the right in the distance is the white dome of the Pennsylvania Monument, topped by a statue. As you face due east, Emmitsburg Road crosses your line of vision some 550 yards away; follow it as it runs along the west edge of the Peach Orchard. Beyond the Peach Orchard and to the right (southeast) is a rocky hill marked by several monuments – Little Round Top. Finally, as you look to your far right, you will see a clearing where a road from the Peach Orchard, bounded by a white picket fence, passes by a white farmhouse belonging to the Snyder family before intersecting with West Confederate Avenue; beyond that you can see an observation tower, hereafter known as Longstreet's Tower.

What Happened

On the morning of July 2 *Lee* ordered *Longstreet* to march the divisions of *Hood* and *McLaws* southward in preparation for an attack against the Union left, which he supposed was located in the vicinity of where the Pennsylvania Monument now stands. *Longstreet* countered by suggesting that he take his men around the south end of the Army of the Potomac and force the enemy to evacuate his position and attack the Confederates. *Lee*, encouraged by reconnaissance reports that there were no Union forces from the Peach Orchard east to the Round Tops, held to his original plan of attack, reminiscent of Stonewall *Jackson's* march and attack on the Union right flank at Chancellorsville exactly two months before. Using the woods and Seminary Ridge to conceal his movement, *Longstreet* was to position *Hood* and *McLaws* astride Emmitsburg Road and launch an attack *en echelon* – with each brigade advancing in a staggered sequence from right to left. Upon hearing of the opening of *Longstreet's* assault, *Ewell's* corps would launch a diversion against Cemetery and Culp's Hills to distract Union commanders and prevent them from sending reinforcements to the endangered left flank.

Longstreet's implementation of *Lee's* instructions proved controversial. Some observers have accused him of moving too slowly, perhaps as a silent protest against the operation. Others criticize his handling of the march itself. As the Confederate columns made their way southward, they came across a clearing visible to Union observers on Little Round Top. Although artillery commander Col. Edward Porter *Alexander* had located a short detour that would shield the Confederates from observation, *Longstreet* chose instead to retrace his steps in a time-consuming countermarch. It was not until midafternoon that his men reached this area and began to deploy in line from this location southward.

What *Longstreet* here encountered was not what he had anticipated—Union infantry and artillery in place in a line running south along Emmitsburg Road to a peach orchard and then eastward toward Little Round Top. These were the two divisions of Sickles's III Corps. Sickles had decided to redeploy his men from their original position that ran roughly from the Pennsylvania Monument to the northern base of Little Round Top because he believed that the strip of woods in front of him interfered with his fields of vision and fire. Reports of Berdan's encounter with Confederate soldiers in the fields north of Pitzer's Woods persuaded him to advance his line again, this time to Emmitsburg Road, hinging his center on the Peach Orchard. Brig. Gen. Andrew A. Humphreys deployed his division north of the orchard and east of Emmitsburg Road; Sickles's other division, commanded by Maj. Gen. David B. Birney, attempted to defend the area from the Peach Orchard to the base of Little Round Top. Meade was not consulted about the move and upon learning of it rode out to countermand Sickles's advance.

Both Meade and *Lee* encountered subordinates with minds of their own whose actions shaped the battle that followed, yet the army commanders contributed to the confusing state of affairs. *Lee's* plan of attack rested on a serious misapprehension of the location of enemy forces and assumed that Meade would make no adjustments for several hours despite the arrival of reinforcements. Meade, concerned about the possibility of a Confederate attack against Cemetery and Culp's Hills, did not devote sufficient time to his left. The removal of one of Buford's cavalry brigades from the area for rest and refitting deprived him of advance information about Confederate activities. Neither general planned what happened that afternoon.

If you look to the south toward the Mississippi Monument, you will see the area where Brig. Gen. William *Barksdale's* four Mississippi regiments deployed on July 2 on the left of *McLaws's* division. *Barksdale's* men soon came under fire from the Union batteries posted at the Peach Orchard but held their position in accordance with *Longstreet's* plan of attack. If you look to the left (north), you will see where Richard *Anderson's* division of A. P. *Hill's Third Corps* deployed in the area of the Berdan Loop with orders to assault the Union center once *McLaws* had engaged the enemy.

Lieutenant General James Longstreet. From a photograph. 3:254

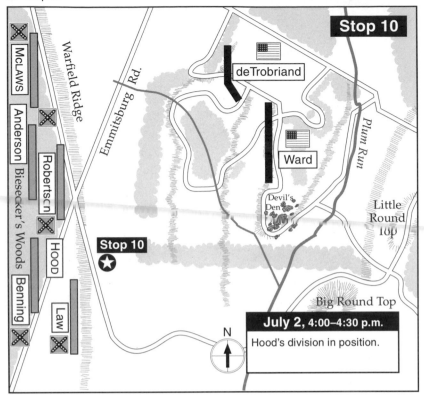

STOP 10   Warfield Ridge   4:00–4:30 P.M.

Directions   Return to your vehicle. Reset your odometer. *Continue south*
                     on WEST CONFEDERATE AVENUE, crossing the MILLERSTOWN
                     ROAD. On your left past the intersection you will see the
                     Longstreet observation tower; to the right a cannon barrel
                     marks *Longstreet's* headquarters. *McLaws's* other brigades de-
                     ployed in this area. *Continue south*, crossing EMMITSBURG ROAD
                     (U.S. 15) (0.75 mile); you are now on SOUTH CONFEDERATE AVE-
                     NUE. In this area *Hood* prepared his division for action. Pull
                     over just before the wooden park gates. You need not leave
                     your vehicle. Look to your left (east).

STOP 10a   4:00 P.M.

                     ***Hood's* Protest**

Orientation   You are on Warfield Ridge, near the extreme right of the Con-
                     federate line. Ahead you will see the wooded summit of Big
                     Round Top and the cleared western slope of Little Round Top
                     to its left (north). Nearer to you a gravel path leads to the
                     Bushman Farm. To your right is a pink granite marker noting

the location of Jerome *Robertson's* brigade, composed primarily of regiments from Texas; *Hood* had once commanded it.

What Happened

Just as *Hood's* lead brigade, under the command of Evander M. *Law*, was about to step off, Confederate scouts reported that Big Round Top was unoccupied. *Law* urged *Hood* to inform *Longstreet*: perhaps there was a chance to swing around the Union left after all. *Hood* agreed. But *Longstreet* refused to alter *Lee's* plan. Having lost his battle with *Lee* over how to proceed, he would not now defy his superior's orders.

Analysis

Law's plan was not as simple as one might think. He had called for the occupation of Round Top during the night of July 2, not a new way to inaugurate the afternoon attack. Commentators overlook this fact. It is doubtful that Little Round Top would have remained unoccupied; indeed, in the absence of an attack Meade might have been able to remedy Sickles's erroneous deployment. *Lee*, aware of the report, did not countermand his original orders.

STOP 10b

3:30–4:30 P.M.

The Alabamians Advance

Directions

Continue driving along SOUTH CONFEDERATE AVENUE. Just beyond the picnic area to your right is the Alabama Monument (1.1 miles). Pull over. You need not leave your vehicle. Look left (northeast).

Orientation

By now the sight of the Round Tops should be familiar to you. Much of the wooded terrain in front of you was clear ground at the time of the battle.

What Happened

Here *Law's* brigade of five Alabama regiments commenced the assault against the Union left on the afternoon of July 2. Eventually three of them would strike the southern slope of Little Round Top. Remember that this brigade had done a good deal of marching and countermarching–approximately 28 miles–to reach this position, much of it under a hot July sun; before the day was over those who survived the coming action would be exhausted.

STOP 11   Little Round Top   3:30–6:30 P.M.

Directions   *Continue driving* along SOUTH CONFEDERATE AVENUE as it makes
its way past the extreme right flank of the Confederate army
and winds up Big Round Top. Ignore the markers in this sector, which refer to the third day's cavalry action in this area.
You are following the general path of advance of *Law's* brigade across the western slope of Big Round Top. At the intersection of Warren, Wright, and Sykes Avenues, *continue
straight* onto SYKES AVENUE and ascend Little Round Top. Park
your car and walk to the sidewalk along the left side of the
road. Take the path at the northern edge of the parking lot to
the statue of a Union officer poised on top of a large rock.
Along the way you will notice a plaque on the side of another
rock that commemorates the activities of the Signal Corps at
Gettysburg.

STOP 11a   3:30–5:00 P.M.

Warren Takes Action

Directions   Face west (the statue faces westward).

Orientation   You are on the northern crest of Little Round Top. The statue
marks the position of Maj. Gen. Gouverneur K. Warren, chief
engineer of the Army of the Potomac. If you look due north
(right), you will see Cemetery Ridge, featuring the white
cylinder of the Cyclorama building; somewhat closer is the
Pennsylvania Monument. As you look west across the cleared
face of Little Round Top, you will see a valley bordered on the
west by a wooded ridge known as Houck's Ridge; the rocks on
the left (south) mark Devil's Den. Running through the valley
from north to south is Plum Run; the field itself would gain
the name of the Valley of Death after the day's action. The
wooded lot directly to your front about 420 yards away belonged to the Rose Farm; beyond it is an open area that after
the events of July 2 would become known simply as the
Wheatfield (although it was also part of the Rose Farm).
Along the north edge of the Wheatfield is Wheatfield Road
(then known as Millerstown Road); as you follow it westward
into the distance you will see the Peach Orchard and then
Pitzer's Woods. Longstreet's Tower is to the left along the
tree line.

What Happened When Sickles decided to deploy his corps along Emmitsburg Road, division commander David Birney stretched his
brigades from Devil's Den through Rose Woods to the Peach

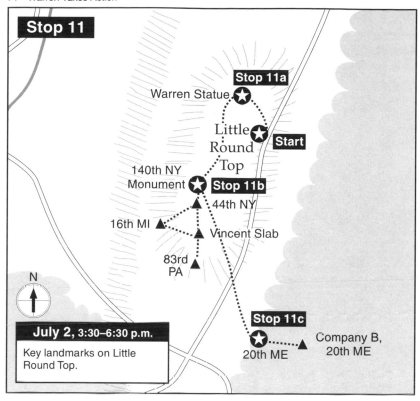

Stop 11

Stop 11a

Warren Statue

Little Round Top

Start

140th NY Monument

Stop 11b

44th NY

16th MI

Vincent Slab

83rd PA

N

Stop 11c

July 2, 3:30–6:30 p.m.

Key landmarks on Little Round Top.

Company B, 20th ME

20th ME

Orchard. This proved to be far too much ground for his men to defend; it also rendered Little Round Top vulnerable to attack by *Hood's* division. Only a signal station held the position.

Warren arrived on Little Round Top just as *Hood* was deploying to go into action. The area beyond Devil's Den leading to Warfield Ridge was much more open than it is now; it was not difficult to see the Confederates go into line. This significantly modifies the import of Warren's later account that he directed the commander of the artillery section to his front (two cannon belonging to Cap. James Smith, 4th Battery, New York Light Artillery, visible in the field due west) to fire a shot into the woods, then watched as the Confederates turned, the sun's reflection on their rifle barrels giving away their position, for this incident (if it did in fact happen) at best confirmed what should have been apparent.

Warren immediately dispatched several staff officers who sought out Meade, Sickles, and V Corps commander George Sykes to request reinforcements to hold Little Round Top. Eventually, two brigades from the V Corps came to the rescue. Col. Strong Vincent's brigade was in the vicinity of Wheatfield Road where Plum Run crosses it, when its commander, learning of Warren's request from one of Sykes's staff officers, ordered his four regiments to take position along the southern face of Little Round Top. The brigade marched eastward along Wheatfield Road, then southward across the eastern (and wooded) face of Little Round Top, its line of advance along a logging trail roughly parallel to the park road you used to get here.

Warren could hear the noise of battle on the south slope, but he could see little if any of Vincent's position, which was in the woods south of the castle at the southern edge of the crest (you can envision Warren's difficulty by looking southward to your left from this spot). Still anxious, he welcomed the arrival of Capt. Charles Hazlett, who promised to place his battery on the summit; while talking with him, Warren was slightly wounded in the neck. Warren then rode down the north slope of Little Round Top and fortuitously intercepted his former brigade, now commanded by Brig. Gen. Stephen H. Weed, which was on its way westward along Wheatfield Road to reinforce the III Corps. He convinced Col. Patrick O'Rorke to take his regiment, the 140th New York, to Little Round Top. Later, the other three regiments of Weed's brigade (the 146th New York and the 91st and 155th Pennsylvania) deployed along the crest in this area, facing westward. As dusk came, Confederate forces, having taking the Wheatfield, approached the northwest slope of Little Round Top (to your left), only to be driven away by Brig. Gen. Samuel Crawford's Pennsylvania Reserves.

Analysis

The quickness of the Union response to protect Little Round Top was owing to the initiative of four men: Warren, Vincent, Hazlett, and O'Rorke. Although the Signal Corps flagmen may have spotted Confederates in the area, it seems that before Warren's arrival their warnings were not heeded. O'Rorke's arrival was especially fortuitous. Had he not known Warren personally, it is less likely that he would have been so agreeable to Warren's request.

Sidelight:
The Signal Station

In the far distance beyond Pitzer's Woods you should be able to make out a cleared slope in which is a large barn with a metallic roof. *Longstreet's* column would have been observed by the signal station had it continued along its original line of approach and passed over that slope.

The signal station detected the presence of *Hill's* corps in the area north of Pitzer's Woods at midday; had *Longstreet* not reversed course, his march would have been detected easily. But the signalmen did see part of the countermarch, and their reports erroneously suggested that *Lee* might be shift-

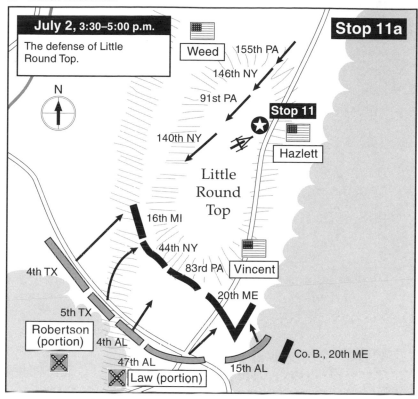

July 2, **3:30–5:00 p.m.**

The defense of Little Round Top.

Stop 11a

Weed
155th PA
146th NY
91st PA
Stop 11
140th NY
Hazlett
Little Round Top
16th MI
44th NY
83rd PA   Vincent
20th ME
4th TX
5th TX
Robertson (portion)
4th AL
47th AL
Co. B., 20th ME
15th AL
Law (portion)

ing men to his left in the vicinity of Gettysburg. Later, they noticed the arrival and deployment of *Longstreet's* two divisions, although this information apparently did not reach Meade in time to influence his plans.

Optional

You may want to explore the area around Warren's statue where Weed's brigade took up position. Perhaps the easiest way is to retrace your path to the parking lot. As you approach the lot, turn to your left, where an open area contains several ways to walk to the monuments of the 146th New York and 155th Pennsylvania–the latter topped by a granite statue of a zouave soldier (of Weed's four regiments only the 146th New York was wearing that uniform that day). Although this area did not come under direct assault during the battle, the final Confederate drive eastward across the Valley of Death threatened it before being repelled by Crawford's counterattack. In the aftermath of Pickett's Charge on July 3, George G. Meade traveled to Little Round Top and viewed the battlefield from the site of the 146th New York Monument–just north of the Warren statue. As you return to the Warren statue, you will notice that it stands behind a low stone wall built by Union soldiers to fortify their line.

STOP 11b   4:30–5:30 P.M.

O'Rorke Saves Vincent's Right

Directions

Walk southward along the paths toward the castle. The ground rises as you approach the tall monument to the 91st Pennsylvania; this rise obstructed Warren's view. If you pause at the observation area by the monument, look to the southwest, beyond Devil's Den (and slightly to the left), to spot the Alabama Monument in the distance. To the left of the path are two artillery pieces marking the position of Hazlett's battery (Battery D, 4th U.S. Artillery); the pieces probably were stationed on the low plateau in front of you. The smaller marker nearby once was located where today stands the main monument to the 91st Pennsylvania. As you approach the castle at the southern crest, you will pass a modest monument marking the position of the 140th New York, with a portrait of O'Rorke on the west face. Stop when you reach the entrance to the castle and face toward the southwest.

What Happened

Vincent deployed his regiments along the south slope of Little Round Top. The 20th Maine held the ground far to your left; then came the 83rd Pennsylvania, the 44th New York, and, on the right, the 16th Michigan, whose monument should be visible to you 25 yards southwest of where you stand, mounted on a boulder along a dirt path. Vincent did not position his men at the south summit of Little Round Top, choosing instead to drape his line along the lower part of the slope–the military crest–to maximize his men's field of fire.

Before long several regiments of *Robertson's* brigade (the *4th* and *5th Texas*) and two regiments of *Law's* brigade (the *4th* and *48th Alabama*) came out of the woods just beyond the road to your front, east of Devil's Den. After initially striking the center of Vincent's position, only to be repulsed, these regiments (minus the *4th Alabama*) shifted their attention to the 16th Michigan. The attackers swung around the right flank of the Michigan regiment, charging up the slope due west of where you stand. Vincent personally tried to rally his men but fell mortally wounded. The 16th Michigan began to give way; for a moment it seemed as if the Confederates would score a major breakthrough. These hopes were dashed by the arrival of the 140th New York, which rushed forward in such haste that many of the men did not have time to load their rifles. O'Rorke fell dead on the spot marked by his regiment's monument, but his men succeeded in driving back the attackers. The subsequent arrival of Weed's other three regiments and Hazlett's guns secured the area; later that afternoon Weed was mortally wounded and Hazlett killed in the vicinity of the main monument to the 91st Pennsylvania.

Optional

You may wish to explore Vincent's position in more detail. One way is to navigate the ground leading to the 16th Michigan Monument; then turn left and walk along the path marking the position of the 44th New York and the 83rd Pennsylvania. The other way is to walk to the southeast corner of the castle, where several paths (some more challenging than others) lead to a path running west along Vincent's line to the 16th Michigan Monument.

Sidelight:
A Colonel
and a Private

A small marble slab topped by a Maltese cross due south of the castle marks where Strong Vincent was mortally wounded – perhaps. In 1910 park historian John P. Nicholson, responding to a request from veterans of the 83rd Pennsylvania (which Vincent had once commanded) who wished to erect a marker where Vincent fell, pointed out that two markers already existed – the marble slab and an inscription cut into a rock – both claiming to be where Vincent was wounded. The rock, with the inscription still visible on top, is just north of the 44th New York Monument, one of three boulders adjacent to the castle; you can see both markers from the top of the castle. Vincent died from his wounds on July 7.

If at the Vincent slab you face south (downhill) and bear to your left for a short distance, you will come upon another path that leads downhill to the base of Little Round Top and the 83rd Pennsylvania Monument, topped by a statue that, though obstensibly of "a Union officer," represents Vincent. The monument is also visible from the path leading to the position of the 20th Maine east of Sykes Avenue (see stop 11c).

Eight men belonging to the 83rd Pennsylvania were killed on July 2; six more later died of wounds. Among the dead was Pvt. Eli Berlin, Company G, who was shot in the heart. The disposition of Private Berlin's remains offers an interesting case study in what happened to the Gettysburg dead. On the evening of July 2 and the morning of July 3 detachments from the regiment searched for wounded and dead comrades. Berlin was buried in the fields of J. Weikert's farm, just to the east of Little Round Top, in a marked grave. Several months later his body was moved to the new battlefield cemetery. Today visitors to the Gettysburg National Cemetery can walk to the Pennsylvania section, row C, lot number 51, where his remains are located. The Pennsylvania State

Monument, which carries the names of all the soldiers of the Keystone State who fought at Gettysburg by regiment, includes a bronze tablet to the 83rd on the northeast base. Next to Berlin's name is a star, signifying he was killed.

STOP 11c   4:00–6:30 P.M.

The Stand of the 20th Maine

Directions   Walk around (or through) the castle–a monument to the 44th New York–and pick up one of the paths that lead to Sykes Avenue. Cross the road toward the Park Service directional marker for the 20th Maine Monument and follow a blacktop path to the monument. If you look over your right shoulder, you may see a regimental monument topped by a statue of a Union officer. It marks the position of the 83rd Pennsylvania–demonstrating how far downslope Vincent established his line–and the officer is none other than Vincent, who had once commanded the regiment. Just after the path crosses a low stone wall, stop. Ahead of you, on a boulder, is the monument to the 20th Maine. Face southeast toward the monument.

What Happened   As Vincent's men formed line of battle on the south slope of Little Round Top, the brigade commander sought out Col. Joshua L. Chamberlain of the 20th Maine and instructed him to "hold that ground at all hazards." Chamberlain detached one company (B) to serve as skirmishers to protect his left, then readied to meet the Confederate attack.

Col. William B. *Oates* led his *15th Alabama* from approximately the area marked by the Alabama Monument across the wooded west face of Big Round Top, reaching that height's summit. Although *Oates* later claimed that he could have rendered the entire Union line vulnerable had he the opportunity to clear Big Round Top, it would have proved difficult to drag artillery to that position and cut down enought trees to open up a satisfactory field of fire. Instead, he headed northward toward the south slope of Little Round Top, only to encounter the Union position. Immediately *Oates* began to shift eastward in an effort to turn Chamberlain's flank; Chamberlain responded by bending his line back at a right angle (called "refusing the flank") and stretched out his regiment to the left, while his right continued to fend off the attack of the *47th Alabama*. You are standing at the approximate point of the center of the regiment's line. Several Confederate assaults failed to crack Chamberlain's line, although they came close to folding Chamberlain's left back on his right; *Oates* later maintained that his last attack actually reached the boulders over your left shoulder (north).

The men from Maine soon found themselves running out of ammunition. Anticipating a final Confederate assault, Chamberlain decided to strike first. Instructing his men to fix bayonets, he prepared to order his left to sweep down and bear right like a gate hinged on the apex of the regiment's position; the right flank would also swing forward, and the two flanks would form a straight line. Much to his surprise, the men on his left flank commenced advancing before the orders were issued; the regiment moved as if its men had read their commander's mind. At the same time, the detached company charged forward, adding to the Confederates' shock and confusion. *Oates's* men were driven back; Chamberlain's men gathered several hundred prisoners.

Analysis

Chamberlain's management of his position remains a classic example of small unit leadership. Extending his line and simultaneously refusing his left flank—a maneuver conducted under fire—enabled him to maintain his position. It is even more remarkable when one remembers that Chamberlain, still struggling to ward off the effects of illness, had just returned to his command; in addition, during the engagement he was twice slightly wounded. The 20th Maine's counterattack proved timely, even though *Oates* may well have already directed his men to withdraw; yet it is worth remembering that the Confederates had come a long way over rugged terrain—and without water, for a detachment sent to refill canteens never rejoined the regiment. Nor should the achievements of the 20th Maine overshadow the contributions of others at Little Round Top. O'Rorke's counterattack proved as critical as Chamberlain's defense to saving the Union left; Vincent and Warren had taken leading roles in establishing the position.

Sidelight: Company B

The experience of Company B proved most trying. In detaching it, Chamberlain was responding to Vincent's initial deployment of the brigade, which placed the 16th Michigan on his left. Capt. Walter Morrill never knew that Vincent revised his deployment by shifting the 16th Michigan to hold the brigade's right; thus he struggled to make contact with a nonexistent force before ordering his men to take cover behind a stone wall over a hundred yards east of the remainder of the regiment. There they encountered a dozen or so Union sharpshooters, who placed themselves under his orders. As the 20th Maine charged down the slope, Morrill's men opened fire on the retreating Confederates; some idea of their impact is reflected in *Oates's* claim that two regiments fired on his rear.

To view the marker at the position of Company B, head east into the woods along paths that lead to a low stone wall running north and south—the western edge of J. Weikert's property. Another trailhead is located off Wright Avenue a short walk from the parking lot by the 20th Maine's monument; bear right at the fork in the paths. Company B's marker is located almost due east of the regimental monument.

Optional

You might want to explore Chamberlain's position in more detail; the remnants of Chamberlain Avenue form a loop from the main regimental monument around the left flank of the 20th Maine before rejoining the path you are now on.

There is another monument to the 20th Maine at the summit of Big Round Top. Late on the evening of July 2, after the end of the struggle for Little Round Top, Chamberlain received orders to occupy Big Round Top. Although his men came under a smattering of fire, they reached their objective and captured 25 Confederates who were scouting the area. You may choose to follow Chamberlain's route and pick up the trail to Big Round Top at Wright Avenue, or you may later retrace your drive along South Confederate Avenue to a trailhead by a parking area.

View from the position of Hazlett's battery on Little Round Top. From a photograph. 3:298

STOP 12   Houck's Ridge   4:50–5:45 P.M.

Directions   *Return to your car. Continue north* on SEDGWICK AVENUE to the WHEATFIELD ROAD and *turn left. Proceed* 0.3 mile to CRAWFORD AVENUE and *turn left.* Stay on the avenue (which becomes SICKLES AVENUE) as it loops around the massive boulders of Devil's Den and rises to the crest of a modest ridge. As you reach the crest, look for four cannon on the right side of the road. Find a convenient place to pull over to the shoulder.

En route you will notice two cannon on Crawford Avenue about 0.2 mile south of the intersection of Crawford Avenue and Wheatfield Road. If you have time, pull over beside the cannon and pause to consider the location. You are in Plum Run valley, dubbed the Valley of Death after the fighting here on July 2. To your left is Little Round Top. To your right is Houck's Ridge—your next destination. Directly ahead is Devil's Den gorge, known after the battle as the Slaughter Pen. When the fighting began on July 2, Houck's Ridge marked the extreme left end of Sickles's line. With insufficient infantry to prolong the line, these two guns—belonging to the 4th New York Battery—were posted here to cover the gorge with fire if the Confederates came from that direction.

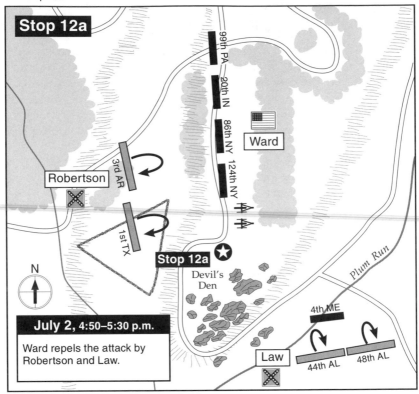

Stop 12a

Robertson

3rd AR

1st TX

99th PA

20th IN

86th NY

124th NY

Ward

N

Devil's Den

Plum Run

4th ME

Law

44th AL   48th AL

July 2, 4:50–5:30 p.m.

Ward repels the attack by
Robertson and Law.

STOP 12a   4:50–5:30 P.M.

Ward's Defense

Directions   Exit your vehicle and walk to the monument to the 4th Battery, New York Light Artillery. Face west, the same direction
the cannon barrels are pointing.

Orientation   You are standing on the summit of Houck's Ridge, the left-
most of the three main infantry positions occupied by the
Union III Corps. The area around you was held by a single
brigade under Brig. Gen. J. H. Hobart Ward, supported by the
4th New York Battery under Capt. James E. Smith. There is
quite a lot to explore in the immediate area if you have the
time; you can usually find paths that will take you wherever
you want to go.

   Directly ahead of you about 30 yards, hidden by the down-
ward slope of the ridge, is a small triangular field enclosed by
a stone fence. The Confederates attacked from that direction.
(The field is too rocky to have been used for crop cultivation;
it was probably a cattle or hog pen.)

If you walk about 20 yards to your left front, you will come upon a sniper's nest used by Confederate marksmen at a later stage of the fighting. A National Park Service interpretive marker describes the famous Gardner photograph made at this site a few days after the battle–a posed image of a dead Confederate.

What Happened   Ward's brigade, about 1,500 men, reached this position about 3:30 P.M. Four guns of the 4th New York Battery took up position probably in front of you–the placing of the four present-day cannon is most likely in error. The two remaining guns of the battery were sited in Plum Run valley facing south so as to cover the left flank of the brigade with fire.

The first Confederate troops–the two wayward regiments from *Robertson's* brigade–appeared to your right front around 4:50 P.M. They shoved back the skirmishers of Ward's brigade but were stopped when they reached the main Union line. Undaunted, the two regiments tried again and soon afterward received fortuitous assistance from two regiments of *Law's* brigade that advanced into Devil's Den, hoping to get behind Ward's brigade and capture the 4th New York Battery. The 4th Maine regiment blocked this attempt.

Vignette   Although Ward's brigade managed to parry the first Confederate blows, the pressure on its front and left flank increased. Additional Southern regiments were coming up, and the 4th New York Battery fired fiercely in an attempt to keep them at bay. The cannoneers soon used up their supply of case shot. "Give them shell!" Captain Smith bellowed, "give them solid shot! Damn them, give them anything!" Feverishly the gunners began firing "canister without sponging"–a truly desperate measure that meant shoving bags of black powder down a barrel that might well contain smoldering residue from the previous discharge, risking an accidental blast that would maim the artillerist loading the round.

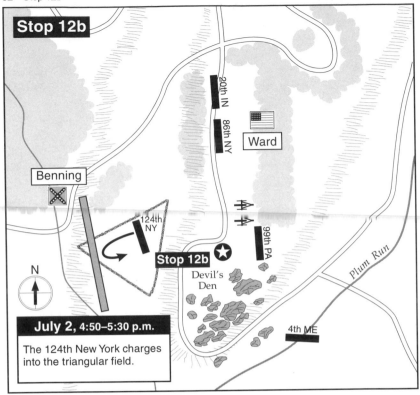

Stop 12b

20th IN

86th NY

Ward

Benning

124th NY

99th PA

Stop 12b

Devil's Den

Plum Run

N

4th ME

July 2, 4:50–5:30 p.m.

The 124th New York charges into the triangular field.

STOP 12b   4:50–5:30 P.M.

The Orange Blossoms

Directions

The next phase of the action is best appreciated by proceeding to the roadway and walking north (to your right) about 50 yards to the 124th New York Monument, which is topped by a statue of the regiment's colonel. Face west toward the stone wall that marks a corner of the triangular field. If you are pressed for time, you may simply walk to the west (straight ahead) to a point from which you can see into the triangular field.

Orientation

This monument marks the approximate center of Ward's line.

What Happened

Created in response to President Lincoln's August 1862 call for 300,000 additional three-year volunteers, the 124th was raised mainly in Orange County, New York. It saw no action until the battle of Chancellorsville in May 1863, where it suffered 40 percent casualties. There the colonel of the 124th,

A. Van Horne Ellis, had affectionately addressed his men as his "Orange Blossoms." The nickname stuck.

The 124th New York fought off repeated attacks by the *1st Texas*. To help steady the men, Ellis and his major, James Cromwell, mounted their horses and were conspicuously visible just behind the firing line. A captain protested— mounted officers were often the first to be picked off in battle—but Ellis dismissed his concerns: "The men must see us to-day."

Cromwell thought the best way to stop the Confederates was by counterattacking. At first Ellis demurred, but presently he agreed. Sword in hand, Cromwell screamed, "Charge!" and the Orange Blossoms swept forward down the slope with bayonets fixed. They broke the Texans' line and forced them to within a hundred feet of the far end of the triangular field. Then the Texans turned and fired, killing or wounding about one-quarter of the men in the 124th, including Cromwell, who fell dead from his saddle. Ellis shouted for the men to save their major, but within moments they were set upon by an entire brigade under Brig. Gen. Henry A. *Benning*. A bullet drilled Ellis through the brain; his men began falling back to the crest of Houck's Ridge in hope of surviving.

Behind them, *Benning* urged his men onward. "Give them hell, boys," he growled repeatedly, "give them hell."

Devil's Den, facing Little Round Top. 3:331

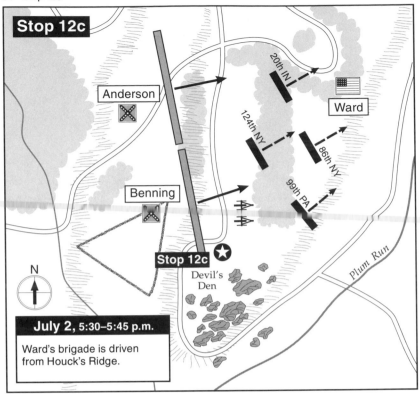

Stop 12c

Anderson

20th IN

Ward

124th NY

86th NY

99th PA

Benning

Stop 12c

Devil's
Den

Plum Run

N

July 2, 5:30–5:45 p.m.

Ward's brigade is driven
from Houck's Ridge.

STOP 12c   5:30–5:45 P.M.

Benning Sweeps the Ridge

Directions   Remain in place.

What Happened   With the arrival of *Benning's* brigade, the situation on Ward's
front became critical. Ward asked for, and got, two regi-
ments from other brigades to help sustain his position. These
units joined with Ward's own in a furious seesaw battle
of charge and countercharge that continued for perhaps
another hour. The 4th New York Battery continued to blast
away at the Confederates, sometimes with little or no infantry support. Captain Smith might have withdrawn the
guns to avoid the risk of their capture, but he decided to keep
them firing. Eventually, when Rebel troops finally overran
the crest of Houck's Ridge, they captured three of Smith's
cannon.

Analysis   The defense of the Houck's Ridge–Devil's Den position was
ably conducted. The Union forces held their ground steadily,
and well-timed counterattacks like the one made by the Or-

ange Blossoms – although extremely expensive in lives lost –
repeatedly threw the Confederate attackers off balance.

The Confederates were also hurt by the fact that *Hood*, the
division commander in this sector, had been wounded early
in the battle and no one seems to have taken his place. Evander *Law*, the next senior general on the field, either did not
learn of *Hood's* wounding until later or else was too far forward to assume effective command of the division. As a result, the Confederate attack, though powerful, was somewhat disorganized. Two regiments from *Robertson's* brigade
struck the right-center of Ward's line, then two more from
Law's brigade struck his left flank. Only later – after Ward understood the threat against him and sent for reinforcements – did an entire Confederate brigade, *Benning's*, attack
in coordinated fashion.

Although the Confederates needed to seize it so as to continue *Longstreet's* main assault, the Houck's Ridge – Devil's
Den position was of little intrinsic importance. Riflemen
took up positions among the boulders from which to blaze
away at Little Round Top, but the open Plum Run valley offered poor ground for a direct attack on that vital Union bas-
tion. The position also had scant effect on the fighting that
continued unabated to the north, in the Wheatfield and
Peach Orchard.

Dead Confederate
sharpshooter in the
Devil's Den. From a
photograph, probably
posed. 3:328

STOP 13   The Wheatfield   5:15–6:30 P.M.

Directions   Return to your car. *Proceed north* on SICKLES AVENUE to the four-way intersection and go straight through. *Continue* about 0.2 mile and pull off at the turnout by the National Park Service interpretive markers.

STOP 13a   5:15–5:45 P.M.

                   The 17th Maine

Directions   Exit your vehicle and face north, in the direction of the two cannon (separated by a large marker) prominently sited in the open field that dominates this area.

Orientation   You are facing the Wheatfield, one of the most famous and confusing parts of the Gettysburg battlefield. The complexity of the fighting here is legendary; this stop will simply provide an overview. More detailed coverage is in the Wheatfield excursion.

The cannon in the field represent the six guns of Battery D, 1st New York Artillery, under Capt. George B. Winslow. This battery provided the sole Union artillery support during the early stages of the fighting here.

Behind you, about 50 yards distant, is a large monument to the 17th Maine regiment, easily identified by the red diamond and the crouching infantryman on top. Just behind it, a low stone wall separates the monument from the woodland beyond. When the fighting began, the area was thinly held by that single Union regiment positioned along the stone wall.

A look to your left, in the direction of Sickles Avenue as it continues west, and you will see a low wooded ridge known as the Stony Hill. Three additional regiments under Brig. Gen. Philippe Regis de Trobriand were posted on the southern end of the hill—the left end from your current point of view. Shortly before the main fighting began on this part of the field, two brigades from Brig. Gen. James Barnes's division of the V Corps arrived to bolster the line on the west side of the Stony Hill.

If Houck's Ridge was the first of the three main positions occupied by the III Corps, the Stony Hill was the second. Beyond the hill and out of your sight about 400 yards away was the third: the Peach Orchard and the line of Brig. Gen. A. A. Humphreys's division along Emmitsburg Road.

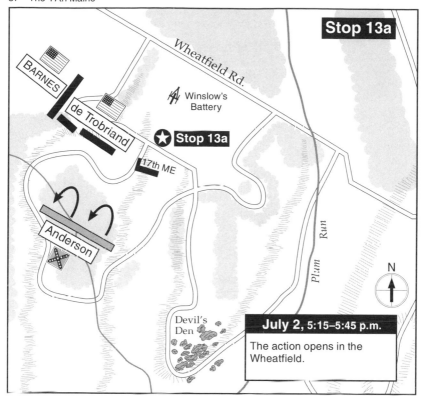

BARNES

de Trobriand

Wheatfield Rd.

Winslow's Battery

Stop 13a

17th ME

Anderson

Devil's Den

Plum Run

N

Stop 13a

July 2, 5:15–5:45 p.m.

The action opens in the Wheatfield.

What Happened

The 17th Maine was at first lightly engaged against the left-most Confederate regiments attacking Houck's Ridge. The real fighting, however, began when a brigade under Brig. Gen. George T. *Anderson,* which had supported the thrusts against Houck's Ridge, extended the main assault north-ward. *Anderson's* troops came at the 17th Maine and the Stony Hill from the woodlands beyond the stone wall.

Winslow's battery threw solid shot directly over the heads of the 17th Maine and into the ranks of the advancing Confederates. The cannon balls splintered trees and rained fragments down among the Rebels. The 17th Maine held steady, but presently its neighboring regiments on the Stony Hill withdrew under the enemy pressure, and the colonel of the 17th had to place three companies of his regiments at right angles to the others to protect his flank and remain in position. But he succeeded in repulsing the first Confederate attack.

Vignette

A soldier in the 17th Maine recalled: "At this point, while shot, shell, spherical case, and cannister filled the air [the soldier was mistaken about the type of artillery ammunition being fired], General de Trobriand, our brigade commander, rode down into the wheatfield and inquired, 'What troops are those that are holding the stone wall so stubbornly?' On learning it was the 17th Maine, one of his regiments, he ordered us to 'Fall back, right away!' . . . It isn't often that an order to fall back in a battlefield is disregarded. The old fellow didn't quite comprehend this state of ours. We had good reason for our action. This stone wall was a great protection and the Rebels were straining every nerve to get possession of it for the same purpose. So, we held it till our ammunition was exhausted and we had used all we could find on the dead and wounded. . . . We knew the fate of the army hung on the result."

STOP 13b   5:30–6:00 P.M.

Kershaw's Attack

Directions   Do an about-face so that you are now looking toward the 17th Maine Monument and the road that runs between it and the Stony Hill.

What Happened   Maj. Gen. Lafayette *McLaws's* division joined the assault around 5:30 P.M., shortly after the collapse of the Houck's Ridge–Devil's Den position. The right-most brigade of this division, under Brig. Gen. Joseph *Kershaw*, advanced across the Emmitsburg Road near the Rose Farmhouse. Two of its regiments peeled off to confront the Union artillery along the south face of the Peach Orchard salient. The others continued into Rose Woods and finally came at the Stony Hill from the woodlands beyond the stone wall.

Advancing in concert with *Anderson's* brigade, *Kershaw's* men placed considerable pressure on the 17th Maine and the Union troops defending the Stony Hill. But Winslow's battery continued to rain solid shot on the Confederates, the 17th Maine stuck doggedly to its position, and the rest of de Trobriand's brigade maintained its battle lines on the Stony Hill. For some reason, however–perhaps because he worried that too great a gap separated his troops from the III Corps infantry in the Peach Orchard–General Barnes withdrew his understrength division about 300 yards to the north, to a new position near Wheatfield Road. De Trobriand and the 17th Maine had to follow suit, and the Stony Hill fell into Confederate hands.

Analysis   Barnes made a serious error in judgment when he withdrew his division. After the battle he was so severely criticized for

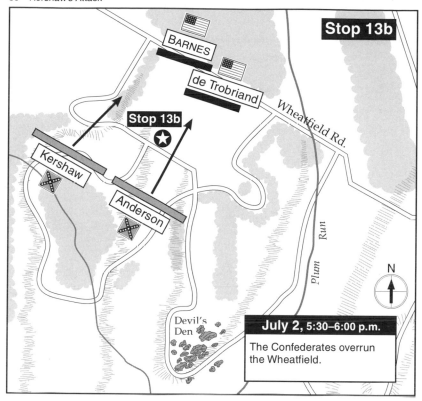

Stop 13b

BARNES

de Trobriand

Stop 13b ★

Wheatfield Rd.

Kershaw

Anderson

Plum Run

Devil's Den

N

July 2, 5:30–6:00 p.m.

The Confederates overrun the Wheatfield.

it that his military career, for all practical purposes, came to an end. The loss of the Stony Hill placed Confederate troops on ground that overlooked the Peach Orchard position to the west and clearly dominated the Wheatfield area. Even if Barnes had remained in place, however, it is possible that the Confederates might have seized the hill. Although nominally a division, Barnes's force mustered fewer than 1,700 men—about the size of an average brigade. De Trobriand referred in his after-action report to Barnes's two understrength brigades as "two regiments."

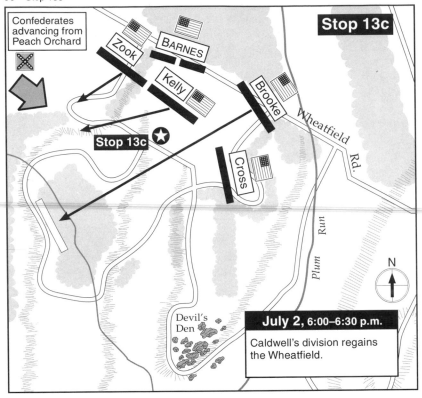

Confederates advancing from Peach Orchard

Stop 13c

Zook

BARNES

Kelly

Brooke

Stop 13c

Cross

Wheatfield Rd.

Plum Run

N

Devil's Den

July 2, 6:00–6:30 p.m.

Caldwell's division regains the Wheatfield.

STOP 13c   6:00–6:30 P.M.

Caldwell's Counterattack

Directions

About-face, so that you are looking once more toward Winslow's battery.

What Happened

The fight for the Wheatfield now began. The victorious Confederates swept over the stone wall and advanced into the Wheatfield behind you. Winslow's battery withdrew to safer ground near Wheatfield Road, but the 17th Maine and other Federal units took position on the reverse slope of the low ridge ahead of you (that is, just beyond the position occupied by the battery) and peppered away at the Rebels. Soon the Federals could see an entire division–four brigades–marching to their support from the direction of Cemetery Ridge.

The division was commanded by Brig. Gen. John C. Caldwell. It belonged to the II Corps and had been en route toward the Wheatfield since shortly after 5 P.M., when II Corps commander Winfield S. Hancock instructed Caldwell to go to the support of the troops "in the direction of Little Round Top." As the division reached the scene of action, three brigades (under Cols. Samuel K. Zook, Patrick Kelly, and Edward E. Cross) moved forward against the Confederates; a fourth, under Col. John R. Brooke, remained in reserve. Zook's and Kelly's brigades drove the Rebels from the Stony Hill. Cross's brigade cleared the Wheatfield, firing so rapidly than within 15 minutes it was running low on ammunition and was replaced by Brooke's men.

By this time the Confederates had fallen back to the edge of Rose Woods. The Federals pursued them, capturing dozens of prisoners and continuing about 500 yards to the far side of the woods. Unfortunately for the Federals, at this time the Union position in the Peach Orchard collapsed. Additional Confederate brigades poured in from that direction, retaking the Stony Hill and flanking the Union forces in the Wheatfield. With Rebels now coming in behind them, Caldwell's brigade in Rose Woods had to retreat at high speed to the east. For reasons beyond their control, their valorous and successful counterattack had turned into a nightmare. The Confederates pursued them, and this area of the battlefield slipped firmly into Southern hands.

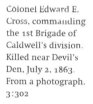

Colonel Edward E. Cross, commanding the 1st Brigade of Caldwell's division. Killed near Devil's Den, July 2, 1863. From a photograph. 3:302

Wheatfield Excursion

Begin the excursion at the National Park Service interpretive marker turnout on SICKLES AVENUE. You may want to review stop 13 of the basic tour before continuing.

STOP A   5:00–5:40 P.M.

Winslow's Battery

Directions   Walk to the 1st New York Light Artillery Monument (the large stone marker, flanked by two cannon in the field to your right [north]). Face back toward your vehicle.

Orientation   You are standing in what was the wheatfield of John P. Rose, whose farmhouse lies just beyond the woods ahead of you. To your right is the Stony Hill, which at the start of the combat in this sector was held by three regiments under Col. Philippe Regis de Trobriand. Out of sight beyond the Stony Hill is the Peach Orchard salient. Directly ahead, just beyond your vehicle, is the stone wall occupied by the 17th Maine.

What Happened   This position was held by Battery D, 1st New York Light Artillery. Commanded by Capt. George B. Winslow, it consisted of six 12-pounder smoothbore Napoleons. Note the constricted range of observation available from this location. Although the ground plainly allowed the artillerists to command the Wheatfield itself, the surrounding woodlands confined vision to little more than 200 yards. The III Corps artillery chief recognized this defect in the position but believed Winslow's battery could provide badly needed fire support to this thinly manned portion of the line.

Once the fighting began, Winslow's limited field of vision forced him literally to "play it by ear": "I was unable from my obscure position to observe the movements of the troops, and was compelled to estimate distances and regulate my fire by the reports of our own and the enemy's musketry." At first the battery fired into the woods with solid shot, aiming just over the heads of the men of the 17th Maine. The intended effect was as much moral as physical; contemporary artillery doctrine maintained that the horrendous sound of cannonballs crashing through trees could frighten an attacking infantry force as badly as any casualties they might inflict. As long as there were friendly troops in front of them, Winslow's artillerists could not use case shot or shell, for the fuses of the day were unreliable, and a premature shell burst would harm their own men.

Eventually, enemy pressure forced the 17th Maine to fall back behind the battery. Winslow ordered the battery to open fire with shell and case shot, with the fuses cut to explode one to one and a half seconds after the rounds left the barrels. In this way Battery D was able to prevent the Confederates from leaving the woods ahead of you. Rebel infantrymen began working their way around the left of Winslow's battery toward covered positions from which they could pick off the cannoneers. Realizing that his gunners were now dangerously exposed and without infantry support, Winslow ordered the battery to withdraw. One at a time, starting with the left-most piece, each cannon in turn was limbered (hitched to horses) and withdrawn. Winslow lost ten horses but no guns during this trying period, and his human casualties were light: just ten men wounded and eight missing.

Analysis

The experience of Battery D suggests how the realties of Civil War combat can differ markedly from accepted generalizations. "Many modern commentators," the British tactical historian Paddy Griffith writes, "have supposed that the short- and medium-range use of artillery in the Civil War was a logical impossibility–or at best an expression of suicidal bravery–simply because the gunners were vulnerable to the new small-arms fire. . . . Hence the only practicable [artillery] gunfire on the Civil War battlefield is often assumed to have consisted of largely useless potshots at ranges of above 1,000 yards" (*Battle Tactics of the Civil War*, 172). In fact, Griffith argues, Civil War artillery routinely fought within 200 to 300 yards of enemy infantry without heavy losses. Far from being dominated by the rifled musket, the artillery– with its steady, lethal blasts–usually dominated whatever position it happened to occupy. From the stone wall 150 yards ahead of you, Confederate infantry in theory should have been able to pick off Winslow's artillerists readily. But Winslow's after-action report states that it was not until enemy infantry approached to within 25 yards–partly shielded by the rock outcroppings to your left front–that he felt obliged to retire.

STOP B

5:40–6:00 P.M.

The Stony Hill: Barnes's Error

Directions

Return to your car and *drive up* the LOOP, which traces roughly the crest of the Stony Hill. Pause when you reach the 140th Pennsylvania Monument on the right side of the road, about 0.2 mile from the Wheatfield turnout (stop A). You need not get out.

En route, observe how the Stony Hill – particularly at the southwestern end of the Loop – dominates the lower ground around it. Many regimental monuments dot the landscape, and corps badges are prominently displayed on most of them. The diamond badges of the III Corps indicate Federal units that were in place when the fighting began. Monuments bearing the Maltese cross of the V Corps indicate the positions of Barnes's division, which arrived soon afterward. The trefoil (three-leaf clover) emblem of the II Corps indicates units belonging to Caldwell's division, which counterattacked and recovered the Stony Hill when it was first overrun by Confederates. (You will make a second transit of the Loop near the end of this excursion.)

Face the open field on the left (west) side of the road, in the direction of the Peach Orchard, about 350 yards distant.

Orientation

Your location corresponds approximately to the right end of the original Union line on the Stony Hill. The III Corps infantry line resumed only at the Peach Orchard; the area in between was covered by Union artillery (indicated by the row of guns along Wheatfield Road, which runs eastward from the Peach Orchard). The "left wing" of *Kershaw's* brigade – two regiments and a battalion – charged across the open field in front of you from left to right.

What Happened

Although the Stony Hill was a strong position that dominated the approaches to the Wheatfield, as well as Rose's Farm to the south, the wide gap between the hill and the Peach Orchard intimidated General Barnes, whose concerns can best be appreciated from this location. Almost from the moment his two brigades reached the Stony Hill, he gave orders for his subordinates to be prepared to fall back. The colonel of the 32nd Massachusetts, admirably posted where the terrain best favored the defense, protested when his brigade commander relayed Barnes's cautionary warning. "I don't want to retire," he declared. "I am not ready to retire; I can hold this place." The 32nd Massachusetts did maintain its position for a time, but presently Barnes – spooked by *Kershaw's* "left wing" of three Confederate regiments assailing the Wheatfield Road gun line – ordered a withdrawal.

Ironically, *Kershaw's* "left wing" was having a bad time of it. The men were exposed to repeated blasts from the massed Union artillery, and a misunderstood command caused the Confederate infantry to veer toward the Stony Hill just as they were about to overrun the Federal gun line, rendering them vulnerable to renewed salvos of enemy shot and shell. After the war, *Kershaw* recalled mournfully that "hundreds of the best and bravest men of [South] Carolina fell, victims of this fatal blunder."

STOP C1
5:30–6:00 P.M.

Caldwell's Counterattack: Deployment

Directions
Continue along the LOOP to the T intersection with WHEAT-FIELD ROAD and *turn right. Proceed* to the next intersection, AYRES AVENUE and *turn right. Drive* 0.1 mile to the first cast-iron tablet on the right, topped by a trefoil and labeled "First Brigade." Pull over at the unimproved turnout in front of it.

En route, just after you turn from the Loop onto Wheat-field Road, you will pass the position occupied by the Union infantry after they withdrew from the Stony Hill. Note the modest stone marker (easily identified by a Maltese cross) standing on the left side of the road. It shows the second position occupied by the 118th Pennsylvania, a unit that had earlier defended the right flank of the Stony Hill position.

Walk to the two small stone flank markers about 20 yards beyond the tablet. Stand at the markers with your back to the bronze tablet.

Orientation
You are standing at approximately the center of the battle line occupied by Col. Edward E. Cross's brigade of Caldwell's division shortly after it began its advance into the Wheat-field. Visualize a line connecting the regimental monuments to your left and right; this will help indicate the frontage held by the brigade. The left-most regiment, the 5th New Hampshire, advanced through the woods to your left; the right-most regiment, the 61st New York, is represented by the smaller and more distant of the two regimental monuments to your right. Somewhat to the right of this line of monuments you will see a tall, obelisk-like monument surmounted by an eagle. This represents the 27th Connecticut, a regiment from Col. John R. Brooke's brigade, which deployed in support of Cross's brigade.

To your front, about 100 yards distant, you will see the by now familiar turnout (stop 13 of the basic tour; stop A of this excursion) near the junction of Brooke and Crawford Avenues. Just beyond and to the left of it is the stone wall, which at this stage of the battle would have been occupied by the Brig. Gen. George T. *Anderson's* Confederate brigade. Additional Confederates (the *1st Texas* and *15th Georgia*) were also in the tree line to the left of the stone wall; *Kershaw's* Confederates had already seized the Stony Hill north of the Wheatfield.

What Happened

From his vantage point on Cemetery Ridge, II Corps commander Maj. Gen. Winfield S. Hancock had earlier watched Sickles's III Corps make its fateful advance to the Houck's Ridge–Peach Orchard position. Shortly after the fighting began, he saw the two brigades from Barnes's division moving up in support of Sickles. Highly dubious about Sickles's new and exposed position, Hancock predicted, "Wait a moment, you'll soon see them falling back." Turning to Brig. Gen. John C. Caldwell, commanding the II Corps division closest to the action, he instructed Caldwell to prepare for action. Caldwell's four brigades (under Cols. Cross, Kelly, Zook, and Brooke) were in reserve behind Cemetery Ridge. To save time, Caldwell simply ordered each brigade to face left and begin marching southwest toward the sound of the firing.

STOP C2

6:00–6:30 P.M.

Caldwell's Division Clears the Wheatfield

Directions

Remain in place.

What Happened

The lead brigade was that of Col. Edward E. Cross, a former businessman from New Hampshire. It rankled Cross that although now a brigade commander, he had not yet been promoted to brigadier general. As his unit advanced into battle, Hancock rode up and assured him, "Colonel Cross, this day will bring you a star." Troubled for several days by a presentiment of death, Cross replied, "No, general, this is my last battle." He proved correct. Soon after the brigade entered the Wheatfield, while visiting the 5th New Hampshire on the extreme left of the line, Cross fell, mortally wounded.

Partly concealed by woodland, the left portion of Cross's brigade advanced as far as the stone wall; the two right-most regiments probably got no farther than where their monuments stand today. Meanwhile, Kelly's brigade (the famed Irish Brigade) charged across the Wheatfield toward the Stony Hill, while Zook's brigade converged on the Stony Hill from a more northerly direction. (Looking to your right, you may be able to discern a small obelisk silhouetted against the tree line near Wheatfield Road. It marks the spot where Zook was mortally wounded early in the charge of his brigade.)

Cross's men held this position until they exhausted their ammunition, which may have occurred in as little as 10 or 15 minutes. Then Brooke's brigade—which Caldwell had been holding in reserve—was ordered to relieve Cross's brigade and continue the advance. It swept across the field, passed through Cross's battle line, and continued to the west end of the stone wall (near present-day Brooke Avenue). For several minutes, Federals and Confederates exchanged volleys at close range. "Fix Bayonets!" Brooke ordered, seeking to break the impasse; his men shouldered their way into Rose's Woods, forcing the Confederates back.

STOP D   6:30–6:45 P.M.

Caldwell's Counterattack Crests

Directions

Return to your car. *Proceed* on AYRES AVENUE to the four-way intersection with SICKLES AVENUE. *Continue* straight through to CROSS AVENUE, which eventually becomes BROOKE AVENUE. *Drive* 0.5 mile to the Kershaw's brigade marker and pull over to the unimproved turnout on the left side of the road. Thirty yards behind you, you will see a line of Union regimental monuments on the right side of the road. They commemorate the regiments of Brooke's brigade, erected at the site of its farthest advance. Walk to the fence line just behind the tablet.

En route, just short of the intersection with Crawford Avenue, you will pass an odd shaped monument composed of an octagonal disk resting on a base of four boulders and surmounted by a fifth. It marks the spot where Colonel Cross was mortally wounded.

Orientation

Beyond the fence line and to the right, you should easily locate the stone farmhouse that belonged in 1863 to John P. Rose and his family. Driven from the Stony Hill by the counterattack of Kelly's and Zook's brigades, *Kershaw* reformed his troops on the farmhouse grounds. Advancing in support of *Kershaw's* brigade, four Georgia regiments under Brig. Gen. Paul J. *Semmes* took a position at a stone wall (no longer extant) and used it as a base from which to contest Brooke's Union regiments.

What Happened

Brooke's Federals drove *Anderson's* Confederates—exhausted by their long approach march to the battlefield and 90 minutes of intense combat—across Rose's Woods, taking prisoners as they went. Reaching the advanced position indicated by the monuments you passed some thirty yards back, the five Union regiments formed a semi-circular line and struggled to hold the ground they had won. *Anderson's* troops, meanwhile, fell back to the vicinity of the triangular field near Houck's Ridge. There they reformed. Soon Brooke found his brigade hotly assailed by *Semmes's* Confederates and bedeviled by skirmishers from *Anderson's* brigade, which was returning to the attack. Realizing that he could not alone hold his new position long, Brooke sent messengers to locate General Caldwell and ask for help. Caldwell, it turned out, was already trying to locate troops to support his own fully committed division, but assistance could not come in time. Within about 15 minutes, Brooke's regiments were down to as little as five rounds per man, and Confederate pressure on their front was increasing. Brooke reluctantly gave the order to fall back.

STOP E

6:45–7:00 P.M.

"I Think We Are Facing in the Wrong Direction"

Directions

Continue along BROOKE AVENUE about 0.3 mile to the 62nd Pennsylvania Monument on the right side of the road. The unit designation is not visible, but it is the second monument before the T intersection and is marked by a Maltese cross (it's also the first monument after the one to the 17th Maine). Pull over momentarily. You need not leave the car. Look toward Winslow's battery, which by this time should be a familiar landmark.

En route, as you cross the small bridge over Rose Run, you will have a good view of the Stony Hill as it appeared to *Kershaw's* Confederates during their several attacks against it.

Orientation

At this stage of the fighting, the brigades of Kelly and Zook had recovered the Stony Hill to your left. Brooke's brigade was still at the far edge of Rose Woods, about 150 yards to your rear.

What Happened

In response to General Caldwell's pleas for reinforcements, Col. Jacob B. Sweitzer's brigade of Barnes's division advanced once again from Wheatfield Road. Passing across the Wheatfield in line of battle, it marched directly toward your current position and deployed behind the stone wall that had been held first by the 17th Maine, then by *Anderson's* brigade; it had recently been retaken by Brooke.

Sweitzer naturally expected any enemy fire to come from Rose Woods beyond the stone wall. Instead, a steady rain of bullets assailed his troops from the Stony Hill. Sweitzer dismissed it as friendly fire until his color bearer told him, "Colonel, I'll be —— if I don't think we are faced the wrong

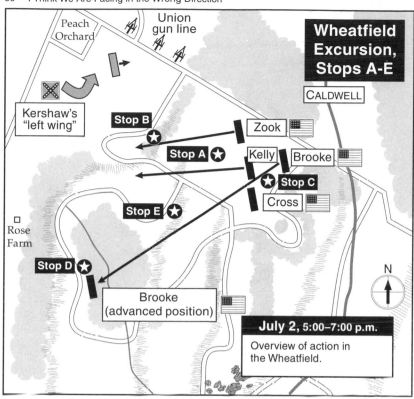

Peach Orchard

Union gun line

Wheatfield Excursion, Stops A-E

CALDWELL

Kershaw's "left wing"

Stop B

Zook

Stop A

Kelly

Brooke

Stop C

Cross

Stop E

Rose Farm

Stop D

Brooke (advanced position)

N

July 2, 5:00–7:00 p.m.

Overview of action in the Wheatfield.

way; the rebs are up there in the woods behind us, on our right."

It was true. The Peach Orchard salient had finally collapsed, permitting Brig. Gen. William T. *Wofford*'s brigade to sweep eastward along Wheatfield Road. Assisted by *Wofford's* advance, *Kershaw* had been able to regain the Stony Hill. Sweitzer shifted two of his three regiments to face the new threat, but it was no use. The Stony Hill completely dominated his position. Worse, Brooke's retreat soon brought *Anderson's* brigade piling in from the direction of Rose Woods. Assailed on two sides, Sweitzer had little choice but to order his troops to retreat in the only direction they could–eastward toward the lower fringe of Cemetery Ridge.

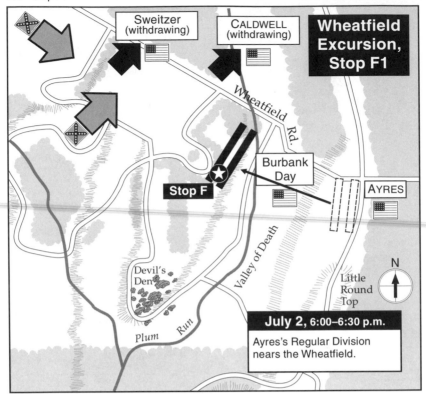

STOP F1   6:00–6:30 P.M.

The Regulars Arrive

Directions

Begin a second circuit of the excursion route by *continuing* to the intersection and *turn left*. *Proceed* via the LOOP to WHEATFIELD ROAD; *turn right* and then *right again* when you reach AYRES AVENUE. About 0.3 mile after the intersection of AYRES AVENUE and WHEATFIELD ROAD you will see, on the left, a cast-iron tablet labeled "First Brigade" (Col. Hannibal Day) (not to be confused with Cross's 1st Brigade tablet at stop C). Walk beyond the tablet to the fence line. Face toward the two cannon, plainly visible in the valley below.

En route, as you drive along Ayres Avenue, you will pass three regimental monuments on the left side of the road. These commemorate units from Brig. Gen. Samuel Crawford's division; keep their location in mind as you read the text for stop F4, below.

Orientation

You are looking down into the so-called Valley of Death. The two cannon commemorate the section of the 4th New York Battery that covered the Devil's Den gorge at the start of the day's fighting. Little Round Top dominates the horizon beyond. Devil's Den lies about 200 yards to your extreme right. Plum Run winds through the valley, from left to right, just beyond Crawford Avenue.

What Happened

In addition to securing aid from Sweitzer's brigade, General Caldwell also sought support from Brig. Gen. Romeyn B. Ayres, who commanded the 2nd Division of the Union V Corps—often called the Regular Division because two of its three brigades were composed of regularly enlisted United States troops, not state volunteers. The division's one volunteer brigade, under Brig. Gen. Stephen H. Weed, was already engaged on Little Round Top, but Ayres had earlier advanced his two Regular brigades—one behind the other—from their initial position on the north shoulder of Little Round Top and across the valley in front of you. During this first advance, which brought them to the woods where you now stand, the Regulars had come under heavy fire from Confederate sharpshooters in Devil's Den, as well as from a few Confederate troops in your current location.

Vignette

Capt. Dudley H. Chase, 17th U.S. Infantry, recalled the initial advance: "As we advanced down the slope of Little Round Top, our officers and men began to fall rapidly, and as we crossed a marsh, called Plum Run, the enemy opened a most destructive fire on my regiment, the Seventeenth Infantry, the extreme left of our line. We were thoroughly wrought up with excitement, and some one yelled out 'double quick.' At this we all cheered and broke into a run towards the enemy, who were firing at us from the cover of a stone wall a short distance to our front, and from the Devil's Den on our left flank. Our cheers were in the nature of shrieks. As we reached a stone wall in our front we were ordered to lie down, but we did not get down quickly enough to avoid a terrible flank fire from the Devil's Den. Within fifteen minutes, 150 officers and men, of our 260 in the regiment, were killed or wounded."

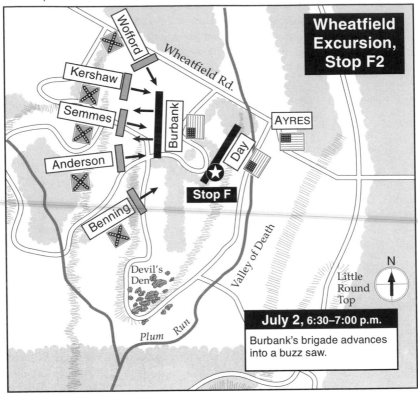

Wheatfield
Excursion,
Stop F2

Wofford

Wheatfield Rd.

Kershaw

Semmes

Burbank

AYRES

Anderson

Day

Stop F

Benning

Devil's
Den

Valley of Death

N

Little
Round
Top

Plum Run

July 2, 6:30–7:00 p.m.

Burbank's brigade advances
into a buzz saw.

STOP F2   6:30–7:00 P.M.

The Regulars Attack

Directions   Do an about-face so that you are looking into the woods.

What Happened   Reaching the knoll where you stand, the rear brigade (under
Col. Hannibal Day) halted. The other (under Col. Sidney Bur-
bank) continued into the woods and halted near the east
edge of the Wheatfield, about 100 yards beyond you. It could
go no farther because Caldwell's division was starting its
initial counterattack across the Wheatfield. The Regulars
watched as first Cross's brigade, then Brooke's brigade,
charged across the Wheatfield. A bit later, searching for reinforcements, Caldwell came upon General Ayres. Ayres ordered Burbank's brigade to wheel into the Wheatfield so as
to support Brooke's brigade. No sooner had the Regulars advanced than Confederates came swarming over the Stony
Hill and through Rose Woods, and the Union position at the
west end of the Wheatfield collapsed. Executing its left wheel
into the Wheatfield, Burbank's brigade suddenly found itself

flanked, as Confederate volleys from the Stony Hill ripped into the Regulars' ranks.

Vignette   The 2nd U.S. Infantry got the very worst of it. Maj. Arthur Lee wrote: "A fresh column of the enemy at this time appeared on our right, we were ordered to retire. The word was scarcely given when three lines of the enemy, elevated one above the other on the slope to our right [the Stony Hill], poured in a most destructive fire, almost decimating my regiment."

Uphill Work. 4:152

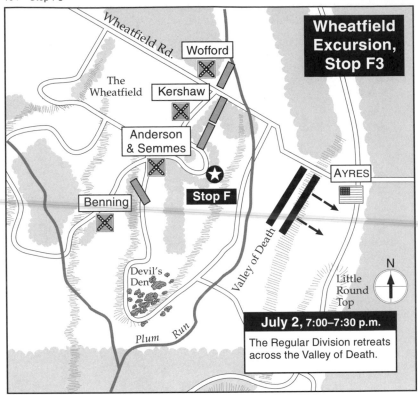

Wheatfield Excursion, Stop F3

Wheatfield Rd.

Wofford

The Wheatfield

Kershaw

Anderson & Semmes

AYRES

Benning

Stop F

Devil's Den

Valley of Death

Little Round Top

N

Plum Run

July 2, 7:00–7:30 p.m.

The Regular Division retreats across the Valley of Death.

STOP F3   7:00–7:30 P.M.

The Regulars Are Destroyed

Directions

Do a second about-face so that you are again facing the two cannon.

What Happened

The Regulars retreated from the Wheatfield, through the woods around you, and back toward the relative safety of Little Round Top. With true Old Army discipline they remained in close formation despite heavy casualties and pursuing Confederates, who soon reached the area where you stand and fired repeatedly into the withdrawing Federals. Confederates in the Devil's Den area did the same.

Vignette

Capt. Richard Robins, 11th U.S. Infantry, remembered: "The few hundred yards to the foot of Little Round Top, already strewn with our disabled comrades, became a very charnel house, and every step was marked by ghastly lines of dead and wounded. Our merciless foes from their vantage ground [at Devil's Den], poured in volley after volley, their sharpshooters picking off with unerring aim many a valuable officer and gallant color-bearer. Their battalions, fresh from the pursuit of Caldwell and Sweitzer, poured in a deadly fire on our other flank [from the stone wall to your left, near Ayres Avenue] until gasping and bleeding, we reached Little Round Top and took position behind Hazlett's guns."

In this relatively brief engagement, the two Regular brigades lost 829 men killed, wounded, or missing out of 2,613 engaged, a loss rate of 31.7 percent.

Dead on the Rose Farm, gathered for burial. From a photograph. 3:342

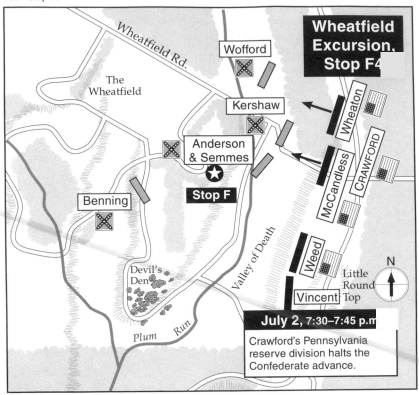

Wheatfield Excursion, Stop F4

Wheatfield Rd.

Wofford

The Wheatfield

Kershaw

Wheaton

Anderson & Semmes

McCandless

CRAWFORD

Benning

Stop F

Weed

Valley of Death

Devil's Den

Little Round Top

Vincent

N

Plum Run

July 2, 7:30–7:45 p.m

Crawford's Pennsylvania reserve division halts the Confederate advance.

STOP F4   7:30–7:45 P.M.

Crawford's Counterattack

Directions   Remain in place but look to your left front.

What Happened   Thus far, two divisions of the Union V Corps had been committed to the fighting. And with the exception of the two brigades deployed to defend Little Round Top (Vincent's and Weed's), both had been thrown back–along with Caldwell's division and Sickles's entire III Corps. Ayres's Regulars took position between Little Round Top and Wheatfield Road; Barnes's division continued the line from Wheatfield Road northward.

The Confederates pressed home their advantage by attacking into the Plum Run valley ahead of you. The brigades of *Anderson*, *Semmes*, and *Kershaw*–now somewhat disordered and considerably exhausted by hours of combat in the summer heat–moved forward toward the northern fringe of Little Round Top. Farther north along Wheatfield Road, *Wofford's* brigade also pressured the beleaguered Union line. Then more fresh Union brigades arrived. As one Confederate later recalled, a hapless question began to bloom in the minds of *Longstreet's* surviving troops: "My God, have we got the whole universe to whip?" The new brigades belonged to the third division of the V Corps, commanded by Brig. Gen. Samuel W. Crawford. As the Confederates reached the lower slopes of Little Round Top (not in front of the summit but along the hill's northern shoulder), Crawford ordered a counterattack–and, as his statue in the field beyond indicates, personally led it, waving the colors of the 1st Pennsylvania Reserves.

Col. William McCandless's brigade spearheaded the attack, supported by a second brigade to the north. The weight of the charge forced the weary Confederates to fall back rapidly–first to the woods around you, then beyond the Wheatfield to the Stony Hill. McCandless's brigade made it all the way across the Wheatfield and took cover behind a fence on its western side. Then, recognizing that the new position was too advanced and exposed, Crawford pulled the brigade back to the east edge of the Wheatfield (the line marked by the regimental monuments you saw on Ayres Avenue).

Analysis

The success of McCandless's attack testifies to the roles played in war by timing and fatigue. The attack occurred just as the Confederates were pursuing Ayres's defeated Regulars back to Little Round Top. The swift reversal of fortune took them by surprise, and the weight of McCandless's attack was the greater for being unexpected. Although his men had been marching much of the day, they had not been fighting or even under fire much before their arrival on the north shoulder of Little Round Top, leaving them relatively fresh. The Confederates, by contrast, had not only endured a lengthy approach march to reach the battlefield, they had also spent the better part of three hours in some of the most intensive combat of the entire war. The surviving commanders were beginning to comprehend that, despite their success at Houck's Ridge, the Peach Orchard, and the Wheatfield, they had really just broken the Union's first defensive line. A second, even more formidable line loomed ahead of them. When McCandless's men burst forth in an energetic counterattack, it is small wonder the Confederates fell back so readily.

This concludes the Wheatfield excursion. Return to your vehicle. *Continue* along AYRES AVENUE; *turn right* onto SICKLES AVENUE, and follow it to WHEATFIELD ROAD; then turn to the directions for stop 14, the Peach Orchard.

STOP 14   The Peach Orchard   3:30–6:00 P.M.

Directions   Return to your vehicle. If you have just completed the Wheat-
                            field excursion, *drive* to the four-way intersection, *turn right*,
                            and *drive* until you reach WHEATFIELD ROAD; otherwise, *resume
                            driving* along SICKLES AVENUE until you reach WHEATFIELD
                            ROAD. *Turn left* onto WHEATFIELD ROAD and *drive* 0.25 mile to
                            BIRNEY AVENUE (on your left); *turn left* onto BIRNEY AVENUE,
                            bear right round the bend, and then park your vehicle. Walk
                            to the two flank markers designating where the left flank of
                            the 3rd Maine Infantry joined the right flank of the 3rd
                            Michigan Infantry. Face south, looking across Birney Avenue.
                                En route, just as you turn onto Wheatfield Road, you will
                            notice a line of cannon along the right (north) shoulder of
                            the road. These batteries were the sole line of Union defense
                            in this area. The first battery marker you will encounter be-
                            longs to the 9th Massachusetts, which had recently joined
                            the army. Note its location for future reference.

Orientation   You are standing at the southern edge of a peach orchard
                            owned by the Sherfy family, whose barn is just north of the
                            intersection of Emmitsburg Road and Wheatfield Road to
                            your right rear. As you face south, you will see the Rose Farm-
                            house to your left and Emmitsburg Road to your right. To the
                            left of the Rose Farmhouse are Rose Woods and the Stony
                            Hill; visible on the horizon are the Round Tops. To the right
                            of Emmitsburg Road is Biesecker's Woods, then (due west of
                            where you stand) Pitzer's Woods, both on Warfield Ridge. The
                            orchard on today's battlefield was part of a larger orchard at
                            the time of the battle, extending to your left and across
                            Wheatfield Road to your rear.

What Happened   Early on the afternoon of July 2, III Corps commander Daniel
                            Sickles, responding to Berdan's report of Confederates mass-
                            ing along the northern edge of Pitzer's Woods, decided to ad-
                            vance his two divisions westward from their positions on
                            Cemetery Ridge south of the Pennsylvania Memorial. Just
                            two months before, at Chancellorsville, Sickles had pressed
                            forward to make contact with another Confederate column
                            marching through the woods across his front–the tail end of
                            Stonewall *Jackson's* flank march. The Union corps comman-
                            der was determined not to fall victim to yet another of Bobby
                            Lee's surprises. He deployed Andrew A. Humphreys's division
                            just east of Emmitsburg Road north of the Peach Orchard;
                            David Birney's division stretched from the Peach Orchard to
                            Devil's Den.

During the afternoon *Longstreet's* two divisions deployed along the woods on Warfield Ridge. *Lee's* plan of attack called for them to sweep north across the Peach Orchard and hit the Union line on Cemetery Ridge—a line he assumed stopped somewhere in the vicinity of the Pennsylvania Memorial. Sickles's new position did not cause *Lee* and *Longstreet* to reconsider their plan; indeed, *Longstreet* assured division commander Lafayette *McLaws*, "There is nothing in your front; you will be entirely on the flank of the enemy." *McLaws* had reason to differ when his men came under artillery fire as they deployed to your right along the edge of Pitzer's Woods.

Major General A. A. Humphreys, Army of the Potomac. From a photograph. 4:115

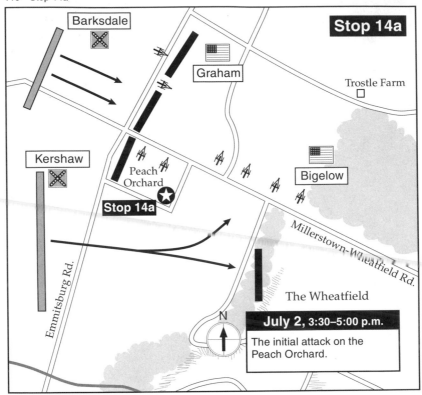

Barksdale

Stop 14a

Graham

Trostle Farm

Kershaw

Peach Orchard

Bigelow

Stop 14a

Millerstown-Wheatfield Rd.

Emmitsburg Rd.

The Wheatfield

N

July 2, 3:30–5:00 p.m.

The initial attack on the Peach Orchard.

STOP 14a   3:30–5:00 P.M.

The Opening Attack

Directions   Walk south to the bend in Birney Avenue. Face east, looking back along Wheatfield Road.

Orientation   You are looking at Rose Woods and Stony Hill; beyond them are the Wheatfield (behind the woods) and Little Round Top. You can recognize several major terrain features along the Union line north of Wheatfield Road. As you look at the line of cannon, recollect the position of the 9th Massachusetts Battery–it was positioned near the intersection of Wheatfield Road and Sickles Road. Beyond the line of artillery batteries are woods, a farmhouse, and a barn belonging to the Trostle family. To your left, beyond the Trostle farm buildings, is the Pennsylvania Memorial.

What Happened   As the fighting opened at the Wheatfield and the Stony Hill, Joseph *Kershaw's* brigade of South Carolinians marched east from Biesecker's Woods, across Emmitsburg Road, and toward the Rose Farmhouse. Union artillery, part of the army's reserve, opened fire on *Kershaw's* left flank; *Kershaw*, anticipating this, ordered two regiments and a battalion to wheel to the left to attack the line of cannon deployed along Wheatfield Road to the east of the Peach Orchard. For a moment it looked as if they might overrun the troublesome guns; then, misinterpreting *Kershaw's* orders, they pivoted back toward the east once more, rendering themselves vulnerable to a killing fire.

Analysis

The line of Union artillery along Wheatfield Road plugged a gap between the Peach Orchard (and Humphreys's left flank) and Rose Woods and the Wheatfield. It enjoyed a good field of fire, but to maintain its position, it had to hope that the infantry on both flanks would hold their ground. Before *Kershaw's* advance, the artillery had been exchanging shots with Confederate guns to the southwest, while suffering some from the Confederate artillery fire from Pitzer's Woods toward the Union batteries at the Peach Orchard.

The battery at the extreme left (eastern edge) of the line of cannon was the 9th Massachusetts. Commanded by Capt. John Bigelow, it consisted of six Napoleons. It took position here at approximately 3:45 P.M., arriving via Trostle's Farm. We will follow this battery's movements later in the day.

Vignette

As *Kershaw's* men crossed the fields near the Rose Farmhouse, a rabbit dashed off toward the Union line. "Go to it, old fellow," cried one of the attackers, "and I would be glad to go with you, if I hadn't a reputation to sustain!" Moments later a rabbit (perhaps the same one) bounded into the ranks of the 118th Pennsylvania (deployed at the western tip of Rose Woods) and pounced onto the neck of one of the privates hugging the ground. The soldier jumped up, yelling: "Oh, I'm shot! I'm a dead man! Shot clean through the neck!"

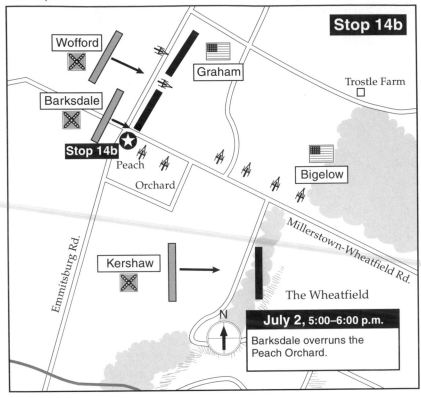

Stop 14b

Wofford

Graham

Trostle Farm

Barksdale

Stop 14b

Peach
Orchard

Bigelow

Millerstown-Wheatfield Rd.

Emmitsburg Rd.

Kershaw

The Wheatfield

N

July 2, 5:00–6:00 p.m.

Barksdale overruns the
Peach Orchard.

STOP 14b   5:00–6:00 P.M.

Barksdale's Charge

Directions   Walk to the northernmost corner of the Peach Orchard at the
junction of Emmitsburg Road and Wheatfield Road. Face
north.

Orientation   Emmitsburg Road runs northward from your immediate left
toward Cemetery Ridge in the distance – marked by the white
cylinder of the Cyclorama Center. The top of the light green
water tower marks Cemetery Hill. Just to your left is the
Sherfy Farm; up the road, its barn marked by three steeples,
is the Codori Farm.

What Happened   You are now looking at the area where Humphreys deployed
his division on the afternoon of July 2. Although he stationed
skirmishers at Emmitsburg Road, he kept his main force
back at Trostle's Farm, minus a brigade which Sickles ordered to reinforce Birney. Sickles then directed Humphreys
to advance toward Emmitsburg Road with his main force;
Humphreys placed his regiments on the eastern slope lead-

ing down from the road to the park road–the northern extension of Sickles Avenue–to protect his men and prepare a defense in depth of the position. As the battle opened, he received orders to go to Little Round Top, but these orders were soon countermanded. "With a firm step with colors flying the bravest men in the army marched into the open field," an observer later recalled. "It was a splendid sight."

Meanwhile, the Peach Orchard was becoming a focal point of Confederate artillery fire from the south and the west. Although the Union batteries gathered here responded effectively, the crossfire was deadly, slackening only as the Confederate infantry advanced.

Directions

Face west toward Pitzer's Woods. You should see the white house–the Snyder House–in the area where the Louisiana Monument is located.

What Happened

As Union artillery and infantry along the Peach Orchard and Wheatfield Road tore holes in *Kershaw's* brigade, William *Barksdale* ordered his Mississippians forward. The general himself led the way, on horseback, waving a sword; a second brigade of Georgians followed. The Union infantry north of the Peach Orchard gave way; artillery commanders hastily gave orders to limber up and withdraw their cannon. The apex of the III Corps position was overrun. Confederate artillerists rushed their guns up to Emmitsburg Road and opened fire on the collapsing Union line.

Directions

Walk east toward the statue of an artilleryman flanked by two cannon (Battery F, Pennsylvania Light Artillery [Hampton's Battery]). Face northeast toward the Trostle Farm.

What Happened

In the fields north of Wheatfield Road Humphreys tried to check the Confederate advance, but before long he found himself under attack from the west as well as from *Barksdale's* Mississippians to the south. Soon Humphreys was forced to pull back in orderly fashion. Meanwhile, one of *Barksdale's* regiments, the *21st Mississippi*, swept east along Wheatfield Road and headed for the guns of the 9th Massachusetts, just as some of *Kershaw's* South Carolinians charged it from the south. Bigelow, aware that he might lose precious moments in attempting to limber up, ordered his men to "retire by prolonge"–that is, drag his guns back while maintaining a rate of fire (the recoil from the shots would make it easier to move the guns). The battery would return to whence it came–the Trostle Farm.

Analysis

When Sickles ordered his men forward, he had no true idea of either the strength or location of the Confederates gathering on his front – in part because he had deployed his men in response to Berdan's report, which placed the Confederate right north of where *Longstreet* deployed. Birney could not hold his line; when it crumbled, Humphreys was too weak (and vulnerable) to maintain his position when the orchard came under Confederate crossfire.

Vignette

If you return for a moment to the corner of Wheatfield Road and Emmitsburg Road, you will notice four rectangular stones with bronze tablets mounted on them. The narrative of events embodied therein is in marked contrast to most other accounts of the battle. It asserts that Sickles changed position to save the day and fought a holding action until reinforcements came up. The account tells us much more about postbattle controversies than it does about what actually happened on July 2; it reflects the fact that Daniel Sickles played a major role in developing Gettysburg as a battlefield park. In later years, when someone pointed out that there was no Sickles statue anywhere on the battlefield, Sickles calmly replied that the whole battlefield was his monument. The narrative on these markers represents the way he wanted to be remembered.

Trostle's Farm, near the scene of the fighting by Bigelow's 9th Massachusetts Battery. From a wartime photograph. 3:306

STOP 15   Trostle's Farm   3:30–6:00 P.M.

Directions   Return to your vehicle. *Exit* BIRNEY AVENUE by *turning right* onto EMMITSBURG ROAD, then *turn right* onto WHEATFIELD ROAD. *Turn left* onto the northern section of SICKLES AVENUE (just after you pass Birney Avenue) and *drive* to UNITED STATES AVENUE. *Turn right. Drive east* on UNITED STATES AVENUE toward the Trostle Barn. When you reach the barn (with two cannon in front), pull over to the shoulder before the road bears left. Exit your vehicle, cross United States Avenue, and walk to the battery (marking the second position of the 9th Massachusetts Artillery). Looking westward, back toward the road you just took, locate a bridle path; follow it as it curls around a fence and runs north to a small marker topped by a diamond.

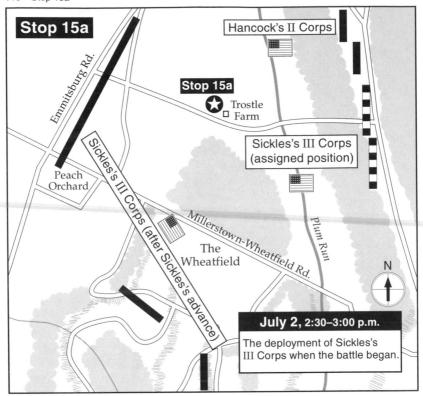

Stop 15a

Hancock's II Corps

Stop 15a

★ Trostle
□ Farm

Sickles's III Corps
(assigned position)

Emmitsburg Rd.

Sickles's III Corps (after Sickles's advance)

Peach
Orchard

Millerstown-Wheatfield Rd.

The
Wheatfield

Plum Run

N

July 2, 2:30–3:00 p.m.
The deployment of Sickles's
III Corps when the battle began.

STOP 15a   2:30–3:00 P.M.

Sickles the Incredible

Directions   Face west toward Emmitsburg Road, visible on the near crest.

Orientation   You are standing just west of Trostle's Farm, to the rear of
                        Sickles's position on the afternoon of July 2. The Peach Or-
                        chard is to the southwest (your left), about 660 yards away,
                        just below Longstreet's Tower; due south across Wheatfield
                        Road is Rose Woods, about 330 yards away.

What Happened   In this vicinity Sickles established his headquarters on the af-
                        ternoon of July 2 (a cannon barrel mounted on a rock by
                        United States Avenue across from the Trostle Barn marks the
                        official location). Standing here, you can follow his reasons
                        for moving his corps forward from its position on Cemetery
                        Ridge east of Weikert Woods. Sickles observed that Weikert
                        and Rose Woods would obstruct his artillery's field of fire
                        westward from Cemetery Ridge. Upon approaching this area,
                        he looked west to the Peach Orchard and Emmitsburg Road.

Aware of Berdan's report of Confederate activity to the west, he decided that the best way to deprive the enemy of the ground in front of him was to occupy it himself. "I took up that line because it enabled me to hold commanding ground," he later explained. In later years he also sought to traduce George G. Meade by claiming that by moving to this position he had forced a battle at a time when Meade (according to the story) was contemplating retreat—one of the best pieces of fiction generated by the conflict.

Sickles would have been on firmer ground had he argued that Meade did not pay sufficient attention to matters on his left flank during the morning and early afternoon of July 2. The absence of a Union cavalry shield and Berdan's reports alarmed Sickles; neither Meade's son George (an aide to his father) nor artillery commander Maj. Gen. Henry J. Hunt succeeded in impressing Meade's intentions on the corps commander, who seemed bent on getting his way. Perhaps he was excited in part because of the lack of supporting units. Waiting for the arrival of the VI Corps to serve as his reserve, Meade was forced to keep the V Corps in reserve instead of dispatching it to his left, leaving the III Corps on its own.

Vignette

Meade rode to the valley in front of you to meet with Sickles on the afternoon of July 2. "General, I am afraid you are too far out," he told Sickles, doing a masterful job of keeping his temper under control. When Sickles justified his choice of ground, Meade tightened. "General Sickles," he replied, "This is in some respects higher ground than to the rear, but there is still higher ground in front of you, and if you keep on advancing you will find constantly higher ground all the way to the mountains." Just as Sickles offered to withdraw; a Confederate artillery ball struck the ground near the feet of Meade's horse. "I only wish you could, sir," Meade replied, struggling to control both his mount and his anger, "but you see those people don't intend to let you." He had barely enough time to add that he would send artillery to support Sickles before his horse began to rear and plunge, forcing Meade to seek safer ground.

Sickles would pay on this spot for his decision to advance his line. He was on horseback directing operations when another Confederate cannonball found its mark, nearly removing the general's right leg below the knee. Aides helped the wounded commander to dismount; Sickles instructed a drummer boy to apply a tourniquet to slow the bleeding. As a stretcher carried him off the field, Sickles, always the showman, lit up a large cigar and puffed it to show his men he was

Major General Daniel
E. Sickles. From a
wartime photograph.
3:296

not dead. A surgeon amputated the severed limb; someone
preserved the bones, and in later years Sickles visited them.
They currently reside at the National Museum of Health and
Medicine in Washington DC.

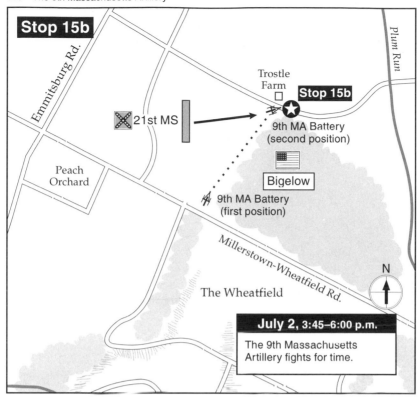

Stop 15b

Emmitsburg Rd.

Trostle
Farm

Stop 15b

⊠ 21st MS

9th MA Battery
(second position)

Peach
Orchard

Bigelow

9th MA Battery
(first position)

Millerstown-Wheatfield Rd.

The Wheatfield

Plum Run

N

July 2, 3:45–6:00 p.m.

The 9th Massachusetts
Artillery fights for time.

STOP 15b   3:45–6:00 P.M.

The 9th Massachusetts Artillery

Directions   Walk back to the two cannon. Face south.

Orientation   If you look due south, you should be able to spot the position
                      of the 9th Massachusetts Battery at the beginning of the en-
                      gagement: it is the battery on the left of the line. To the
                      southeast is the northern slope of Little Round Top and the
                      Valley of Death. Due east is Weikert Woods, also about 330
                      yards away. Plum Run runs just to the east of the farm.

What Happened   The 9th Massachusetts Artillery paid a high price for Sickles's
                      decision to occupy the Peach Orchard. Its six guns formed
                      part of a line of cannon facing south along Wheatfield Road
                      on July 2. When the Union line at the Peach Orchard started
                      to give way at 6:00 P.M., Col. Freeman McGilvery, in charge of
                      the 1st Volunteer Brigade of the Army of the Potomac's ar-
                      tillery reserve, decided that it was time to pull back the three
                      batteries still in action. At first they made a stand in the fields
                      just south and west of the Trostle Farm until McGilvery, see-

ing the Confederates concentrate their fire on the artillery-men, decided on another withdrawal across Plum Run. An inspection of the condition of the Union line east of Weikert Woods altered his plans, in large part because there was no line to speak of, although Union infantrymen, dazed by battle, were attempting to regather their wits. McGilvery needed time to form a new line of cannon to block the enemy attack; he rode up to Bigelow and ordered him to hold his position just south of the Trostle Farm "at all hazards."

Directions

Cross United States Avenue. Look to your left and locate a low stone wall that breaks just short of the fence in front of you. It borders a depressed section of the farm.

What Happened

Bigelow's battery was pinned against the corner of a stone wall, making it difficult to continue moving his guns back. He held the Confederates at bay with canister, but eventually the attackers closed in. "Sergeant after sergt. was struck down, horses were plunging and laying all around, bullets now came in on all sides for the enemy had turned my flanks," Bigelow later recalled. "The air was dark with smoke. . . . The enemy were yelling like demons, yet my men kept up a rapid fire, with their guns each time loaded to the muzzle." Eventually Bigelow had to abandon four of his guns, for enemy fire had cut down most of the battery's horses, and the stone wall proved too much of an obstacle. Bigelow was wounded; bugler Charles W. Reed led a successful rescue of the captain (for which he received the Medal of Honor). The battery bought the time necessary for McGilvery to plug the gap with batteries just east of Plum Run. A marker just east of the cannon commemorates the efforts of the 150th New York in recovering several of Bigelow's guns late that day.

STOP 16   South Cemetery Ridge   7:00–9:00 P.M.

Directions

Return to your vehicle. *Continue driving* east along UNITED STATES AVENUE until it terminates at the junction of Hancock and Sedgwick Avenues. *Turn left* (north) onto HANCOCK AVE-NUE, and *drive* to the parking lot to the right of the Pennsylvania Memorial. (You may wish to take advantage of the rest room facilities.) Walk to the Pennsylvania Memorial, ascend the stairway to the landing opposite Hancock Avenue, and walk to the western-most corner of the landing (marked by statues of Meade and Lincoln).

En route you will cross Plum Run and pass the George Weikert Farm—the area where McGilvery formed his final line. Several cannon north of the road help mark that line. The advance of the *21st Mississippi* ended south of this area, when it launched one final attack against yet another Union battery, capturing it before Union infantry forced the attackers to relinquish their prize. On Hancock Avenue, the first monument on the right commemorates Father William Corby, who granted absolution to the soldiers of the Irish Brigade before they were ordered to advance into the Wheatfield.

Orientation

You are standing just east of the northern edge of Plum Run (which runs along the wood line to the west). To the north you should be able to see the Cyclorama Center; the Round Tops are plainly visible to the south. Due west, along Emmitsburg Road, you should be able to locate a large diamond-shaped white granite marker, denoting Humphreys's right flank on the afternoon of July 2.

Hand-to-hand for Ricketts's guns on the evening of the second day. 3:369

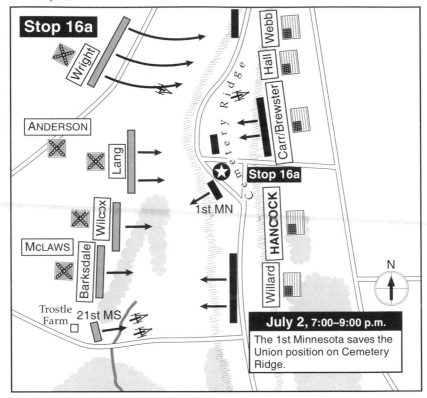

Stop 16a

Wright

ANDERSON

Lang

Wilcox

McLAWS

Barksdale

Trostle Farm   21st MS

Webb

Hall

Carr/Brewster

Cemetery Ridge

Stop 16a

1st MN

HANCOCK

Willard

N

July 2, 7:00–9:00 p.m.
The 1st Minnesota saves the Union position on Cemetery Ridge.

STOP 16a   7:00–9:00 P.M.

The Charge of the 1st Minnesota

Directions   Remain in place but face south. Among the monuments you should see is a shaft topped by a running infantryman, bayonet at the ready. It marks the point at which the 1st Minnesota commenced its charge.

What Happened   Late on the afternoon of July 2 Confederate infantry surged eastward in one final thrust against the Union line. To the south, west of the Weikert Farm, McGilvery struggled to hold his line against *Barksdale's* brigade, still sweeping eastward (although *Barksdale* fell mortally wounded). The appearance of reinforcements from the II and XII Corps proved sufficient to deter the exhausted Mississippi attackers. The same could not be said for the area between this monument and McGilvery's line. Humphreys's division had occupied this area on the morning of July 2; now it was vulnerable. Only one battery of six cannon held the line. As Brig. Gen. Cadmus M. *Wilcox's* brigade of Richard *Anderson's* division, having overrun Humphreys's right flank, approached this area from the west, Winfield Scott Hancock, who had assumed command of this sector of the Union line, looked about for reinforcements. He found the 1st Minnesota. Commanded by Col. William Colvill Jr., the regiment numbered 262 officers and men. Hancock pointed at the flag of one of the Alabama regiments and cried, "Advance, Colonel, and take those colors!"

The Minnesotans, bayonets fixed, smashed into the startled Alabamians and drove them across Plum Run. Rallying, the Confederates delivered a withering fire, but they did not counterattack. Eventually the 1st Minnesota withdrew. According to some accounts, 40 men had been killed; another 175 had been wounded – a casualty rate of 82 percent. Although the Confederate attack was already beginning to stall, the gallant charge – plus the fire from the artillery battery deployed just southwest of this monument – put an end to the promise of a Rebel breakthrough in this sector.

There is a path toward Plum Run from the 1st Minnesota's monument that allows you to explore this area of the field in more depth. By the way, the monument just south of the 1st Minnesota marks the position of the 88th Pennsylvania (of Oak Ridge fame) later in the battle.

Major General Cadmus M. Wilcox, C.S.A. From a photograph. 3:364

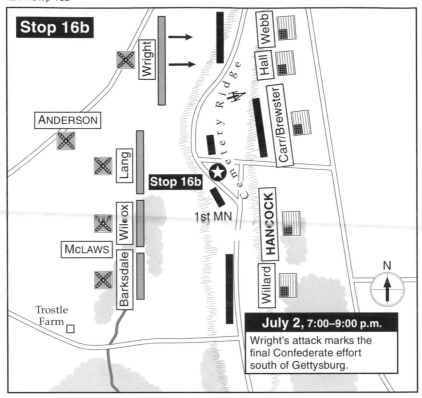

July 2, 7:00–9:00 p.m.

Wright's attack marks the final Confederate effort south of Gettysburg.

STOP 16b   7:00–9:00 P.M.

Wright's Attack

Directions   Remain in place but face northwest. You will see Emmitsburg Road in the middle distance; the Codori Barn stands alongside it. As you look to the right, just behind a tall obelisk, you will see the copse of trees that visitors usually associate with the action of July 3.

What Happened   Dusk was not far away when Brig. Gen. Ambrose R. *Wright's* brigade of Georgians advanced across the fields between Seminary Ridge and Emmitsburg Road toward the Codori Farm, held by forward units of the *Second Corps*. The Confederates swept over the position and continued onward toward Cemetery Ridge. The Union brigades that had held this sector at the beginning of the afternoon's action had marched southward to stop the opening thrusts of *Longstreet's* attack. Although *Wright's* left flank soon came under telling fire from Union regiments and batteries at the copse of trees, his right encountered little opposition. For a few moments the only Federals in the sector were George Meade and his staff.

They waited anxiously for reinforcements to arrive. The 13th Vermont appeared (in the vicinity of the tall pillar topped by a statue of an officer) and struck the Georgians' right, driving it back. The remnants of Humphreys's division joined in a counterattack against what remained of *Anderson's* force, reaching Emmitsburg Road as dusk came.

Analysis

In years to come *Wright* and other Confederates thought that they had come close to victory. But Union reinforcements were on their way, and any deeper Rebel penetration would have been short-lived. At least as important was that there were no Confederate forces available to exploit initial opportunities. The failure to provide adequate support for attack forces would characterize Confederate operations against Cemetery Ridge on both July 2 and 3. In contrast, Meade's ability to shift reserve forces skillfully to contain breakthroughs negated whatever chance the Confederates had of following through on their assaults.

Confederates waiting for the end of the artillery duel. 3:361

STOP 17   Culp's Hill   6:00 A.M.–9:30 P.M.

Directions   Return to your car. The next segment of the tour route requires several turns, so take an extra moment to familiarize yourself with the map before going on.

Drive to the T intersection with PLEASONTON AVENUE and turn right. Continue to the T intersection with TANEYTOWN ROAD (PA 134) and turn left. Drive 0.5 mile to HUNT AVENUE (near the Visitor Center) and turn right. Go to the T intersection with BALTIMORE PIKE (PA 97) and turn right. Then proceed not quite 0.4 mile to CARMAN AVENUE and turn left. A National Park Service sign will help you identify the turnoff.

CARMAN AVENUE soon makes a sharp bend to the left, becomes COLGROVE AVENUE, and eventually changes its name to SLOCUM AVENUE. Watch your odometer. At 0.8 mile from the turnoff from BALTIMORE PIKE, you will reach the second intersection with GEARY AVENUE (which begins and ends at Slocum Avenue). Pull off into the turnout on the right just beyond the intersection, a few feet past the marker on your right denoting the location of Brig. Gen. Thomas L. Kane's brigade.

En route you will pass three sites worth noting. At the turnoff from Taneytown Road to Hunt Avenue is a small white cottage, the Lydia Leister House, that served as Meade's headquarters during the battle. (You will have a better chance to examine the house when you reach stop 20.) The point where Carman Avenue bends to the left to become Colgrove Avenue marks the approximate location of MacAllister's Woods, the extreme right end of the Union line on July 2. Spangler's Spring is 0.5 mile from Baltimore Pike, easily identifiable because of the National Park Service marker and the adjacent parking lot. A well-known bit of Gettysburg lore relates how soldiers from both sides filled their canteens from this spring on the night of July 2, but this tale is not well supported by the evidence.

STOP 17a   6:00 A.M.–7:00 P.M.

Greene Holds the Line

Directions   Exit your vehicle and face northeast, directly toward the 109th Pennsylvania Monument (it has what appear to be stone urns carved into its corners).

Orientation   You are standing in the "saddle" between the upper and lower crests of Culp's Hill, just behind the position held by the Union XII Corps on July 2. If you look just beyond the

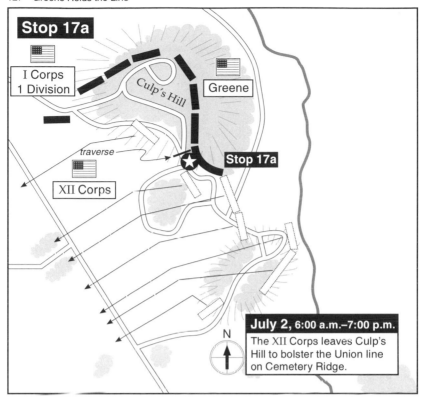

Stop 17a

I Corps
1 Division

Culp's Hill

Greene

traverse

XII Corps

Stop 17a

July 2, 6:00 a.m.–7:00 p.m.
The XII Corps leaves Culp's Hill to bolster the Union line on Cemetery Ridge.

N

109th Pennsylvania Monument, you will see a low but distinct mound of earth that runs like a serpent along the ground, the remnant of a Union trench constructed here on the afternoon of July 2. To your left, you will see a large boulder a few yards from where the trench line makes a sharp bend (it is further identified by a plaque commemorating the 14th Brooklyn Regiment). The boulder marks the approximate location of a large breastwork called the "traverse" that extended from the bend in the trench line, across the present-day roadbed, and on toward a ravine over your left shoulder. No trace of the traverse remains today.

Turning left, you will face the intersection of Geary and Slocum Avenues and, beyond it, an open area known as Pardee Field. Just across Slocum Avenue and to the left of Geary Avenue, you should be able to discern the remnants of a stone wall. The traverse and the stone wall both figure prominently in the discussion that follows.

What Happened   Led by Maj. Gen. Henry W. Slocum, the XII Corps began filing into its Culp's Hill position around 6 A.M. and by midmorning occupied a line stretching from the upper crest of the hill to MacAllister's Woods, down by Rock Creek. Around

5:30 P.M., in response to the crisis at the Peach Orchard and Little Round Top, most of the corps was sent to reinforce the Union left. Only a single brigade, under Brig. Gen. George S. Greene, remained to hold Culp's Hill.

Greene had earlier urged his superiors to fortify the line and had put his own men to work constructing entrenchments. Within three or four hours his troops had prepared extensive fieldworks consisting of rifle pits, breastworks, and abatis. (Pronounced *ah-bah-tee*, these were trees felled so that the branches faced toward the enemy.) When complete, the fieldworks were nearly five feet thick and capable of stopping an artillery shell. On the right flank of their initial position, Greene's men also constructed a traverse at right angles to the main line. Perhaps this was done to support a weak point in the line—as you can see, the ground in this area is low—but it may also have been built because Greene worried at first that the brigade on his right would *not* entrench, and he wanted protection from that direction.

In any event, once the rest of the corps pulled out, Greene extended his line to occupy the now empty trenches on his right and left. His soldiers spread out until nearly a foot separated each man—something almost unheard-of during the Civil War era. The 137th New York crossed over the traverse and took up the position formerly occupied by the 109th Pennsylvania, in front of you. Greene would have extended his line even more, but at that point he received word that Confederate forces were launching a strong attack against the upper slope of Culp's Hill.

Brevet Major General George S. Greene. From a photograph. 3:372

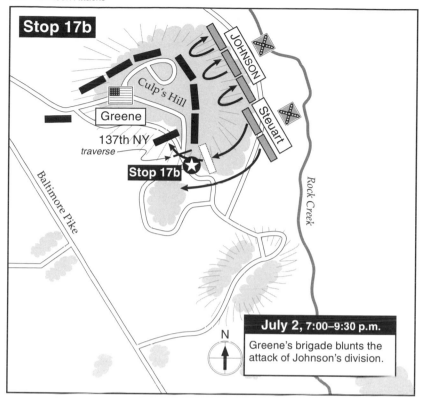

Stop 17b

Culp's Hill

JOHNSON

Steuart

Greene

137th NY

traverse

Stop 17b

Baltimore Pike

Rock Creek

July 2, 7:00–9:30 p.m.

Greene's brigade blunts the attack of Johnson's division.

N

STOP 17b   7:00–9:30 P.M.

Johnson Attacks

Directions   Remain in position.

What Happened   The Confederate division of Maj. Gen. Edward "Allegheny Ed" *Johnson* had spent most of the day some 600 yards northeast of your current location, just beyond Rock Creek beneath the crest of Benner's Hill. At about 7:00 P.M., *Second Corps* commander *Ewell* ordered the division to advance against Culp's Hill. The timing of the attack makes it tempting to believe that *Ewell* somehow knew the Union XII Corps had largely vacated the hill, but there is no evidence that he did. Apparently he was just following *Lee's* suggestion to convert his demonstration (see stop 7c) into a real attack once *Longstreet* was heavily engaged.

Johnson's division–four brigades totaling nearly 6,000 men–handily outnumbered Greene's 1,424 Federals. Several factors combined to reduce this seemingly forbidding edge. Reports of Union cavalry to the east forced *Johnson* to detach one brigade to guard his flank and rear. The slope of Culp's

Hill and the onset of twilight made it difficult for the Confederates to reach the Union lines, particularly along the steep, boulder-strewn upper crest of the hill. Finally, the Union entrenchments enabled the defenders to keep up a harrowing fire while suffering few casualties of their own.

The Confederates made the best progress in the area where you are standing. A brigade under Brig. Gen. George H. "Maryland" *Steuart* eventually pressured the 137th New York out of the entrenchments to your right, but the 137th was able to fall back to the safety of the traverse and maintain a heavy flanking fire against the Rebel troops. Meanwhile, about 755 Federals arrived from Cemetery Hill to bolster Greene's line, and eventually one division from the XII Corps countermarched to Culp's Hill and stopped *Johnson's* advance for good.

Analysis

In his novel *The Killer Angels*, author Michael Shaara makes Joshua Lawrence Chamberlain, whose 20th Maine held the extreme left of the Union line, wonder briefly about his counterpart on the extreme right. For all practical purposes that counterpart was General Greene. Both defended key terrain features the Union army *had* to control to maintain its position at Gettysburg. Greene's performance was as capable as Chamberlain's and he faced even greater odds. But it does Greene no disservice to point out that the Confederates at Culp's Hill enjoyed no opportunity like the one at Little Round Top. With nightfall upon them, few troops not already committed to the fight, and a division from the XII Corps en route back to Culp's Hill, *Johnson's* men could not have exploited any breakthrough they might have achieved.

STOP 17c

July 3, 4:30 A.M.–noon

Fighting on the Third Day

Directions

Cross the intersection and walk along the left shoulder of Geary Avenue until you have a clear view of the open field, called Pardee Field.

Orientation

After the return of Brig. Gen. John Geary's division around 9:30 P.M. on July 2, one of his brigades, under Brig. Gen. Thomas L. Kane, occupied the traverse. Col. Charles Candy's brigade (of which the 5th Ohio was a part) held a line beginning at the traverse and extending roughly along the tree line at the right (northern) edge of Pardee Field. No Union troops occupied the area to your left; it was covered by Union artillery batteries placed on Powers Hill and along the Baltimore Pike. (In 1863 the ground to your west was open as far as Powers Hill, not wooded as it is today.) A second Union division, under Brig. Gen. Thomas Ruger, occupied a position just south of Spangler's Spring out of sight to your extreme left. The Confederates occupied a portion of the Union trench line in the direction of Spangler's Spring and also retained footholds on the lower slopes of Culp's Hill. Notice the remnants of a low stone wall to your immediate left; it figured prominently in the fighting on July 3.

What Happened   Both sides received orders to attack the next morning. The XII Corps, commanded by Brig. Gen. Alpheus S. Williams, had orders to drive the Confederates out of the Union trench line. *Johnson*, now reinforced by an additional brigade from his own division, two from *Rodes's* division, and one from *Early's* division, was instructed to seize Culp's Hill and push onward to the Baltimore Pike. Originally *Johnson's* attack was supposed to have been part of a two-pronged offensive in conjunction with an assault on Cemetery Ridge by *Longstreet's* corps, but unknown to *Ewell* and *Johnson* until too late, the two-pronged offensive was canceled.

Fighting on July 3 began at 4:30 A.M., when Union artillery bombarded the Confederate line for 15 minutes. In response, *Johnson's* reinforced division launched the first of three assaults it would make that morning. In the last of these assaults, *Steuart's* brigade advanced across Pardee Field from your left and pressed toward the 5th Ohio and 147th Pennsylvania in this area. A small marker–visible if you look to your left rear between the "Do Not Enter" sign and the stone wall–commemorates the most advanced point gained by the *1st Maryland Battalion* (C.S.A.).

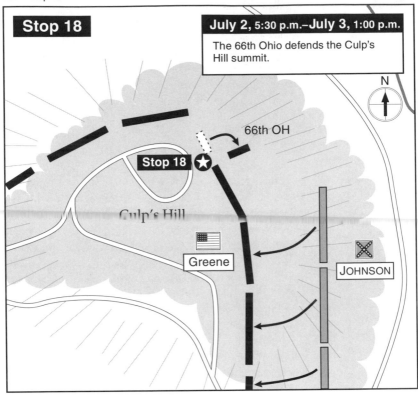

Stop 18

July 2, 5:30 p.m.–July 3, 1:00 p.m.

The 66th Ohio defends the Culp's Hill summit.

N

66th OH

Stop 18 ★

Culp's Hill

Greene

JOHNSON

STOP 18   Culp's Hill Summit   July 2, 5:30 P.M.–July 3, 1:00 P.M.

Directions   Return to your car. *Proceed north* on SLOCUM AVENUE, *bearing right* at the next fork in the road. *Turn right* at the next T intersection, which will take you to the summit of Culp's Hill. Park in one of the spaces provided and walk to the 95th New York marker, a small stone block directly in front of the parking lot (two monuments to the left of the statue of Gen. George S. Greene). Incidentally, the cannon near the observation tower were here for only an hour (5 to 6 P.M.) on July 2, when they engaged in counterbattery fire against Benner's Hill. They played no role in the infantry struggle for Culp's Hill.

Stand directly by the marker and face downhill.

Orientation   You may recall the 95th New York because of its involvement in the action at the railroad cut (stop 3). Late on July 2 it was sent to this location to assist in the final stages of Greene's repulse of *Johnson's* attack, but it arrived too late to play much of a role. You are standing at its marker merely because it offers a convenient reference point.

Similarly, the 7th Indiana Monument to your left rear (the sizable rectangular stone surmounted by a pyramid) is also useful mainly as a reference point. The 7th was part of Cutler's brigade, Wadsworth's division, I Corps. Unlike the other regiments in Cutler's brigade, it arrived too late to play a role in the fighting on July 1 and was sent to this spot to secure Culp's Hill on the evening of the first day. At that time it formed the right flank of the Union line. Subsequently the XII Corps came up and extended the flank to your right, back to Spangler's Spring and beyond. The 7th remained in this area throughout the battle and was engaged here on July 2 and 3, but through a happy accident it faced away from the main Confederate attacks and suffered only ten casualties for all three days.

As the experience of the 7th Indiana attests, most of the fighting on Culp's Hill occurred to your right and somewhat down the slope from where you now stand. If you walk about to the next monument to the right (Knap's Battery) and then about 15 yards down the steep, unimproved path that leads downhill, you will reach the regimental monument of the 66th Ohio. You may take that walk now or read about what happened from your current position.

What Happened

Part of Candy's brigade, Geary's division, XII Corps, the 66th Ohio was one of the many regiments pulled out of the Culp's Hill trench works around 6 P.M. on July 2 and sent to reinforce the beleaguered Union left. Upon its return to the Culp's Hill sector late that night, the commander of the 66th, Lt. Col. Eugene Powell, received orders to take his regiment to the summit of Culp's Hill, face right so as to enfilade the Confederate infantry on Greene's front, and thereby assist in the recovery of the lost entrenchments.

Powell got his regiment to the top of the hill while it was still dark and reported to the "commanding officer"–probably Greene. When he explained his instructions, the officer was taken aback. "My God, young man, the enemy are right out there. I am expecting an attack every moment; if you go out there with your reg[imen]t, they will simply swallow you."

Powell nevertheless did as directed. When the Union artillery bombardment began at 4:30 A.M. on July 3, he took his regiment over the crest–probably starting off not far from where the 7th Indiana Monument now stands–faced to the right, and began working the regiment along the upper slope of Culp's Hill. A couple of the men were shot at the outset, but after a "close hot fight" the 66th managed to drive away

Gettysburg from
Culp's Hill. From a
photograph of about
1886. 3:373

the few Confederates in the area and continued to a rocky
shelf directly in front of the 95th New York marker. There the
regiment maintained its position with a loss of only 17 casualties. One of them, Maj. J. G. Palmer, a former dentist, who
was mortally wounded, is commemorated by a stone tablet a
short distance beyond the 66th Ohio Monument. The tablet
also marks the approximate left flank of the 66th in its unusual early morning foray.

Before returning to your car, you may want to climb the observation tower, which affords a good view of the surrounding area.

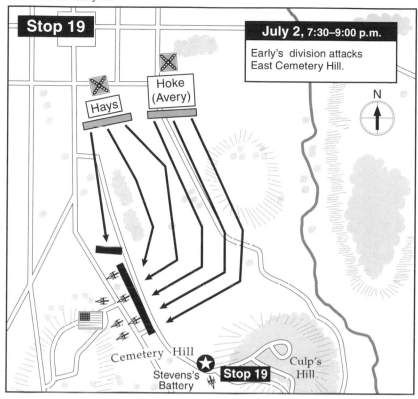

STOP 19

East Cemetery Hill   July 2, 7:30–9:00 P.M.

Directions

Return to your car and *proceed* about 0.2 mile on SLOCUM AVE-NUE to a turnout on the right side of the road directly oppo-site a large equestrian statue of General Slocum. Exit your ve-hicle and face the large field beyond the fence (north).

Orientation

To your left is East Cemetery Hill, the Confederate objective. (A green water tower is prominent on the hill's northern shoulder.) Near the crest are remnants of the Union artillery positions that protected the hill. At the foot of the hill you will see a narrow lane (now called Wainwright Avenue). Union infantry were positioned behind the stone wall bor-dering the lane. The Confederate attack swept across the field in front of you from right to left (east to west).

What Happened

Early's attack consisted of 2,300 men in two brigades, led by Brig. Gen. Harry T. *Hays* and Col. Isaac E. *Avery*. If you look carefully at the field in front, you will see a ridge line 150 yards away (clearly outlined by the trees beyond). *Hays's* brigade advanced on the far side of the ridge line, beyond your line of sight. *Avery's* brigade advanced across the ground in front of you.

Avery's brigade came under Union artillery fire from East Cemetery Hill even before it would have become visible to you from this position. As the Confederates crossed the field in front of you, the guns immediately behind you fired canister. Though many rounds apparently overshot *Avery's* men, large holes were torn in their ranks. But five of the nine Union infantry regiments at the stone wall fled as soon as the attackers reached them. Both Confederate brigades surged up East Cemetery Hill. Union cannoneers remained at their guns, and Union generals Oliver O. Howard and Carl Schurz were able to rally enough troops to block the Confederate attack as it neared the summit. Severe fighting, some of it hand-to-hand, occurred among the Union gun positions near the crest, but the Confederate attackers were too few. As Union counterattacks struck their left and front, *Hays*, the senior Confederate officer present, ordered a withdrawal. Covered by nightfall, the surviving Confederates fell back across the field in front of you.

Analysis

Ewell has been criticized for not attacking sooner, but had he done so *Johnson's* division would have struck an entire Union corps on Culp's Hill, whereas the evening attack caught the Federals after they had sent most of the corps to bolster their left. *Ewell's* principal mistake was his failure to marshal enough troops for the assault. He had more than 5,000 men available, but they were spread in a wide arc west and east of Gettysburg and *Ewell* failed to coordinate them in time. (*Rodes's* division briefly attacked the west face of Cemetery Hill, for instance, but only after *Early's* attack had failed.)

It is thus surprising that *Early's* understrength attack got as far as it did. Three factors help to explain its success. First, the two Confederate brigades maintained excellent cohesion. *Avery's* brigade executed a difficult maneuver—a right oblique—in textbook fashion while under heavy artillery fire. Second, many Union infantry defenders at the stone wall simply ran. Third, as the attackers advanced up the hill the slope of the ground temporarily shielded them from the guns at the summit.

Why did many Union infantry run? The best answer may be that they were units of the XI Corps, which had taken severe losses in the previous day's fighting. The cannoneers, however, stayed at their posts. Veterans from many wars report observing that troops manning crew-served weapons are often the last to break, probably because the mechanical demands of handling the weapons, coupled with the close teamwork involved, helps distract them from their danger while fostering a heightened cohesiveness.

Vignette

As his brigade neared the stone wall, a ball struck Colonel *Avery* in the neck, knocking him off his horse. In the smoke and gathering darkness no one saw him fall; his men pressed on across the wall without him. Knowing his wound was mortal, he took some paper and a stub of pencil and scribbled a note to his friend Major *Tate*. The note, still preserved in the North Carolina Department of Archives and History, reads: "Major— Tell my father I died with my face to the enemy. I. E. Avery."

Uphill Work, detail. 4:152

Overview of the Third Day, July 3

Initially Robert E. *Lee* hoped to renew his assaults on both Union flanks at daybreak; however, fighting on Culp's Hill commenced before dawn, eventually resulting in a Confederate withdrawal (stop 17c). This necessitated a change in his instructions to *Longstreet*, which originally called on him to continue to press forward east of Emmitsburg Road toward the Union center on Cemetery Ridge–a plan fraught with dangerous consequences, for it would have exposed the attackers to fire on their right flank from Little Round Top and other Union positions. *Longstreet* argued in favor of a move against the Federal left flank along the Round Tops, featuring another (although shorter) flank march south around Big Round Top toward Taneytown Road, which would endanger the Union rear. In light of the failure of *Lee* and *Longstreet* to ensure that George *Pickett's* fresh division was in place to participate in a morning attack, however, it was impossible to do much during the morning hours. Faced with this situation, *Lee* decided to strike the Union position on Cemetery Ridge with a massive frontal assault preceded by an artillery bombardment. He placed *Longstreet* in charge of preparing for the blow. *Pickett's* three brigades, plus six brigades of *Hill's Third Corps* that had fought on the first day, were to spearhead the attack; it remains unclear what plans, if any, either *Lee* or *Longstreet* made for infantry support, although apparently *Longstreet's* other two divisions were to remain in place. At the same time, *Lee* made provisions for *Stuart's* cavalry to swing east of Culp's Hill and threaten the Union rear (East Cavalry Battlefield excursion).

Aside from a few artillery exchanges as the Confederates under the supervision of Edward Porter *Alexander* shifted cannon into position east of Seminary Ridge, the only fighting west of Cemetery Ridge occurred when several Union regiments decided to oust enemy marksmen from the Bliss Farm, west of Emmitsburg Road. At noon it grew quiet; many Union soldiers ate lunch, while the Confederates moved into place for their assault. Then, at 1:00 P.M., two Rebel cannons fired, signaling the start of the massive artillery barrage. Union cannon along Cemetery Ridge boomed in reply, although artillery chief Henry J. Hunt wanted to conserve ammunition for use in breaking up the infantry assault to follow (stop 20a). The Confederate cannonade caused more chaos in the Union rear than it did damage to the front lines; eventually, as Hunt ordered his batteries to taper off their fire and replaced damaged units, *Alexander* thought he had done what he could to soften up the enemy for a successful infantry assault.

At approximately 3:00 P.M. the Confederate lines began to advance. Nine brigades converged on the area between Ziegler's Grove and a smaller copse of trees. The rolling terrain afforded them some cover from artillery fire; Union infantry waited until they were in close range to deliver their volleys (Pickett's Charge excursion). The II Corps would absorb the brunt of the assault, although elements of the I and III Corps as well as the reserve artillery offered support. To the north the Confederates found it hard to make it past Emmitsburg Road; although a few regiments reached the Union line, other Rebel brigades faltered rendering the remainder vulnerable to a flank attack (stops 20b and 20c). To the south portions of *Pickett's* command actually broke through the Union line at the Bloody Angle, only to be mowed down by Federal reinforcements (stops 20c and 20d); elsewhere the Union line held and counterattacked the Confederate flanks (stops 20e and 20f). By 4:00 P.M. it was all over. As what remained of the attack column made its way back to Seminary Ridge, *Lee* rode out to meet it, consoling his men. "It is all my fault," he admitted.

Back on Cemetery Ridge, the Union survivors broke out in cheers when they saw George G. Meade ride up to inspect the situation. His men had decisively repulsed *Lee's* infantry assault; Union cavalry had checked *Stuart* several miles to the east. The commander then made his way to Little Round Top with ideas of mounting a counterattack but eventually decided against it. A sharp cavalry action at the base of Round Top (South Cavalry Field excursion) ended the battle of July 3.

STOP 20 The High Water Mark   9:00 A.M.–4:15 P.M.

Directions

Return to your vehicle. *Continue* along SLOCUM AVENUE until it ends at the Greenwood Cemetery along BALTIMORE PIKE. *Turn left; drive* approximately 0.75 mile to HUNT AVENUE, where you will *turn right; turn right* again when you reach TANEYTOWN ROAD. Park in either the Visitor Center, the Cyclorama Center, or the overflow parking areas.

Spangler's Spring, east of Culp's Hill. 3:375

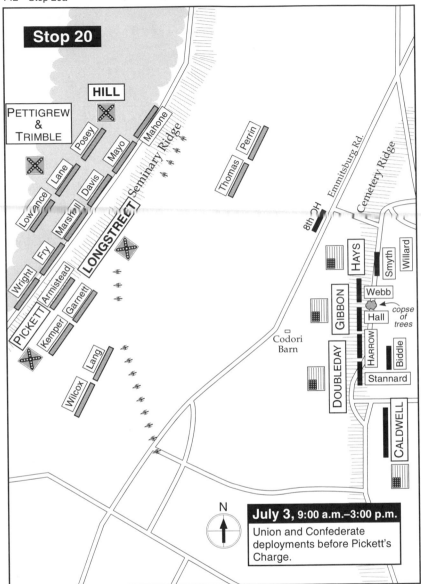

July 3, 9:00 a.m.–3:00 p.m.

Union and Confederate deployments before Pickett's Charge.

STOP 20a   9:00 A.M.–3:00 P.M.

Overview of the Union Position

Directions

Leave your vehicle and walk toward the east entrance to the Cyclorama building. Look for a flagpole along the sidewalk near the entrance to the building; there you will pick up a blacktop path that runs north of the Cyclorama Center through a wooded area and winds its way toward Hancock

Avenue. This is Ziegler's Grove. Note the monument erected by the Sons of Union Veterans to the oldest surviving Union veteran, Albert Woolson. Just past this point the path divides; take the right fork. Ahead you should see two white buildings, one on each side of Hancock Avenue. That is the farm of Abraham Bryan, a free black man; it marks the northern part of the Union line that came under direct assault by the Confederates on July 3. As you walk along the path you will encounter a stone marker between two cannon representing the position of the 9th Massachusetts Artillery on July 3 – the same battery that had played such a key part in the previous day's battle east of the Peach Orchard. When you reach the Bryan Farmhouse, cross Hancock Avenue. The bronze Union soldier on the west side of the street by the barn marks the position of the 111th New York. Walk to the stone viaduct just to the right (north) of the monument and face west.

Orientation   Ahead you will see Emmitsburg Road. In the near (southeast) corner of the first commercial building (a hotel) bordering the open field on the far side of the road you may be able to make out a monument dedicated to the 8th Ohio Infantry – although the regiment was initially located beyond this monument to the west. Note its location now for future reference.

Directions   Walk to the monument to the 111th New York Infantry. Stand to the left (south) of the infantryman and face west.

Orientation   You are looking toward the Confederate position on Seminary Ridge. The orchard midway across the valley to the heavily forested tree line marks the location of the Bliss Farm, which both sides struggled to possess before Union officers ordered the buildings burned on the morning of July 3.

The tree line marks the location of the *Army of Northern Virginia* on July 3. As you look southward (to the left) along that tree line, you should be able to see the white base of the Virginia Monument. The divisions of James J. *Pettigrew* (formerly Henry *Heth's*) and Maj. Gen. Isaac *Trimble* (formerly William *Pender's*) formed to the right (north) of that monument; George E. *Pickett's* division formed to its left (south). In front of the area where *Pickett's* men prepared to go into action, you should see a row of Confederate cannon. To the left, along Emmitsburg Road, are the red walls and three steeples of the Codori Barn, partially obscured by trees; beyond it lies the Peach Orchard. Due south (left) of where you stand, just above Hancock Avenue, are the Round Tops. You may wish to face south to examine the heart of the Union center, distinguished by a copse of trees – the focal point of the Confederate attack.

What Happened

The only action worthy of note in this sector on the morning of July 3 was an expedition by the 14th Connecticut Infantry to burn down the buildings on the Bliss Farm. Brig. Gen. Alexander Hays, who commanded the 3rd Division of Hancock's II Corps, desired to remove any possible obstacle to his artillery should the Confederates attack. Although the mission proved a success, it sparked a short-lived artillery duel.

As noon came and passed, soldiers rested, wrote letters, and cooked lunch. General Meade, his staff, and some guests sat down to eat near his headquarters, a white house on Taneytown Road to your left. Then, at 1 P.M., two Confederate cannon posted near the Peach Orchard fired. Within moments approximately 170 cannon joined in, showering the area in front of you with metal. Officers and soldiers scrambled for cover along the stone wall or hugged the ground. "All we had to do was flatten out a little thinner," one soldier recalled, "and our empty stomachs did not prevent that." The noise of the bombardment proved far more alarming than the damage it caused, for the enemy shells tended to overshoot their mark and land in the rear of the Union line. Still, there was chaos enough, and the shells forced Meade to shift his headquarters elsewhere. Union batteries returned fire: caissons exploded and horses fell wounded or dead. Brig. Gen. Alexander S. Webb, commanding the brigade holding the area north of the copse of trees, later recalled that it seemed as if the majority of the Confederate fire was aimed at him, adding that several times he was hit by debris from the shells. Henry J. Hunt, in charge of the Army of the Potomac's artillery, supervised the work of his cannoneers. At approximately 2:30 P.M. he ordered his batteries to cease fire at staggered intervals to give the Confederates the impression that their cannonade had succeeded in silencing the Federal guns. The move allowed him to conserve ammunition and to replace those batteries that had suffered extensive damage – including several of the batteries in this vicinity.

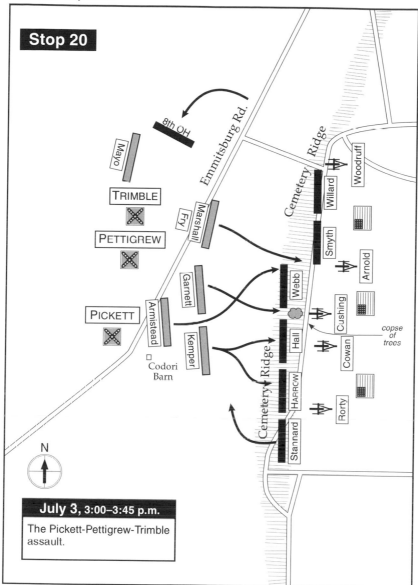

Stop 20

8th OH

Emmitsburg Rd.

Cemetery Ridge

Mayo

TRIMBLE ✖

PETTIGREW ✖

Fry

Marshall

Woodruff

Willard

Smyth

Arnold

Garnett

Webb

PICKETT ✖

Armistead

Cushing

copse of trees

☐ Codori Barn

Kemper

Hall

Cowan

Cemetery Ridge

HARRCW

Rorty

N

Stannard

July 3, 3:00–3:45 p.m.

The Pickett-Pettigrew-Trimble assault.

STOP 20b   3:00–3:45 P.M.

"Here They Come!"

Directions   Walk southward along the path parallel to the stone wall marking Hays's line; note the top of the middle regimental monument to the 12th New Jersey, a buck and ball – the 12th New Jersey was still armed with smoothbore muskets. Cross the stone wall where it meets a fence. Travel along the path leading to the lone tree located at the juncture of two stone walls. Note a short rose-colored stone monument on the near side of the stone wall along Hancock Avenue. It marks the advance point of the *26th North Carolina Infantry*. Stop at the tree at the juncture of the path with the corner formed by the two stone walls. This point bears the name of the Bloody Angle. Look west toward the Virginia Monument. Most of the discussion that follows concerns the area to your right, from the Virginia Monument across Emmitsburg Road to the stone wall just west of Hancock Avenue.

What Happened

At approximately 3:00 P.M., Union soldiers noticed that the Confederate artillery fire had tapered off. Moments later they saw lines of Confederate infantry begin to move forward from their staging positions. From where you stand – a piece of ground about to win the name of the Bloody Angle – three brigades of *Pickett's* division appeared to the left of the Virginia Monument, while to the right another division and two brigades from a third division stepped off – a total of nine brigades. Neither division to the right had its original commander: Henry *Heth*, wounded on July 1, had given way to James J. *Pettigrew*, while Isaac *Trimble* replaced William *Pender*, wounded on July 2, and directed two of *Pender's* brigades.

The main assault is best understood if we divide it into three parts (and discuss the first two here). The first concerns the three brigades on the Confederate left (your right) – those of Col. Robert M. *Mayo* and Joseph *Davis* (*Pettigrew*) and of *Lane* (*Trimble*). Both *Mayo* and *Davis* were sorely understrength – and *Davis's* men had suffered serious losses on July 1 at the railroad cut. *Mayo's* men advanced but a short distance before coming under heavy artillery fire from Cemetery Hill. Moments later the 8th Ohio, which had been left in advance of the Union line while the rest of its brigade hurried to Cemetery Hill on the evening of July 2, opened fire on the dazed brigade, which soon returned to its starting point. The 8th Ohio then turned its attention to *Davis's* battered brigade, swinging about to hit it in the flank with a volley. This proved one surprise too many for *Davis's* men: they retreated as well. In a matter of minutes some 250 Buckeyes had played a major role in disrupting the advance of two (admittedly undersized) Confederate brigades. *Lane's* brigade proved more successful. It made its way across the ruins of the Bliss Farm to Emmitsburg Road (north of where the monument to the 8th Ohio stands, opposite the position of the 9th Massachusetts Battery) before one of Hays's brigades, aided by another flank attack, drove it away. Several Confederates sought cover in the Bryan Farm, but the 111th New York surrounded it and quickly eliminated the threat.

Meanwhile, three more brigades–Col. B. D. *Fry* and Col. J. G. *Marshall* (Pettigrew) and Col. W. Lee J. *Lowrance* (Trimble)– advanced against the Union position along the stone wall along Hancock Avenue. *Lowrance's* men veered north of the Bryan Farm and were repulsed; *Fry* and *Marshall*, however, moved straight ahead and assaulted the Union line at and south of the Bryan Farm. Most remarkable was the advance of *Fry's* brigade, for it had been mauled by the Iron Brigade on July 1 and had lost its commander, James *Archer*. Reaching Emmitsburg Road, the lines staggered under the impact of enemy fire; many Confederates sought cover and returned fire. Parts of both brigades reached the stone wall, but neither could penetrate the Union position. The 12th New Jersey used its smoothbores as shotguns (thus the buck and ball on the monument); two companies of the 14th Connecticut, armed with breechloading rifles, sustained a rapid rate of fire (the regiment's monument can be located to your right rear; it stands behind the stone wall by Hancock Avenue, topped by the trefoil [clubs] of the II Corps). At last the Confederates retreated.

The notion that Pickett's Charge was composed solely of Virginians is false. The majority of the units engaged to your right came from North Carolina; regiments from Mississippi, Tennessee, and Alabama also participated in the assault, while the only four Virginia regiments in this sector belonged to *Mayo's* unfortunate brigade. Indeed, it is a misnomer to call the July 3 assault Pickett's Charge, although that name has persisted in the popular mind, for George *Pickett's* three brigades formed perhaps slightly less than half of the assault force.

Ground over which Pickett, Pettigrew, and Trimble charged. From a photograph taken after the war. 3:388

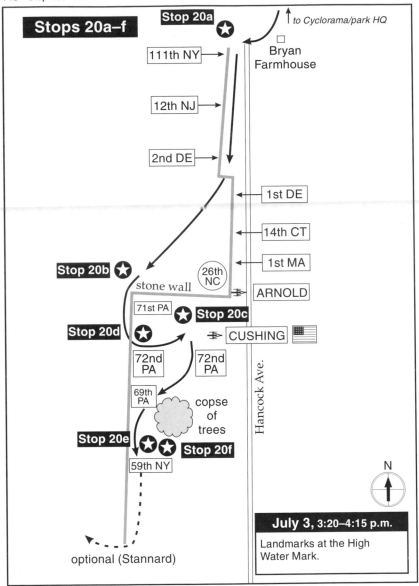

Stops 20a–f

Stop 20a

↑ to Cyclorama/park HQ

□ Bryan Farmhouse

111th NY →

12th NJ →

2nd DE →

← 1st DE

← 14th CT

← 1st MA

26th NC

stone wall

Stop 20b

ARNOLD

71st PA   Stop 20c

Stop 20d

CUSHING

72nd PA   72nd PA

69th PA

copse of trees

Hancock Ave.

Stop 20e   Stop 20f

59th NY

N

July 3, 3:20–4:15 p.m.

Landmarks at the High Water Mark.

optional (Stannard)

STOP 20c   3:20–3:30 P.M.

The Confederate Breakthrough

Directions

You may first want to walk a dozen yards or so along the path leading toward Emmitsburg Road to gain some idea of how the Union line looked to the advancing Confederates as they moved forward in a final surge. Either from there or from the Bloody Angle, walk south alongside the stone wall to the statue of a soldier swinging his rifle like a club–marking the forward position of the 72nd Pennsylvania Infantry—and face west toward the Virginia Monument.

Orientation

You are now standing at the focal point of *Pickett's* assault, the third part of the overall main attack. This position was held by Webb's brigade of Pennsylvanians, part of Brig. Gen. John Gibbon's division of the II Corps. Behind you four cannon mark the position of Battery A, 4th U.S. artillery, commanded by Lt. Alonzo Cushing. The red barn to your left is the Codori Barn.

What Happened

Pickett deployed his division with Brig. Gen. Richard B. *Garnett's* brigade to the north (your right) and Brig. Gen. James L. *Kemper's* brigade to the south (your left), and Brig. Gen. Lewis A. *Armistead* formed behind them. They moved forward as part of the main assault at 3:00 P.M. At first it appeared as if *Pickett's* men would hit the Union lines several hundred yards south of where you stand, but through a series of maneuvers (described in more detail in the Pickett's Charge excursion) he wheeled his command to strike this position. The most significant shift in direction occurred at the Codori Farm; *Pickett* (quite properly) remained there to direct the final assault. *Kemper's* brigade struck the Union line to your south, an area marked by rough and uneven terrain; *Garnett* and *Armistead* attacked here.

Cushing's battery had suffered significant damage during the cannonade preceding the assault; moreover, the battery commanders had exhausted their long-range ammunition, and in the rush to move ammunition out of range of the bombardment no provision had been made to replenish their supply. In later years Hunt claimed that he could have broken up the assault long before it reached the Union infantry had he been allowed to use his artillery as he saw fit. Nevertheless, as *Pickett's* men reached Emmitsburg Road they came under artillery fire from the southern end of Cemetery Ridge and from Little Round Top, where artillerists found themselves knocking down rows of Rebels with "fearful effect, sometimes as many as 10 men being killed and wounded by the bursting of a single shell." The Union infantry occupying this position watched as *Pickett's* line dipped, then appeared again as it crossed several swales.

Webb decided to hold the stone wall in front of you with two regiments: the 69th Pennsylvania to your left, the 71st Pennsylvania to your right. He kept the 72nd Pennsylvania in reserve to your rear. He directed Cushing to move three cannon to the area you now occupy, and, like Hays to the north, instructed his infantry to collect and load the rifles scattered about on the ground to increase their initial rate of fire. To maximize their killing power, however, they were not to open fire until the Confederates were approximately 100 yards away.

Rounds of canister and bullets ripped through the attack column, but the Confederates kept on coming. *Garnett*, mounted, fell; *Armistead*, a black hat poised on the tip of his sword, led on foot. As Cushing yelled an order to fire, a bullet struck his mouth and killed him. As the Rebel wave hit the stone wall, the Union line buckled, then started to give way.

STOP 20d	3:30–3:45 P.M.

"Boys, Give Them the Cold Steel!"

Directions

Turn around and walk back to Cushing's battery. Position yourself by the marker in the middle of the four cannon. Face west toward the previous stop.

What Happened

"Come on, boys, give them the cold steel! Who will follow me?" With those words, *Armistead* led several hundred men over the wall and past Cushing's battery. For a moment it seemed as if they had succeeded in breaking the Union center.

Understandably, *Armistead* and his men were intent on the job before them: the smoke and noise of battle rendered it difficult to assess the situation around them. In fact, the Virginians were alone. To the north Hays's brigade was beating back the brigades of *Pettigrew* and *Trimble*; to the south *Kemper's* men found themselves under fire from front and flank. No support columns were in sight to exploit any Confederate breakthrough, while Union infantry and cavalry were moving into position. With some difficulty Webb hurried forward the 72nd Pennsylvania, which formed in line and opened fire to your left; other regiments also moved to seal the crack. The bravery of the Virginians could not overcome the fact that they were doomed. *Armistead* fell mortally wounded; the small stone scroll in front of you marks the spot. Those of his soldiers who were not killed or wounded surrendered.

Due south (left) of the battery is a marker topped by a stone knapsack denoting the true location of the 72nd Pennsylvania during the charge–not the monument that you stood by minutes before. The regiment refused to obey Webb's orders to charge and instead opened fire on the attacking Confederates. The monument topped by the statue offers the misleading impression that the regiment met the attackers at the stone wall. Nevertheless, its veterans won a court case against the Gettysburg Battlefield Memorial Association and erected it in 1891.

STOP 20e   3:30–3:45 P.M.

"Double Canister at Ten Paces!"

Directions

Walk toward the copse of trees, then veer to the right. To your right, by the stone wall, a series of ten markers flanking an obelisk marks the location of the 69th Pennsylvania. South of it you will encounter the monument to the 59th New York, topped by a pyramid. Face west toward Emmitsburg Road.

Orientation

Here *Kemper's* brigade struck the Union position. The rough ground immediately in front of you hampered the Confederates' progress. To the left, you will see a black iron Confederate brigade marker in the field. It belongs not to *Kemper's* brigade but to *Wright's* brigade of Richard *Anderson's* division, which reached this point on July 2. The following morning *Wright* told artillery commander Edward P. *Alexander*, "The trouble is not in going there There is a place where you can get breath and re-form. The problem is to stay there after you get there, for the whole Yankee army is there in a bunch."

What Happened

The Union soldiers holding this portion of the line, members of the other two brigades of Gibbon's division of the II Corps, had seen some action on July 2 – especially the 1st Minnesota. At first glance they might well have thought that *Pickett's* division was headed straight for them, but as the Confederates maneuvered across the field, it became apparent that only *Kemper's* Virginians would make contact with them. General Hunt had moved a fresh artillery battery under Capt. Andrew Cowan just south of the copse. Unlike the other batteries in the area, Cowan's still had long-range ammunition. Other batteries also targeted *Kemper's* brigade; as the Confederates in this sector approached the Union line, a brigade of Vermonters opened fire on their right flank. *Kemper* fell seriously wounded (although he was the only one of *Pickett's* brigade commanders to survive). Although a few Confederates continued forward under the cover of the rough ground in front of you, the combination of terrain and enemy fire forced survivors to make their way to the Bloody Angle. Where you stand marks the southern limit of where Confederates made contact with the Union line. The 59th New York's right flank did not join with the left flank of the 69th Pennsylvania to preserve Cowan's field of fire. Several Confederates penetrated this gap and headed for the guns. Cowan ordered one final blast of canister at ten paces as Hunt emptied his revolver at the attackers. The smoke cleared: no Confederates remained on their feet.

As *Armistead* led his men across the stone wall, the Union regiments to the south, having broken the attack to their front, began shifting northward toward the copse of trees to contain the Confederate breakthrough.

Vignette

If you look to the south along the Union position, you will see a regimental monument topped by a large, rough, brown rock. It marks the position of the 20th Massachusetts. One of its officers, Capt. Henry L. Abbott, described the final moments of the charge: "The moment I saw them I knew we should give them Fredericksburg. So did everybody. We let the regiment in front of us get within 100 feet of us, & then bowled them over like nine pins, picking out the colors first. In two minutes there were only groups of two or three men running around wildly, like chickens with their heads off."

STOP 20f

3:30–4:15 P.M.

Vermonters on the Flank

Directions

Stay in place but face southwest, left of the Codori Farm.

What Happened

Three regiments of Vermonters who had enlisted for 90 days had been assigned to the I Corps but had missed the battle on July 1. It seemed that they might never see action, for their enlistments would expire in a few days. On July 2 they had participated in checking *Wright's* attack; still, they had appeared somewhat nervous during the artillery bombardment. They were some 100 yards in front of the main battle line. Although they fired at the advancing Confederates, they watched as the attackers passed them to the right (north). Their commander, Brig. Gen. George J. Stannard, and II Corps commander Winfield Scott Hancock decided to order the Vermonters to swing north, just south of the rough ground, and fire into the flank of the Rebel line. Their volleys tore through *Kemper's* men. "Glory to God, glory to God!" cried Abner Doubleday. "See the Vermonters go at it!" Thus those Confederates who actually made it to the Union line found themselves under fire from three sides.

The battle was not over for the Vermonters. To the south two Confederate brigades advanced toward the Union line, heading for the area just north of the woods. These brigades, totaling some 1,500 men, were supposed to support *Pickett's* division, but they failed to bear to the left. They were too few, too late to reverse what had happened. Union artillery shelled them; then some of the Vermonters turned around, faced southward, advanced, and opened fire on the Confederate flank. It proved too much for the Rebel brigades, who never posed a serious threat to the Union line.

To examine the flanking movement in more detail, walk south to the paved path, turn right, and then follow the gravel path. If you look to the north to see where *Kemper's* men struck the Union line, you will see the cover this area afforded the Vermonters. If you look due south toward another clump of woods at the southern end of the Union center, you may notice a small obelisk in front of the trees to the right of the Union line. At that spot Winfield Scott Hancock was wounded; the wound's effects lingered on throughout the 1864 campaigns and eventually compelled Hancock to relinquish command of the II Corps.

This ends the tour of the High Water Mark. You can return to your car by walking north on Hancock Avenue. As you pass the Bloody Angle. you might want to look to your right (east) to see the white farmhouse along Taneytown Road (PA 134) that served as Meade's headquarters. A path leads down to it for those who want a closer look. You will also see a monument to Meade, whose cool head and steadiness served the Union cause so well at Gettysburg.

Brigadier General Lewis A. Armistead, C.S.A. Killed July 3, 1863. From a photograph. 3:347

Pickett's Charge Excursion

For this excursion, sturdy walking shoes or hiking boots (preferably waterproofed) are recommended.

Directions

Begin at the Virginia Memorial on WEST CONFEDERATE AVENUE. Park in the area provided and walk down to the National Park Service interpretive marker at the end of the paved pathway that parallels the tree line. (The marker is further identified by a row of cannon.)

STOP A   The Confederate Deployment

Directions

Face east toward the copse of trees on Cemetery Ridge about 1,400 yards away.

Orientation

The copse of trees marks the objective of *Lee's* intended attack. The Confederate brigades were intended to converge at that point. All available Confederate cannon were aimed at that section of the Union line for the preassault bombardment. Only a few Confederate troops were deployed where you stand. *Pickett's* division was about 200 yards to your right (south), mostly in front of the woods. The rising ground (swale) in front of their position–visible to your left–hid them from Federal observation and partially shielded them from Union artillery fire. The remaining troops involved in the attack–six brigades under *Pettigrew* and *Trimble*–were deployed to your left (north), in the vicinity of the North Carolina Memorial (out of sight to your far left and slightly behind you).

Take a moment to locate Big Round Top and Little Round Top, clearly visible about 1.6 miles to your right; the Peach Orchard, closer and slightly to the right of Little Round Top, visible about 1,300 yards distant; the Codori Farm, visible near Emmitsburg Road about 880 yards distant (the Codori Barn is red and surmounted by three white steeples); and Cemetery Hill, visible to your left front about 1.25 miles distant, behind the modern fast-food restaurants and motels on Steinwehr Avenue (Emmitsburg Road). A cylindrical water tower will help you confirm its location. These landmarks all figure in the course of the excursion. You may wish to review the discussion of the events preceding the charge (stop 20a).

What Happened

You are standing near the spot from which *Lee* inspected the Union lines on the morning of July 3, formulated the attack on the enemy center, and observed both the assault preparations and the charge itself. If you had been here that morn-

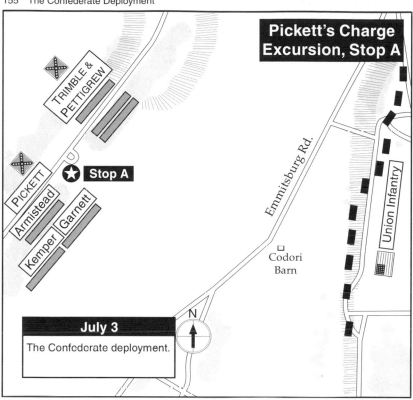

Pickett's Charge Excursion, Stop A

July 3

The Confederate deployment.

ing, you would have discerned a large body of troops to your left, partially hidden in the tree line. The six brigades in this sector belonged to A. P. *Hill's Third Corps* and had been heavily engaged in the fighting on July 1. Although they were not committed to the second day's battle, several units had skirmished with Union infantry for possession of the Bliss Barn, which would have been located to your left front, about halfway between Seminary and Cemetery Ridges. Federal troops burned it on the morning of July 3; its ashes still smoldered as the Confederates prepared for the assault.

To your right, you would have seen *Pickett's* division, with two of its brigades (led by *Garnett* and *Kemper*) positioned in the open field, while the third (under *Armistead*) was posted in the tree line. The all-Virginian division had made a forced march to Gettysburg from Chambersburg, 28 miles to the west, and had bivouacked for the night about three miles short of the battlefield. Resuming its march at daybreak, it reached the jump-off point for the assault around 9 A.M.

For the next four hours, the infantry waited, while *Longstreet's* chief of artillery, Lt. Col. E. Porter *Alexander*, supervised the posting of the artillery pieces that would soften up the enemy position with a preliminary bombardment. The guns belonging to *Longstreet's* corps were concentrated mainly in the Peach Orchard; they were supported by additional cannon from the corps of *Hill* and *Ewell* posted on Seminary Ridge. The early morning preparations were accompanied by a steady crash of musketry and artillery fire from the fighting around Culp's Hill. Around 10 A.M. or so the fighting died out. Quiet descended over the battlefield.

At about 1 P.M., two Confederate guns near the Peach Orchard barked, one after another: a signal for the bombardment to begin. For the next two hours, 170 cannon pounded the Union line in an effort to disable enough of the Federal batteries on Cemetery Ridge to give the infantry an optimal chance to attack successfully. At 3 P.M. the firing ceased. The men of *Pickett's* division rose, aligned their ranks, and began moving forward. On the left, those of *Pettigrew* and *Trimble* soon did the same.

Vignette

Lt. Col. Rawley *Martin, 53rd Virginia, Armistead's* brigade, recalled the moment the attack began: "Soon after the cannonade ceased, a courier dashed up to General Armistead, who was pacing up and down in front of the 53rd Virginia, his battalion of direction . . . and gave him the order from General Pickett to prepare for the advance. At once the command 'Attention, battalion!' rang out clear and distinct. Instantly every man was on his feet and in his place; the alignment was made with as much coolness and precision as if preparing for dress parade. Then Armistead went up to the color sergeant and said 'Sergeant, are you going to put those colors on the enemy's works to-day?' The gallant fellow replied: 'I will try, sir, and if mortal man can do it, it shall be done.'"

General Meade's headquarters on the Taneytown Road. From a wartime photograph. 3:294

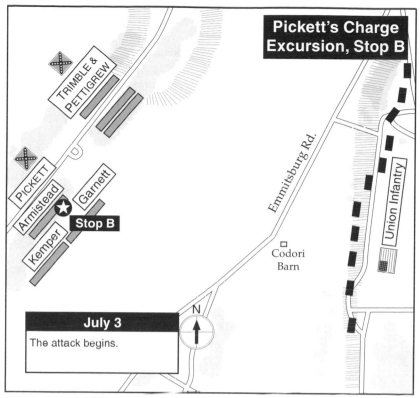

Pickett's Charge
Excursion, Stop B

Stop B

TRIMBLE &
PETTIGREW

PICKETT

Armistead

Garnett

Kemper

July 3

The attack begins.

N

Emmitsburg Rd.

Codori
Barn

Union Infantry

STOP B   *Pickett's* **Advance**

Several trails crisscross the area over which Pickett's Charge occurred, but only one, a horse trail, is permanently maintained. The others are more informal and vary from year to year and season to season. When the fields are not in cultivation, it is possible to trace *Pickett's* direct line of march. The excursion instructions assume that you may walk freely throughout the area. Be prepared to exercise some flexibility and adapt your route according to the conditions that prevail at the time of your visit. The main terrain feature of this walking tour–the swale that alternately shielded and exposed the attacking Confederates to Federal observation and fire–is characteristic of the entire area between Seminary and Cemetery Ridges.

Directions   Walk south along the tree line to a point from which you can easily see a red barn in front of you and can see only the very tops of the cannon at the National Park Service interpretive marker. You should not be able to see the Pennsylvania Memorial on Cemetery Ridge. Turn left (east), so that you face the open ridge, with the tree line behind you.

Orientation

You now occupy approximately the same ground from which *Garnett's* brigade of *Pickett's* division began the attack. You can easily see why it was possible for *Pickett* to deploy much of his infantry in the open: the ridge line in front shielded the troops from Union observation. Walk forward (east) until you reach the crest of the ridge.

What Happened

At this point–about three minutes after their advance began–*Pickett's* troops first became visible to the Federals. Some Union artillery began to open fire on the attacking column– but not much, because the Union artillery commander wished to preserve his remaining ammunition. The Federal infantry did not fire at all; the attacking column was still much too far away for effective musketry (indeed, one Union colonel even instructed his men not to fire until they saw the whites of the Confederates' eyes).

Vignette

William *Wood*, a lieutenant in the *19th Virginia*, *Garnett's* brigade, recalled: "'Forward, guide center, march!' and we moved forward to the top of the hill–just in front of our artillery, and halted. Here we formed a beautiful line of battle and were in full view of the enemy. Glancing my eyes over the field I felt, 'That hill must fall' still applied to the future. Forward again! and, look yonder! Kemper's brigade in splendid array, moving steadily forward. To the left and rear is Armistead's brigade seemingly more hurried as they come into line. What a line of battle! How they keep together! 'That hill must fall.'"

Route Step. 2:530

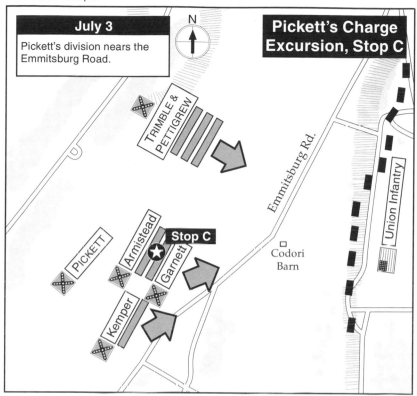

July 3

Pickett's division nears the Emmitsburg Road.

Pickett's Charge Excursion, Stop C

TRIMBLE & PETTIGREW

Emmitsburg Rd.

Union Infantry

PICKETT

Armistead

Stop C

Garnett

Kemper

Codori Barn

STOP C   **"Left—Oblique!"**

Directions   Begin walking toward the copse of trees on Cemetery Ridge. If you pace yourself so as to take 110 steps per minute, each step a 30-inch stride, you will match the speed of *Pickett's* advance. At that rate the Confederates crossed the ground at just over 90 yards per minute. Pause when you reach a bridle trail that runs perpendicular to your line of march. A 5-foot-high monument resembling a tombstone should be visible to your left; the Spangler Farmhouse should be visible to your right. (The monument marks the right flank of the 1st Massachusetts skirmish line, which was posted here to screen Sickles's battle line on July 2.)

What Happened   *Pickett's* division began its advance on a direct east-west line. Had it continued in that direction, it would have reached the Union lines in the vicinity of the present-day Pennsylvania Memorial, not the copse of trees. To maneuver toward the copse of trees without sacrificing a proper line-of-battle formation, *Longstreet's* instructions called for *Pickett's* division to carry out a series of "left obliques" that would gradually bring the division into contact with *Pettigrew's* and *Trimble's* brigades on the left. *Pickett* ordered the first left oblique at about this stage in the advance. At the command, "Left–oblique!," each man in the division turned 45 degrees to his left so that the entire line of battle shifted to the left while still maintaining its north-south orientation.

Major General George E. Pickett, c.s.a. From a photograph. 3:350

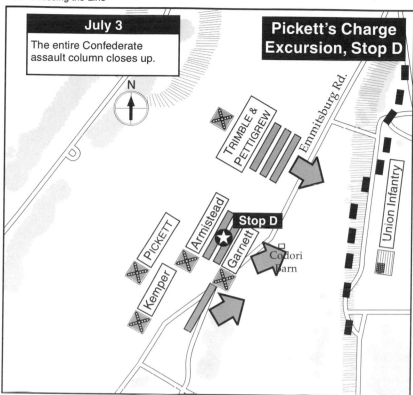

July 3

The entire Confederate assault column closes up.

Pickett's Charge Excursion, Stop D

STOP D — Dressing the Line

Directions

Adjust your line of march toward the copse of trees and continue until you reach a low point in the ground, about 100 yards or so before Emmitsburg Road.

Orientation

Notice what is *not* visible from this location. You can see only the statue that surmounts the Pennsylvania Memorial. You cannot see the slope of Little Round Top or Cemetery Hill (except the tops of the trees).

What Happened

In this swale, shielded from direct Union fire, *Pickett* stopped to dress his line; that is, he took a minute or two to halt the division and have his colonels get the men of their respective regiments closed up and carefully aligned. To some extent, Confederate officers and men had done this throughout the advance up to this point. When soldiers were wounded or otherwise fell out of line, their comrades closed ranks to fill the gap, and when it seemed that one part of the line was outpacing another, shouted orders attempted to keep everyone moving in tandem. Despite these ad hoc efforts, however, inevitably the battle lines had become slightly disorganized during the initial advance. Since this swale offered the last opportunity to restore the line before the final assault on the Federal position, *Pickett* prudently took advantage of it.

Brigadier General J. Johnston Pettigrew, c.s.a. Killed in action at Falling Waters MD on July 14, 1863. From a photograph. 3:429

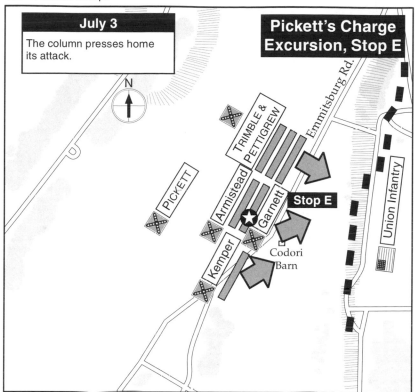

STOP E

A Tactical Triumph

Directions

Continue your walk toward the copse of trees. Stop when you reach the last rise in the ground before crossing Emmitsburg Road. You should be standing on an imaginary line that runs between the Virginia Monument (on Seminary Ridge) and the U.S. Regulars Monument (a large, obelisk-shaped monument on Cemetery Ridge).

What Happened

You are now standing at approximately the spot where *Pickett's* division linked up with *Pettigrew's* brigades for the final charge against the Union position. The Confederates had successfully completed a complex tactical movement under enemy fire. The entire attacking column–originally spread out along nearly a mile of front–was now massed directly in front of its objective, the copse of trees on Cemetery Ridge.

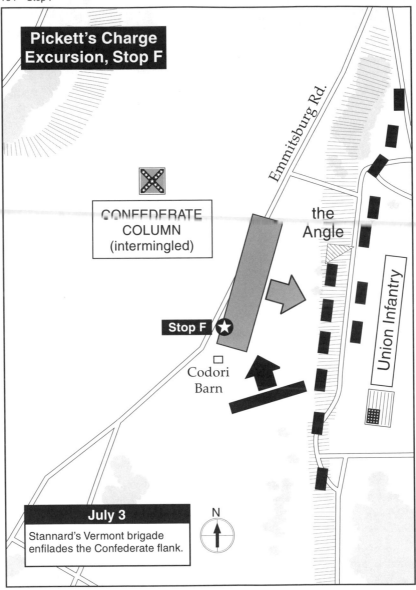

Pickett's Charge Excursion, Stop F

Emmitsburg Rd.

CONFEDERATE COLUMN (intermingled)

the Angle

Stop F

Codori Barn

Union Infantry

July 3

Stannard's Vermont brigade enfilades the Confederate flank.

N

STOP F **Closing with the Enemy**

Directions Proceed to Emmitsburg Road via one of the gaps in the rail fence line that parallels the road. Cross to the other side. Be careful! High-speed traffic is on the road. Continue about 10 yards and halt. Face the copse of trees.

Orientation The stone wall and regimental monuments in front of you obviously indicate the Union position. About 30 yards to your right front, note an area of rough ground (rock outcroppings and brush). The rough ground divided *Kemper's* brigade during the final charge—some of the troops attacking on one side of it, some on the other. About 100 yards farther to the right you will see the Vermont Monument, a large fluted column surmounted by a standing figure. This indicates the position of Brig. Gen. George J. Stannard's Vermont Brigade, which advanced from that area and attacked the right flank of *Kemper's* brigade at the height of the charge.

Looking to the left of the copse of trees, you will see a 90-degree angle in the stone wall marked by a large, lone tree. *Garnett's* brigade struck the line in approximately that spot. Just to the right of it—between the Bloody Angle and the copse of trees—is where *Armistead's* brigade breached the Union position. Still farther to the left (north of the Angle), is where the *Pettigrew-Trimble* column approached—but did not quite breach—the Union line.

What Happened

At about this point—200 yards from the Union line—the attacking column began to come under steady small-arms fire from the Union defenders, as well as canister from the Union artillery in the immediate area. Worse than the fire, however, was the disorganization that occurred as the units of *Pickett's* division intermingled. And worst of all, Union troops—the Vermont Brigade—struck the exposed right flank of the division.

Vignette

Capt. Henry Owen, *18th Virginia*, describes the desperation and confusion of these moments: "There off on our right was the grandest sight I have ever seen—A body of Yankees 800 or 1000 yards away [an exaggeration] coming at a double quick 'right shoulder shift.'. . . Their line was perpendicular to our own and they were hastening to strike us before we reached the stone wall. I saw at once it was to be a race and as Genl. Garnet[t] came along saying several times 'faster, faster men.' I put my men to the doublequick and each time was ordered on guide time [i.e., ordered by his colonel to slow down]. I have always thought that Garnet[t] perhaps saw this flanking party but there is no way now of ever deciding that point. . . . I saw [the Vermont brigade] deliberately fire into our whole line. In a few minutes all was confusion and companies belonging in the 8th Va. were in a few minutes fighting on my left while I found myself with a part of my company upon the left of Capt. Cocke and a part of his Co. E. and we on the right advanced upon the stone wall 15 or 20 deep. I saw men turn deliberately and coolly commmence [firing] upon this new enemy while others shot to the front. At one time I saw two men cross their muskets one fired to our right the other to our left."

This concludes the Pickett's Charge excursion. To continue the story, walk to the Bloody Angle and turn to stop 20c.

Cemetery Ridge after Pickett's Charge. From a wartime sketch. 3:389

East Cavalry Battlefield Excursion

Directions   Drive east from Gettysburg along HANOVER ROAD (PA 116). You will drive under U.S. 15 bypass. Drive 0.6 mile beyond the bypass, then *turn left* onto HOFFMAN ROAD. *Drive* 1.5 miles north on HOFFMAN ROAD to CAVALRY FIELD ROAD; *turn right* (east). *Drive* 0.4 mile, then *bear right* onto CONFEDERATE CAVALRY AVE-NUE. Park and walk to the third artillery battery marker.

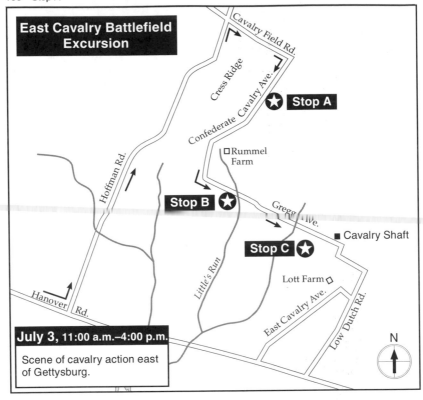

East Cavalry Battlefield Excursion

Stop A

Rummel Farm

Stop B

Gregg Ave.

■ Cavalry Shaft

Stop C

Lott Farm

Hanover Rd.

Little's Run

East Cavalry Ave.

Low Dutch Rd.

N

July 3, 11:00 a.m.–4:00 p.m.

Scene of cavalry action east of Gettysburg.

STOP A

11:00 A.M.–2:00 P.M.

Cress Ridge

Directions

Face southeast toward the open fields – where the cannon point.

Orientation

You are about 3.5 miles east of Gettysburg's town square. Due south (to your right) is the Rummel Farm. The cannon to your front are pointed at the Union position: you should be able to see two white shafts in the distance. To the left is the Cavalry Shaft; the Michigan Cavalry Monument is to the right.

What Happened

On the afternoon of July 2, Confederate cavalry commander James Ewell Brown ("Jeb") *Stuart* arrived at *Lee's* headquarters on the Chambersburg Pike. *Lee* was unhappy with the cavalryman's tardiness in rejoining the *Army of Northern Virginia*, for it deprived *Lee* of *Stuart's* skills at reconnaissance and gathering information (although *Lee* failed to use the three cavalry brigades *Stuart* left behind effectively). Nevertheless, *Lee* decided to incorporate *Stuart* in his attack plan for July 3. Either *Stuart* would sweep down upon a disorganized Union rear already reeling from successful Rebel infantry assaults or he would divert Meade's attention from the main field of battle.

On the morning of July 3 *Stuart* led four brigades east along the York Pike, then along Cavalry Field Road to this location, known as Cress Ridge. Two brigades (Brig. Gen. A. G. *Jenkins* and Col. J. R. *Chambliss*) formed south of this area; two others (Brig. Gen Wade *Hampton* and Brig. Gen. Fitzhugh *Lee*) arrived north of this area. Although he had hoped to keep his movement concealed from Union scouts, *Hampton* and *Lee* deployed in the open, alerting the Federals to their presence. Efforts by *Stuart* to map out a plan of battle in a timely fashion suffered further disruption because of a communication breakdown that delayed *Hampton's* arrival in this area to receive instructions. In the meantime, *Stuart* ordered a cannon to fire four shots—one in each compass direction. Perhaps this was a way to notify the main Confederate army that he was in place; it also served to notify the enemy of his presence.

These delays allowed Union cavalry to disrupt *Stuart's* plans. Division commander Brig. Gen. David McM. Gregg had stationed his men just north of the Hanover Road on July 2 to protect the army's rear. Late that day his troopers had pressed westward and skirmished with Confederate infantry preparing to assault Culp's Hill, persuading Gregg of the importance of his position. On July 3, Gregg decided not to obey orders that would have transferred his command south of Culp's Hill; he also ordered one brigade of Brig. Gen. Judson Kilpatrick's cavalry division to join him rather than to ride to the vicinity of Big Round Top. That brigade was commanded by Brig. Gen. George A. Custer. Custer was on the point of leaving when the action began. The appearance of *Hampton* and *Lee* confirmed the message of a Union signal station that had noted the movement of an enemy force beyond the Confederate left opposite Culp's Hill.

Just as the main cannonade that preceded Pickett's Charge commenced, *Stuart* ordered one brigade (known as *Jenkins's* brigade but headed that day by Col. M. F. *Ferguson*) to move southeast from the Rummel Farm to develop the Federal position, while his artillery along Cress Ridge would shell the enemy position. Union counterbattery fire from the southeast silenced some of the Confederate cannon; dismounted Union horsemen moved forward to meet the Rebel skirmishers by the Rummel Farm.

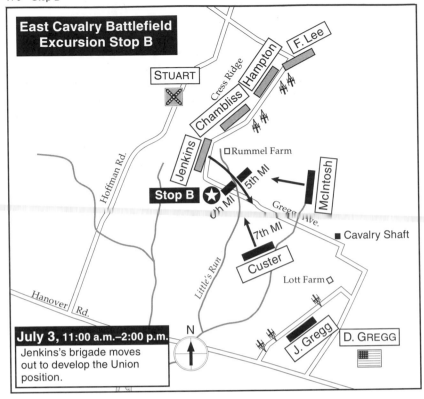

East Cavalry Battlefield Excursion Stop B

STUART

F. Lee

Hampton

Cress Ridge

Chambliss

Jenkins

Hoffman Rd.

Rummel Farm

5th MI

McIntosh

Stop B ★

6th MI

Gregg Ave.

■ Cavalry Shaft

7th MI

Custer

Lott Farm □

Little's Run

Hanover Rd.

July 3, 11:00 a.m.–2:00 p.m.
Jenkins's brigade moves out to develop the Union position.

N

J. Gregg

D. GREGG

STOP B   2:00–3:00 P.M.

The Struggle for Rummel's Farm

Directions   Return to your vehicle. Set your odometer to zero. *Continue* south along CONFEDERATE CAVALRY AVENUE past the Rummel Farm on your left. As the road bears to the left, it becomes GREGG AVENUE. As you approach a dip in the road (0.65 mile on your odometer), you will see a line of trees on the banks of a small stream, named Little's Run. Pull over. You need not leave your vehicle, although you may choose to do so. In either case, face left (north).

Orientation   You are due south of Cress Ridge, in the fields of the Rummel Farm.

What Happened   Dismounted Union cavalrymen from the 5th and 6th Michigan advanced to this area after hearing the four shots *Stuart* fired. Soon reinforcements arrived; *Ferguson's* skirmishers inflicted serious damage on the 5th Michigan, then withdrew when they ran out of ammunition. The firefight escalated as Gregg deployed more cavalry and artillery in the area, while *Stuart* sent forward reinforcements from *Chambliss* and *Hampton*. Finally, the Confederate commander pulled back his men and regrouped for another thrust.

Fitzhugh *Lee's* brigade spearheaded *Stuart's* next effort to take this position. In response, Custer fed more men into the fight, leading the 7th Michigan in a full-fledged charge with the cry, "Come on, you Wolverines!" The troopers smashed through one Virginia regiment, then swerved to the west when it came under carbine fire. Part of the 7th Michigan then engaged in a dismounted firefight with the *1st Virginia*, while the rest headed toward the Rummel Farm. The dismounted Confederates stood firm; a countercharge sent the Union horsemen reeling back.

In the Van. 3:1

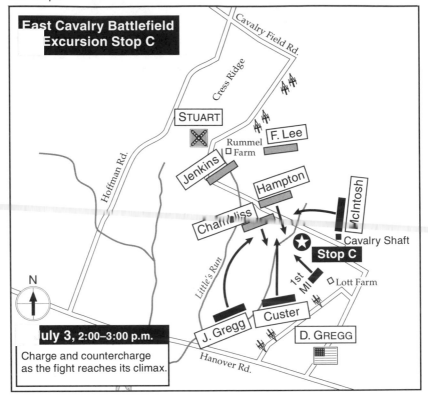

East Cavalry Battlefield
Excursion Stop C

Cavalry Field Rd.

Cress Ridge

STUART

F. Lee

Rummel
Farm

Jenkins

Hampton

Hoffman Rd.

Chambliss

McIntosh

Cavalry Shaft

Stop C

Little's Run

1st MI

Lott Farm

N

July 3, 2:00–3:00 p.m.

J. Gregg   Custer

D. GREGG

Charge and countercharge
as the fight reaches its climax.

Hanover Rd.

STOP C   3:00–4:00 P.M.

Confederates Checked

Directions   *Continue driving* east on GREGG AVENUE to CUSTER AVENUE (1.25 miles). Pull off to the side and exit your vehicle. To the south is the Michigan Cavalry Monument; to the north are markers denoting the position of Col. John B. McIntosh's brigade of Gregg's division and the Cavalry Shaft. Walk to the Michigan Monument. Standing in front of it (the west face), look to the northwest.

Orientation   From here you should see Cress Ridge to the north, where *Stuart* deployed his artillery. To the left is the Rummel Farm. The Confederate attack came toward you from the northwest.

What Happened   The Confederate counterattack against Custer gained momentum, much to *Hampton's* chagrin. Hoping at first to rein in his men, *Hampton* relented when he saw that other Rebel horsemen were joining in the advance. "They marched with well-aligned fronts and steady reins," noted one Union officer. "Their polished saber-blades dazzled in the sun." Federal artillery stationed behind you to your left near the Lott Farm opened fire. Then Custer, who had posted the 1st Michigan by the Lott Farm, led it into action and smashed into *Hampton*. Other units joined in the melee. *Hampton's* charge was stopped; the Confederates pulled back to Cress Ridge and the Rummel Farm. Union efforts at pursuit proved short-lived, and before long the Federal horsemen returned to this area.

Analysis

Stuart's maneuver had no impact on the battle south of Gettysburg. The Confederate assault on Cemetery Ridge was already under way as *Hampton* readied his final charge; by the time Custer checked him, the main battle was over. Nevertheless, the performance of the Union cavalry, less than one month after Brandy Station, demonstrated yet again the ability of the Federal cavalry to hold its own against *Stuart*. It also showed how effective dismounted cavalry could be in combat: the 5th Michigan carried Spencer rifles, which could fire multiple rounds, during the battle.

This ends the East Cavalry Battlefield excursion. *Return to your vehicle. Continue east* along GREGG ROAD until it meets LOW DUTCH ROAD (1.3 miles). *Turn right.* Travel 0.2 mile to EAST CAVALRY AVENUE (1.5 miles) and *turn right.* You will see the Lott Farm ahead of you; as you follow EAST CAVALRY ROAD you will pass the Union artillery positions. *Exit right* onto HANOVER ROAD (PA 116; 2.1 miles) and return to Gettysburg.

Union cavalry scouting in front of the Confederate advance. 3:244

South Cavalry Battlefield Excursion

Directions

Drive south on EMMITSBURG ROAD (Business Route U.S. 15) past the intersection with WEST CONFEDERATE and SOUTH CONFEDERATE AVENUES. Stay on EMMITSBURG ROAD; 0.1 mile beyond the intersection you will pass a National Park Service rest area on the left (east) side of the road. Watch your odometer; 1.1 miles beyond the rest area is a large tablet commemorating the 6th U.S. Cavalry. Like the rest area, it is on the left (east) side of the road. As soon as you can safely do so, find a place to *turn around* and pull to the berm of the road near the tablet.

STOP A

noon–3:00 P.M.

Merritt's Position

Directions

You may remain in your vehicle or, if you like, exit and walk about 30 yards beyond the 6th U.S. Cavalry tablet to the two cannon marking the position of Battery K, 1st U.S. Artillery. Stand behind the cannon and look in the direction they are facing (north).

Orientation

Your current position was occupied on July 3 by the Reserve Brigade of the 1st Division, Cavalry Corps, Army of the Potomac. Commanded by Brig. Gen. Wesley Merritt, its mission was to attack the right and rear of *Longstreet's* corps in cooperation with a second cavalry brigade under Brig. Gen. Elon J. Farnsworth, which then occupied a position southwest of Big Round Top. The main strength of the Confederates on this part of the battlefield faced the Union lines on Little Round Top and Cemetery Ridge. Only a thin screen composed of two infantry regiments guarded the southern approach, which ran from east to west and crossed Emmitsburg Road about where the roadside rest area now stands.

What Happened

The attack against the Confederate right flank was ordered by Maj. Gen. Alfred Pleasonton, commander of the Cavalry Corps of the Army of the Potomac. He hoped to put pressure on the Confederates while simultaneously screening the left flank of the Union army, but the attack was neither well conceived nor well executed. Merritt's brigade came up from Emmitsburg, deployed in this area around noon, and advanced dismounted toward the Confederate line west of the Emmitsburg Road. The Confederate commander in this sector, Brig. Gen. Evander M. *Law*, observed the threat and diverted several infantry regiments, as well as 250 cavalry un-

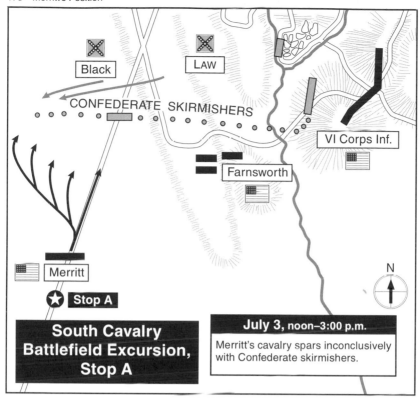

Black

LAW

CONFEDERATE SKIRMISHERS

VI Corps Inf.

Farnsworth

Merritt

N

⭐ **Stop A**

South Cavalry Battlefield Excursion, Stop A

July 3, noon–3:00 p.m.

Merritt's cavalry spars inconclusively with Confederate skirmishers.

der Col. John L. *Black*, to bolster his right flank. One battery of artillery went with them in support.

Merritt's basic tactic was to extend his cavalry regiments steadily to the west, hoping to attenuate and eventually turn the thin Confederate line. *Black's* cavalry shifted westward to prevent this. Shortly after the commencement of the cannonade that preceded Pickett's Charge, *Black* sent word to *Law* that Union cavalry were advancing in force on his right flank. *Law* assembled two additional infantry regiments (the *11th* and *58th Georgia*) and led them in person toward the endangered sector. Just before they arrived, Merritt's troopers succeeded in turning the Confederate line and sent *Black's* cavalry in retreat. *Law* promptly counterattacked and propelled Merritt's cavalry all the way back to Emmitsburg Road.

Analysis

As *Law* pointed out in a postwar article, Merritt erred by choosing to fight dismounted. "It is not an easy task to operate against cavalry with infantry alone, on an extended line, and in an open country where the former, capable of moving much more rapidly, can choose its own points of attack and can elude the blows of its necessarily more tardy adversary. But Merritt's brigade was now dismounted and deployed as skirmishers, and I lost no time in taking advantage of this temporary equality as to means of locomotion." The success of the Confederate counterattack, *Law* added, "reduced my front to manageable dimensions and left some force at my disposal to meet any concentrated attack that the enemy might make."

STOP B

5:30 P.M.

Farnsworth's Charge

Directions

Drive north about 1.2 miles to SOUTH CONFEDERATE AVENUE and *turn right*. Continue about o.8 mile to a turnout on the left side of the road. Pull into the turnout and get out. Face the large farmhouse visible about 250 yards distant (it is the only farmhouse in the area).

En route you may wish to pause in the parking lot of the National Park Service rest area (1.1 miles north of stop A). It offers a good view of the fields–easily visible to the west– over which Merritt's dismounted cavalry advanced.

Orientation

You are looking at the Slyder Farm. On July 3, this farm lay just west of the southern terminus of the main Confederate battle line, which actually ended about 300 yards to your right front. Behind you, a thin screen of Confederate infantry covered the extreme right end of the Rebel line. Beyond it to the south was Farnsworth's brigade of Union cavalry.

What Happened

Farnsworth's division commander, Brig. Gen. Judson Kilpatrick, was present with him in this sector. (The division's other brigade, under Brig. Gen. George A. Custer, remained with the bulk of the Union cavalry and fought on the East Cavalry Field.) During Merritt's dismounted attack little occurred in this area, with the exception of two separate, quickly repulsed charges by the 1st West Virginia and 1st Vermont Cavalry. But around 5:15 P.M. an orderly reported that a massive Confederate attack on Cemetery Ridge had been repelled. "We turned the charge," he enthused; "nine acres of prisoners!"

Kilpatrick turned to Farnsworth and instructed him to charge with his entire brigade. Believing that the repulse of Pickett's Charge had put the Confederates in disarray, he hoped that a cavalry charge would disrupt the Confederate right flank, pave the way for a Union infantry attack in this sector, and create the conditions for a total rout of *Lee's* army. This was visionary to say the least, and Farnsworth objected.

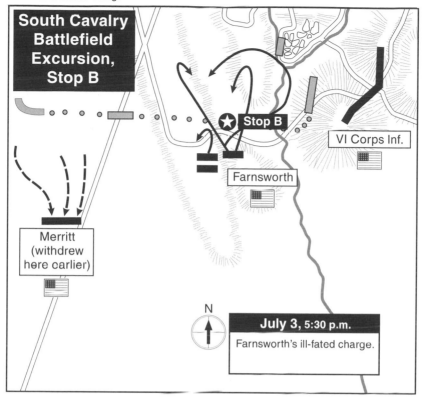

South Cavalry Battlefield Excursion, Stop B

Stop B

VI Corps Inf.

Farnsworth

Merritt (withdrew here earlier)

N

July 3, 5:30 p.m.
Farnsworth's ill-fated charge.

Vignette

Capt. H. C. Parsons, 1st Vermont Cavalry, narrates: "I was near Kilpatrick when he gave the order to Farnsworth to make the last charge. Farnsworth spoke with emotion: 'General, do you mean it? Shall I throw my handful of men over rough ground, through timber, against a brigade of infantry? The 1st Vermont has already been fought half to pieces; these are too good men to kill.' Kilpatrick said: 'Do you refuse to obey my orders? If you are afraid to lead this charge, I will lead it.' Farnsworth rose in his stirrups – he looked magnificent in his passion – and cried, 'Take that back!' Kilpatrick returned his defiance, but, soon repenting, said, 'I did not mean it; forget it.' For a moment there was silence, when Farnsworth spoke calmly, 'General, if you order the charge, I will lead it, but you must take the responsibility.' I did not hear the low conversation that followed, but as Farnsworth turned away he said, 'I will obey your order.' Kilpatrick said earnestly, 'I take the responsibility.'"

The next stop is optional and requires a walk of about 400 yards through uneven terrain. If you choose not to make the walk, remain where you are and simply read the text of stop C.

Brigadier General
Elon J. Farnsworth.
From a photograph.
3:395

STOP C

5:45 P.M.

Farnsworth's Death

Directions

Return to your car and *drive* about 0.3 mile until you see a rail fence on the left side of the road. Pull over on the left side near the far (northern) end of the fence. Exit your vehicle and walk about 200 yards down a narrow trail that leads from the fence to the 1st Vermont Cavalry Monument.

En route you will pass a statue commemorating Maj. William Wells, who led one battalion of the 1st Vermont and received the Medal of Honor for his part in Farnsworth's charge. (The statue is also plainly visible from stop B.)

Orientation

You stand where Farnsworth was killed while leading the charge that Kilpatrick had ordered. Look around and note the woodlands, undergrowth, and rocky ground. Small wonder Farnsworth made the charge under protest.

What Happened

Three cavalry regiments, the 1st West Virginia, 1st Vermont, and 18th Pennsylvania, made the charge and—despite the rough terrain—made it on horseback. The West Virginia and

Pennsylvania units struck the Confederate infantry screen at its strongest point and made little headway, but the 1st Vermont, accompanied by Farnsworth, pierced the Rebel skirmish line and plunged deep into the Confederate rear. Organized into two battalions, the 1st Vermont went by somewhat different routes. Farnsworth, with the 2nd Battalion, took a route that carried him close behind the *15th Alabama*, which turned and fired a volley into them. The 2nd Battalion continued to a point about 160 yards north of the Slyder Farmhouse, where Farnsworth's horse was killed. Most of the battalion continued onward; a trooper offered Farnsworth his own horse, and Farnsworth with a small party tried to return the same way they had come. At the spot where you now stand, Farnsworth's party was caught in a crossfire between Confederate infantry, and Farnsworth fell dead, riddled by five bullets.

Analysis

Most of the other participants made it back unhurt, with 100 prisoners in tow, the only positive gain from what was, on the whole, a tragic misadventure. Kilpatrick afterward complained that much would have come of the charge if only the Union infantry on Big Round Top had joined in, but since Kilpatrick apparently made no effort to coordinate his charge with the infantry commanders, it is hard to see how this was a real possibility.

Civil War cavalry seldom attacked infantry. The attacks by Merritt and Farnsworth were only the fifth time in two years that horsemen from the Army of the Potomac had even ventured such a feat, and their experience was no better than those of their predecessors. The failure of all five attacks stemmed from very much the same causes: the improvised, poorly coordinated nature of the charges, the inadequate numbers, and—in the case of Farnsworth's charge—the fact that the terrain was poorly suited to mounted operations.

This ends the South Cavalry Field excursion. Return to your car and *continue* along SOUTH CONFEDERATE AVENUE to its intersection with SYKES and WARREN AVENUES. From this point you may *turn right* (toward Taneytown Road (PA 134)), *left* (toward the Devil's Den), or *proceed* straight ahead (Little Round Top).

Major General George G. Meade. From a photograph. 4:102

Heavy rains drenched the armies on the night of July 3; although the downpour let up the next day, neither army seemed ready to move. Meade refitted and rested his men, while *Lee* pulled *Ewell's* corps back to Seminary Ridge in anticipation of a Federal counterattack. For a while that afternoon, as the V Corps units probed west of the Round Tops, it looked as if the two sides would renew the contest, but another rainstorm cut short that opportunity. Supported by a majority of his corps commanders, Meade decided to wait and see what *Lee* would do next.

Lee commenced his retreat on the afternoon of July 4. Fortunately for him, Union cavalry had failed to occupy Fairfield, opening a fairly direct southward route. Upon discovering that the Confederates were pulling out, Meade first contemplated pursuing them over the mountain passes; then he decided to swing south into Maryland in hopes of catching *Lee* before the Rebels recrossed the Potomac. The destruction of *Lee's* pontoon bridge at Williamsport by a Union expedition enhanced the chance of doing so, as did the high waters of the Potomac River. Nevertheless, the pursuit seemed late in starting; moreover, the wording of Meade's congratulatory order to his army – especially the phrase that it had driven the enemy "from our soil" – irked Lincoln greatly.

On July 7 Meade reached Frederick, Maryland; five days later his army, having crossed South Mountain, confronted *Lee's* men, who had established a fortified perimeter around Williamsport. That evening Meade held yet another council of war: this time only two corps commanders seconded his preference to assault the next morning. More rain on July 13 discouraged any notion of an attack: when lead elements of the Army of the Potomac pushed forward the next morning, they found that, aside from a rear guard, *Lee's* army had made it across the river. That further inspection convinced Meade's staff officers that the Confederates had erected strong defenses around Williamsport, rendering dubious the chances of a successful assault, did little to quell criticism from others; Lincoln never quite got over what he believed to be an opportunity to end the war that summer. "We had them within our grasp," he sighed. "We had only to stretch forth our hands & they were ours." Eventually, he accepted the fact that while Meade might be competent enough not to lose to *Lee*, it would take another general to defeat the Confederates in Virginia. For *Lee*, who may have lost as much as a third of his army during the campaign, his escape offered him a chance to fight another day, but he could never completely make up what he had lost on those Pennsylvania fields on the first three days of July 1863.

Goodbye! 3:423

For differing interpretations of Meade's pursuit, see Gabor Boritt, "Unfinished Work," in Boritt, ed., *Lincoln's Generals* (New York: Oxford University Press, 1994), and A. Wilson Greene, "From Fredericksburg to Falling Waters: Meade's Pursuit of Lee," in Gary W. Gallagher, ed., *The Third Day at Gettysburg and Beyond* (Chapel Hill: University of North Carolina Press, 1994).

Appendix A: Organization, Weapons, and Tactics

You will get much more from your battlefield tour if you take a few minutes to become familiar with the following information and then refer to it as necessary.

The Organization of Civil War Armies

Following is a diagram of the typical organization and range of strength of a Civil War army:

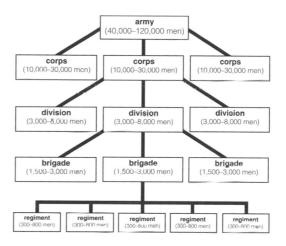

The Basic Battlefield Functions of Civil War Leaders

In combat environments, the duties of Civil War leaders were divided into two main parts: decision making and moral suasion. Although the scope of the decisions varied according to rank and responsibilities, they generally dealt with the movement and deployment of troops, artillery, and logistical support (signal detachments, wagon trains, and so on). Most of the decisions were made by the leaders themselves. Their staffs helped with administrative paperwork but in combat functioned essentially as glorified clerks; they did almost no sifting of intelligence or planning of operations. Once made, the decisions were transmitted to subordinates either by direct exchange or by courier, with the courier either carrying a written order or conveying the order verbally. More rarely, signal flags were used to send instructions. Except in siege operations, when the battle lines were fairly static, the telegraph was almost never used in tactical situations.

Moral suasion was the art of persuading troops to perform their duties and dissuading them from a failure to perform them. This was often done by personal example, and conspicuous bravery was a vital attribute of any good leader. It is therefore not surprising that 8 percent of Union generals–and 18 percent of their Confederate counterparts–were killed or mortally wounded in action. (By contrast, only about 3 percent of Union enlisted men were killed or mortally wounded in action.)

Although any commander might be called upon to intervene directly on the firing line, army, corps, and division commanders tended to lead from behind the battle line, and their duties were mainly supervisory. In all three cases, their main ability to influence the fighting, once it was under way, was by the husbanding and judicious commitment of troops held in reserve.

Army commanders principally decided the broad questions– whether to attack or defend, where the army's main effort(s) would be made, and when to retreat (or pursue). They made most of their key choices before and after an engagement rather than during it. Once battle was actually joined, their ability to influence the outcome diminished considerably. They might choose to wait it out or they might choose, temporarily and informally, to exercise the function of a lesser leader. In various Civil War battles army commanders conducted themselves in a variety of ways: as detached observers, "super" corps commanders, division commanders, and so on, all the way down to de facto colonels trying to lead through personal example.

Corps commanders chiefly directed main attacks or supervised the defense of large, usually well-defined sectors. It was their function to carry out the broad (or occasionally specific) wishes of the army commander. They coordinated all the elements of their corps (typically infantry divisions and artillery battalions) to maximize its offensive or defensive strength. Once battle was actually joined they influenced the outcome by feeding additional troops into the fight–sometimes by preserving a reserve force (usually a division) and committing it at the appropriate moment, sometimes by requesting additional support from adjacent corps or from the army commander.

Division commanders essentially had the same functions as corps commanders, but on a smaller scale. When attacking, however, their emphasis was less on feeding a fight than keeping the striking power of their divisions as compact as possible. The idea was to strike one hard blow rather than a series of lesser ones.

The commanders below were expected to control the actual combat–to close with and destroy the enemy:

Brigade commanders principally conducted the actual business of attacking or defending. They accompanied the attacking force in person or stayed on the firing line with the defense. Typically they placed about three of their regiments abreast of one another with about two in immediate support. Their job was basically to maximize the fighting power of their brigades by ensuring that these regiments had an unobstructed field of fire and did not overlap. During an attack it often became necessary to expand, contract, or otherwise modify the brigade frontage to conform with the vagaries of terrain, the movements of adjacent friendly brigades, or the behavior of enemy forces. It was the brigade commander's responsibility to shift his regiments as needed while preserving, if possible, the unified striking power of the brigade.

Regiment commanders were chiefly responsible for making their men do as the brigade commanders wished, and their independent authority on the battlefield was limited. For example, if defending they might order a limited counterattack, but they usually could not order a retreat without approval from higher authority. Assisted by *company commanders*, they directly supervised the soldiers, giving specific, highly concrete commands: move this way or that, hold your ground, fire by volley, forward, and so on. Commanders at this level were expected to lead by personal example and to display as well as demand strict adherence to duty.

Civil War Tactics

Civil War armies basically had three kinds of combat troops: infantry, cavalry, and artillery. Infantrymen fought on foot, each with his own weapon. Cavalrymen were trained to fight on horseback or dismounted, also with their own individual weapons. Artillerymen fought with cannon.

INFANTRY

Infantry were by far the most numerous part of a Civil War army and were chiefly responsible for seizing and holding ground.

The basic Civil War tactic was to put a lot of men next to one another in a line and have them move and shoot together. By present-day standards the notion of placing troops shoulder-to-shoulder seems insane, but it still made good sense in the mid-nineteenth century. There were two reasons for this technique: first, it allowed soldiers to concentrate the fire of their rather limited weapons; second, it was almost the only way to move troops effectively under fire.

Most Civil War infantrymen used muzzle-loading muskets capable of being loaded and fired a maximum of about three times a minute. Individually, therefore, a soldier was nothing. He could affect the battlefield only by combining his fire with that of other infantrymen. Although spreading out made them less vulnerable, infantrymen very quickly lost the ability to combine their fire effectively if they did so. Even more critically, their officers rapidly lost the ability to control them.

For most purposes, the smallest tactical unit on a Civil War battlefield was the regiment. Theoretically composed of about 1,000 officers and men, in reality the average Civil War regiment went into battle with about 300 to 600 men. Whatever its size, however, all members of the regiment had to be able to understand and carry out the orders of their colonel and subordinate officers, who generally could communicate only through voice command. Since in the din and confusion of battle only a few soldiers could actually hear any given command, most got the message chiefly by conforming to the movements of the men immediately around them. Maintaining "touch of elbows"–the prescribed close interval– was indispensable for this crude but vital system to work. In addition, infantrymen were trained to "follow the flag"–the unit and national colors were always conspicuously placed in the front and center of each regiment. Thus, when in doubt as to what maneuver the regiment was trying to carry out, soldiers could look to see the direction the colors were moving. That is one major reason why the post of color-bearer was habitually given to the bravest men in the unit. It was not just an honor; it was insurance that the colors would always move in the direction desired by the colonel.

En route to a battle area, regiments typically moved in a column formation, four men abreast. There was a simple maneuver whereby regiments could very rapidly change from column to line once in the battle area, that is, from a formation designed for ease of movement to one designed to maximize firepower. Regiments normally moved and fought in line of battle–a close-order formation actually composed of two lines, front and rear. Attacking units rarely "charged" in the sense of running full tilt toward the enemy; such a maneuver would promptly destroy the formation as faster men outstripped slower ones and everyone spread out. Instead, a regiment using orthodox tactics would typically step off on an attack moving at a "quick time" rate of 110 steps per minute (at which rate it would cover about 85 yards per minute). Once the force came under serious fire, the rate of advance might be increased to a so-called double-quick time of 165 steps per minute (about 150 yards per minute). Only when the regiment was within a few dozen yards of the defending line would it be ordered to advance at a "run" (a very rapid pace but still not a sprint). Thus a regiment might easily take about ten minutes to "charge" 1,000 yards, even if it did not pause for realignment or execute any further maneuvers en route.

In theory an attacking unit would not stop until it reached the enemy line, if then. The idea was to force back the defenders through the size, momentum, and shock effect of the attacking column. (Fixed bayonets were considered indispensable for maximizing the desired shock effect.) In reality, however, the firepower of the defense eventually led most Civil War regiments to stop and return the fire—often at ranges of less than 100 yards. And very often the "charge" would turn into a stand-up firefight at murderously short range, until one side or the other gave way.

It is important to bear in mind that the above description represents a simplified idea of Civil War infantry combat. As you will see as you visit specific stops, the reality could vary significantly.

ARTILLERY

Second in importance to infantry on most Civil War battlefields was the artillery. Not yet the "killing arm" it would become during World War I, when 70 percent of all casualties were inflicted by shellfire, artillery nevertheless played an important role, particularly on the defense. Cannon fire could break up an infantry attack or dissuade enemy infantry from attacking in the first place. Its mere presence could also reassure friendly infantry and so exert a moral effect that might be as important as its physical effect on the enemy.

The basic artillery unit was the *battery*, a group of between four and six fieldpieces commanded by a captain. Early in the war, batteries tended to be attached to infantry brigades. But over time it was found that they worked best when massed together, and both the Union and Confederate armies presently reorganized their artillery to facilitate this. Eventually both sides maintained extensive concentrations of artillery at corps level or higher. Coordinating the fire of 20 or 30 guns on a single target was not unusual, and occasionally (as in the bombardment that preceded Pickett's Charge at Gettysburg) concentrations of well over 100 guns might be achieved.

Practically all Civil War fieldpieces were muzzle-loaded and superficially appeared little changed from their counterparts in the seventeenth and eighteenth centuries. In fact, however, Civil War artillery was quite modern in two respects. First, advances in metallurgy had resulted in cannon barrels that were much lighter than their predecessors but strong enough to contain more powerful charges. Thus, whereas the typical fieldpiece of the Napoleonic era fired a 6-pound round, the typical Civil War era fieldpiece fired a round double that size, with no loss in ease of handling. Second, recent improvements had resulted in the development of practical rifled fieldpieces that had significantly greater range and accuracy than their smoothbore counterparts.

Civil War fieldpieces could fire a variety of shell types, each with its own preferred usage. *Solid shot* was considered best for battering down structures and for use against massed troops (a single round could sometimes knock down several men like tenpins). *Shell*—rounds that contained an explosive charge and burst into fragments when touched off by a time fuse—were used to set buildings afire or to attack troops behind earthworks or under cover. *Spherical case* was similar to shell except that each round contained musket balls (78 in the case of a 12-pound shot, 38 for a 6-pound shot); it was used against bodies of troops moving in the open at ranges of from 500 to 1,500 yards. At ranges of below 500 yards, the round of choice was *canister*, essentially a metal can containing about 27 cast-iron balls, each 1.5 inches in diameter. As soon as a canister round was fired, the sides of the can would rip away and the cast-iron balls would fly directly into the attacking infantry. In desperate situations double and sometimes even triple charges of canister were used.

As recently as the Mexican War, artillery had been used effectively on the offensive, with fieldpieces rolling forward to advanced positions from which they could blast a hole in the enemy line. The advent of the rifled musket, however, made this tactic dangerous—defending infantry could now pick off artillerists who dared to come so close—and so the artillery had to remain farther back. In theory the greater range and accuracy of rifled cannon might have offset this a bit, but rifled cannon fired comparatively small shells of limited effectiveness against infantry at a distance. The preferred use of artillery on the offensive was therefore not against infantry but against other artillery—what was termed "counterbattery work." The idea was to mass one's own cannon against a few of the enemy's cannon and systematically fire so as to kill the enemy's artillerists and dismount his fieldpieces.

CAVALRY

"Whoever saw a dead cavalryman?" was a byword among Civil War soldiers, a pointed allusion to the fact that the battlefield role played by the mounted arm was often negligible. For example, at the battle of Antietam—the single bloodiest day of the entire war—the Union cavalry suffered exactly 5 men killed and 23 wounded. This was in sharp contrast to the role played by cavalry during the Napoleonic era, when a well-timed cavalry charge could exploit an infantry breakthrough, overrun the enemy's retreating foot soldiers, and convert a temporary advantage into a battlefield triumph.

Why was cavalry not used to better tactical advantage? The best single explanation might be that for much of the war there was simply not enough of it to achieve significant results. Whereas cavalry had made up 20 to 25 percent of Napoleonic armies, in Civil War armies it generally averaged 8 to 10 percent or even less. The paucity of cavalry may be explained, in turn, by its much greater expense compared with infantry. A single horse might easily cost ten times the monthly pay of a Civil War private and necessitated the purchase of saddles, bridles, stirrups, and other gear as well as specialized clothing and equipment for the rider. Moreover, horses required about 26 pounds of feed and forage per day, many times the requirement of an infantryman. In addition, remounts were needed to replace worn-out horses, it took far more training to make an effective cavalryman than an effective infantryman, and there was a widespread belief that the heavily wooded terrain of America would limit opportunities to use cavalry on the battlefield. All in all, it is perhaps no wonder that Civil War armies were late in creating really powerful mounted arms.

Instead, cavalry tended to be used mainly for scouting and raiding, duties that took place away from the battlefields. During major engagements their mission was principally to screen the flanks or to control the rear areas. By 1863, however, the North was beginning to create cavalry forces sufficiently numerous and well armed to play a significant role on the battlefield. At Gettysburg, for example, Union cavalrymen armed with rapid-fire, breech-loading carbines were able to hold a Confederate infantry division at bay for several hours. At Cedar Creek in 1864 a massed cavalry charge late in the day completed the ruin of the Confederate army, and during the Appomattox campaign in 1865 Federal cavalry played a decisive role in bringing Lee's retreating army to bay and forcing its surrender.

Appreciation of the Terrain

The whole point of a battlefield tour is to see the ground over which men actually fought. Understanding the terrain is basic to understanding almost every aspect of a battle. Terrain helps to explain why commanders deployed their troops where they did, why attacks occurred in certain areas and not in others, why some attacks succeeded and others did not.

When defending, Civil War leaders often looked for positions with as many of the following characteristics as possible:

First, it obviously had to be ground from which they could keep the enemy from whatever it was they were ordered to defend.

Second, it should be elevated enough to provide good observation and good fields of fire—they wanted to see as far as possible and sometimes (though not always) to shoot as far as possible. The highest ground was not necessarily the best, however, for it often afforded an attacker defilade—areas of ground which the defenders' weapons could not reach. For that reason leaders seldom placed their troops at the very top of a ridge or hill (the "geographical crest"). Instead they placed them a bit forward of the geographical crest at a point from which they had the best field of fire (the "military crest"). Alternatively, they might choose to place their troops behind the crest so as to conceal the size and exact deployment of the defenders from the enemy and offer protection from long-range fire. It also meant that an attacker, upon reaching the crest, would be silhouetted against the sky and susceptible to a sudden, potentially destructive fire at close range.

Third, the ground adjacent to the chosen position should present a potential attacker with obstacles. Streams and ravines made good obstacles because they required an attacker to halt temporarily while trying to cross them. Fences and boulder fields could also slow an attacker. Dense woodlands could do the same, but they offered concealment for potential attackers and were therefore less desirable. In addition to its other virtues, elevated ground was also prized because attackers moving uphill had to exert themselves more and got tired faster. Obstacles were especially critical at the end of a unit's position—the flank—if there were no other units beyond to protect it. That is why commanders "anchored" their flanks, whenever possible, on hills or the banks of large streams.

Fourth, it had to offer ease of access for reinforcements to arrive and, if necessary, for the defenders to retreat.

Fifth, a source of drinkable water—the more the better—should be immediately behind the position if possible. This was especially important for cavalry and artillery units, which had horses to think about as well as men.

When attacking, Civil War commanders looked for different things:

First, they looked for weaknesses in the enemy's position, especially "unanchored" flanks. If there were no obvious weaknesses, they looked for a key point in the enemy's position–often a piece of elevated ground whose loss would undermine the rest of the enemy's defensive line.

Second, they searched for ways to get close to the enemy position without being observed. Using woodlands and ridge lines to screen their movements was a common tactic.

Third, they looked for open, elevated ground on which they could deploy artillery to "soften up" the point to be attacked.

Fourth, once the attack was under way they tried, when possible, to find areas of defilade in which their troops could gain relief from exposure to enemy fire. Obviously it was almost never possible to find defilade that offered protection all the way to the enemy line, but leaders could often find some point en route where they could pause briefly to "dress" their lines.

Making the best use of terrain was an art that almost always involved trade-offs among these various factors–and also required consideration of the number of troops available. Even a very strong position was vulnerable if there were not enough troops to defend it. A common error among Civil War generals, for example, was to stretch their line too thin in order to hold an otherwise desirable piece of ground.

Estimating Distance

When touring Civil War battlefields it's often helpful to have a general sense of distance. For example, estimating distance can help you estimate how long it took troops to get from point A to point B or to visualize the points at which they would have become vulnerable to different kinds of artillery fire. There are several easy tricks to bear in mind.

Use reference points for which the exact distance is known. Many battlefield stops give you the exact distance to one or more key points in the area. Locate such a reference point, then try to divide the intervening terrain into equal parts. For instance, say the reference point is 800 yards away. The ground about halfway in between will be 400 yards; the ground halfway between you and the midway point will be 200 yards, and so on.

Use the football field method. Visualize the length of a football field, which of course is about 100 yards. Then estimate the number of football fields you could put between yourself and the distant point in which you're interested.

Use cars, houses, and other common objects that tend to be roughly the same size. Most cars are about the same size and so are many houses. Become familiar with how large or small such objects appear at various distances–300 yards, 1,000 yards, 2,000 yards, and so on. This is a less accurate way of estimating distance, but can be *helpful if the lay of the land makes it otherwise hard to tell whether a point is near or far. Look for such objects that seem a bit in front of the point. Their relative size can give you a useful clue.*

Maximum Effective Ranges of Common Civil War Weapons

Rifled musket	400 yds.
Smoothbore musket	150 yds.
Breech-loading carbine	300 yds.

Napoleon 12-pounder smoothbore cannon

Solid shot	1,700 yds.
Shell	1,300 yds.
Spherical case	500–1,500 yds.
Canister	400 yds.

Parrott 10-pounder rifled cannon

Solid shot	6,000 yds.

3-inch ordnance rifle (cannon)

Solid shot	4,000 yds.

Further Reading

Coggins, Jack. *Arms and Equipment of the Civil War.* 1962. Reprint. Wilmington NC: Broadfoot Books, 1990.

The best introduction to the subject, engagingly written, profusely illustrated, and packed with information.

Griffith, Paddy. *Battle Tactics of the Civil War.* New Haven: Yale University Press, 1989.

Griffith argues that in a tactical sense the Civil War was more nearly the last great Napoleonic war than the first modern war. In his view, the impact of the rifled musket on Civil War battlefields has been exaggerated; the carnage and inconclusiveness of many Civil War battles owed less to the inadequacy of Napoleonic tactics than to a failure to understand and apply them.

Jamieson, Perry D. *Crossing the Deadly Ground: United States Army Tactics, 1865–1899.* Tuscaloosa: University of Alabama Press, 1994.

The early chapters offer a good analysis of the tactical lessons learned by U.S. army officers from their Civil War experiences.

Linderman, Gerald F. *Embattled Courage: The Experience of Combat in the American Civil War.* New York: Free Press, 1987.

A thoughtful, well-written study of how Civil War soldiers understood and coped with the challenges of the battlefield.

McWhiney, Grady, and Perry D. Jamieson. *Attack and Die: Civil War Military Tactics and the Southern Heritage.* Tuscaloosa: University of Alabama Press, 1982.

Confederate prisoners on the Baltimore Pike. From a wartime sketch. 3:384

Although unconvincing in its assertion that their Celtic heritage led Southerners to take the offensive to an inordinate degree, this is an excellent tactical study that emphasizes the revolutionary impact of the rifled musket. Best read in combination with Griffith, above.

The retreat from Gettysburg. 3:426

Appendix B: Orders of Battle

Union Forces

ARMY OF THE POTOMAC (Meade)

I Army Corps (Reynolds, Doubleday, Newton)

1st Division (Wadsworth)

1ST BDE	2ND BDE
(Meredith, Robinson)	(Cutler)
19th IN	7th IN
24th MI	76th NY
2nd WI	84th NY
6th WI	(14th Militia)
7th WI	95th NY
	147th NY
	56th PA (nine companies)

2nd Division (Robinson)

1ST BDE	2ND BDE
(Paul, Leonard, Root, Coulter, Lyle	(Baxter)
16th ME	12th MA
13th MA	83rd NY (9th Militia)
94th NY	97th NY
104th NY	11th PA
107th PA	88th PA
	90th PA

3rd Division (Rowley, Doubleday)

1ST BDE	2ND BDE	3RD BDE
(Biddle, Rowley)	(Stone, Wister, Dana)	(Stannard, Randall)
80th NY (20th Militia)	143rd PA	12th VT
121st PA	149th PA	13th VT
142nd PA	150th PA	14th VT
151st PA		15th VT
		16th VT

ARTILLERY (Wainwright): ME Light, 2nd Battery (B): ME Light, 5th Battery (E); 1st NY Light, Battery L; 1st PA Light, Battery B; 4th U.S., Battery B

II Army Corps (Hancock, Gibbon)

1st Division (Caldwell)

1ST BDE	2ND BDE	3RD BDE	4TH BDE
(Cross, McKeen)	(Kelly)	(Zook, Fraser)	(Brooke)
5th NH	28th MA	52nd NY	27th CT
61st NY	63rd NY	57th NY	(two companies)
81st PA	(two companies)	66th NY	2nd DE
148th PA	69th NY	140th PA	64th NY
	(two companies)		53rd PA
	88th NY		145th PA
	(two companies)		(seven companies)
	116th PA		
	(four companies)		

2nd Division (Gibbon, Harrow)

1ST BDE	2ND BDE	3RD BDE
(Harrow, Heath)	(Webb)	(Hall)
19th ME	69th PA	19th MA
15th MA	71st PA	20th MA
1st MN	72nd PA	7th MI
82nd NY	106th PA	42nd NY
(2nd Militia)		59th NY
		(four companies)

Unattached MA S.S. 1ST Co.

3rd Division (Hays)

1ST BDE	2ND BDE	3RD BDE
(Carroll)	(Smyth, Pierce)	(Willard, Sherrill, Bull)
14th IN	14th CT	39th NY
4th OH	1st DE	(four companies)
8th OH	12th NJ	111th NY
7th WV	10th NY	125th NY
	(battalion)	126th NY
	108th NY	

ARTILLERY (Hazard): 1st NY Light, Battery B; 1st RI Light, Battery; 1st RI Light, Battery B; 1ST U.S., Battery I; 4TH U.S., Battery A

III Army Corps (Sickles, Birney)

1st Division (Birney, Ward)

1ST BDE	2ND BDE	3RD BDE
(Graham, Tippin)	(Ward, Berdan)	(de Trobriand)
57th PA (eight companies)	20th IN	17th ME
	3rd ME	3rd MI
63rd PA	4th ME	5th MI
68th PA	86th NY	40th NY
105th PA	124th NY	110th PA (six companies)
114th PA	99th PA	
141st PA	1st U.S. S.S.	
	2nd U.S. S.S. (eight companies)	

2nd Division (Humphreys)

1ST BDE	2ND BDE	3RD BDE
(Carr)	(Brewster)	(Burling)
1st MA	70th NY	2nd NH
11th MA	71st NY	5th NJ
16th MA	72nd NY	6th NJ
12th NH	73rd NY	7th NJ
11th NJ	74th NY	8th NJ
26th PA	120th NY	115th PA
84th PA		

ARTILLERY (Randolph, Clark): NJ Light, 2nd Battery; 1st NY Light, Battery D; NY Light, 4th Battery; 1st RI Light, Battery E; 4TH U.S., Battery K

V Army Corps (Sykes)

1st Division (Barnes)

1ST BDE	2ND BDE	3RD BDE
(Tilton)	(Sweitzer)	(Vincent, Rice)
18th MA	9th MA	20th ME
22nd MA	32nd MA	16th MI
1st MI	4th MI	44th NY
118th PA	2nd PA	83rd PA

2nd Division (Ayres)

1ST BDE	2ND BDE	3RD BDE
(Day)	(Burbank)	(Weed, Garrard)
3rd U.S. (six companies)	2nd U.S. (six companies)	140th NY
		146th NY
4th U.S. (four companies)	7th U.S. (four companies)	91st PA
		155th PA
6th U.S. (five companies)	10th U.S. (three companies)	
12th U.S. (eight companies)	11th U.S. (six companies)	
14th U.S. (eight companies)	17th U.S. (seven companies)	

3rd Division (Crawford)

1ST BDE	3RD BDE
(McCandless)	(Fisher)
1st PA Reserves (nine companies)	5th PA Reserves
	9th PA Reserves
2nd PA Reserves	10th PA Reserves
6th PA Reserves	11th PA Reserves
13th PA Reserves	12th PA Reserves (nine companies)

ARTILLERY (Martin): MA Light, 3rd Battery (C); 1st NY Light, Battery C; 1st OH Light, Battery L; 5th U.S., Battery D; 5th U.S., Battery I

VI Army Corps (Sedgwick)

1st Division (Wright)

1ST BDE	2ND BDE	3RD BDE
(Torbert)	(Bartlett)	(Russell)
1st NJ	5th ME	6th ME
2nd NJ	121st NY	49th PA (four companies)
3rd NJ	95th PA	119th PA
15th NJ	96th PA	5th WI

2nd Division (Howe)

2ND BDE	3RD BDE
(Grant)	(Neill)
2nd VT	7th ME (six companies)
3rd VT	
4th VT	33rd NY (detachment)
5th VT	43rd NY
6th VT	49th NY
	77th NY
	61st PA

3rd Division (Newton, Wheaton)

1ST BDE	2ND BDE	3RD BDE
(Shaler)	(Eustis)	(Wheaton, Nevin)
65th NY	7th MA	62nd NY
67th NY	10th MA	93rd PA
122nd NY	37th MA	98th PA
23rd PA	2nd RI	102nd PA
82nd PA		139th PA

ARTILLERY (Tompkins): MA Light, 1st Battery (A); NY Light, 1st Battery; NY Light, 3rd Battery; 1st RI Light, Battery C; 1st RI Light, Battery G; U.S., Battery D; 2nd U.S., Battery G; 5th U.S., Battery F

XI Army Corps (Howard)

1st Division (Barlow, Ames)

1ST BDE	2ND BDE
(von Gilsa)	(Ames, Harris)
41st NY (nine companies)	17th CT
	25th OH
54th NY	75th OH
68th NY	107th OH
153rd PA	

2nd Division (von Steinwehr)

1ST BDE	2ND BDE
(Coster)	(Smith)
134th NY	33rd MA
154th NY	136th NY
27th PA	55th OH
73rd PA	73rd OH

3rd Division (Schurz)

1ST BDE	2ND BDE
(Schimmelfennig, von Amsberg)	(Krzyzanowski)
82nd IL	58th NY
45th NY	119th NY
157th NY	82nd OH
61st OH	75th PA
74th PA	26th WI

ARTILLERY (Osborn): 1st NY Light, Battery I; NY Light, 13th Battery; 1st OH Light, Battery I; 1st OH Light, Battery K; 4th U.S., Battery G

XII Army Corps (Slocum, Williams)

1st Division (Williams, Ruger)

1ST BDE	2ND BDE	3RD BDE
(McDougall)	(Lockwood)	(Ruger, Colgrove)
5th CT	1st MD, Potomac Home Bde.	27th IN
20th CT		2nd MA
3rd MD	1st MD, Eastern Shore	13th NJ
123rd NY	150th NY	107th NY
145th NY		3rd WI
46th PA		

2nd Division (Geary)

1ST BDE	2ND BDE	3RD BDE
(Candy)	(Cobham, Kane)	(Greene)
5th OH	29th PA	60th NY
7th OH	109th PA	78th NY
29th OH	111th PA	102nd NY
66th OH		137th NY
28th PA		149th NY
147th PA (eight companies)		

ARTILLERY (Muhlenberg): 1st NY Light, Battery M; PA Light, Battery E; 4th U.S., Battery F; 5th U.S., Battery K

Cavalry (Pleasonton)

1st Division (Buford)

1ST BDE	2ND BDE	RESERVE BDE
(Gamble)	(Devin)	(Merritt)
8th IL	6th NY	6th PA
12th IL (four companies)	9th NY	1st U.S.
3rd IN (six companies)	17th PA	2nd U.S.
8th NY	3rd WV (two companies)	5th U.S.
		6th U.S.

2nd Division (Gregg)

1ST BDE	2ND BDE	3RD BDE
(Mcintosh)	(Huey)	(Gregg)
1st MD (eleven companies)	2nd NY	1st ME (ten companies)
Purnell (MD) Legion [Co. A]	4th NY	10th NY
1st MA	6th OH (ten companies)	4th PA
1st NJ	8th PA	16th PA
1st PA		
3rd PA		
3rd PA Heavy Artillery, Battery H (section)		

3rd Division (Kilpatrick)

1ST BDE	2ND BDE
(Farnsworth, Richmond)	(Custer)
	1st MI
5th NY	5th MI
18th PA	6th MI
1st VT	7th MI
1st WV	(ten companies)
(ten companies)	

Horse Artillery

1ST BDE	2ND BDE
(Robertson)	(Tidball)
9th MI Battery	1st U.S., Batteries E and G
6th NY Battery	1st U.S., Battery K
2nd U.S., Batteries B and L	2nd U.S., Battery A
2nd U.S., Battery M	3rd U.S., Battery C
4th U.S., Battery E	

Artillery Reserve (Tyler, Robertson)

1ST REGULAR BDE	1ST VOLUNTEER BDE	2ND VOLUNTEER BDE	3RD VOLUNTEER BDE	4TH VOLUNTEER BDE
(Ransom)	(McGilvery)	(Taft)	(Huntington)	(Fitzhugh)
1st U.S., Battery H	MA Light, 5th Battery (E)	1st CT Heavy, Battery B	NH Light, 1st Battery	ME Light, 6th Battery (F)
3rd U.S., Batteries F and K	MA Light, 9th Battery	1st CT Heavy, Battery M	1st OH Light, Battery H	MD Light, Battery A
4th U.S., Battery C	NY Light, 15th Battery	CT Light, 2nd Battery	1st PA Light, Batteries F and G	NJ Light, 1st Battery
5th U.S., Battery C	PA Light, Batteries C and F	NY Light, 5th Battery	WV Light, Battery C	1st NY Light, Battery G
				1st NY Light, Battery K

Confederate Forces

ARMY OF NORTHERN VIRGINIA (Lee)

First Army Corps (Longstreet)

McLaws's Division

KERSHAW'S BDE	BARKSDALE'S BDE	SEMMES'S BDE	WOFFORD'S BDE
2nd SC	(Barksdale, Humphreys)	(Semmes, Bryan)	(Wofford)
3rd SC	13th MS	10th GA	16th GA
7th SC	17th MS	50th GA	18th GA
8th SC	18th MS	51st GA	24th GA
15th SC	21st MS	53rd GA	Cobb's (GA) Legion
3rd SC BN			Phillips's (GA) Legion

ARTILLERY (Cabell): 1st NC Artillery, Battery A; Pulaski (GA); 1st Richmond Howitzers; Troup (GA) Artillery

Pickett's Division

GARNETT'S BDE (Garnett, Peyton)	KEMPER'S BDE (Kemper, Mayo)	ARMISTEAD'S BDE (Armistead, Aylett)
8th VA	1st VA	9th VA
18th VA	3rd VA	14th VA
19th VA	7th VA	88th VA
28th NA	11th VA	53rd VA
56th VA	24th VA	57th VA

ARTILLERY (Dearing): Fauquier (VA) Artillery; Hampden (VA) Artillery; Richmond Fayette Artillery; VA Battery

Hood's Division (Hood, Law)

LAW'S BDE (Law, Sheffield)	ROBERTSON'S BDE (Robertson)	ANDERSON'S BDE (Anderson, Luffman)	BENNING'S BDE (Benning)
4th AL	3rd AK	7th GA	2nd GA
15th AL	1st TX	8th GA	15th GA
44th AL	4th TX	9th GA	17th GA
47th AL	5th TX	11th GA	20th GA
48th AL		59th GA	

ARTILLERY (Henry): Branch (NC) Artillery; German (SC) Artillery; Palmetto (SC) Light Artillery; Rowan (NC) Artillery

Artillery Reserve (Walton)

ALEXANDER'S BN (Alexander)	WASHINGTON (LA) ARTILLERY (Eshleman)
Ashland (VA) Artillery	1st CO.
Bedford (VA) Artillery	2nd CO.
Brooks (SC) Artillery	3rd CO.
Madison (LA) Light Artillery	4th CO.
VA Battery (Parker)	
VA Battery (Taylor)	

Second Army Corps (Ewell)

Early's Division

HAYS'S BDE	SMITH'S BDE	HOKE'S BDE (Avery, Godwin)	GORDON'S BDE
5th LA	31st VA	6th NC	13th GA
6th LA	49th VA	21st NC	26th GA
7th LA	52nd VA	57th NC	31st GA
8th LA			38th GA
9th LA			60th GA
			61st GA

ARTILLERY (Jones): Charlottesville (VA) Artillery; Courtney (VA); LA Guard Artillery; Staunton (VA) Artillery

Johnson's Division

STEUART'S BDE	STONEWALL BDE (Walker)	NICHOLLS'S BDE (Williams)	JONES'S BDE (Jones, Dungan)
1st MD	2nd VA	1st LA	21st VA
1st NC	4th VA	2nd LA	25th VA
3rd NC	5th VA	10th LA	42nd VA
10th VA	27th VA	14th LA	44th VA
23rd VA	33rd VA	15th LA	48th VA
37th VA			50th VA

ARTILLERY (Latimer, Raine): 1st MD Battery; Allegheny (VA) Artillery; Chesapeake (MD) Artillery; Lee (VA) Battery

Rodes's Division

DANIEL'S BDE	DOLES'S BDE	IVERSON'S BDE	RAMSEUR'S BDE	O'NEAL'S BDE
32nd NC	4th GA	5th NC	2nd NC	3rd AL
43rd NC	12th GA	12th NC	4th NC	5th AL
45th NC	21st GA	20th NC	14th NC	6th AL
53rd NC	44th GA	23rd NC	30th NC	12th AL
2nd NC BN				26th AL

ARTILLERY (Carter): Jeff Davis (AL) Artillery; King William (VA) Artillery; Morris (VA) Artillery; Orange (VA) Artillery

Artillery Reserve (Brown)

1ST VA ARTILLERY (Dance)	NELSON'S BN
2nd Richmond (VA) Howitzers	Amherst (VA) Artillery
3rd Richmond (VA)	Fluvanna (VA) Artillery
Powhatan (VA) Artillery	GA Battery (Milledge)
Rockbridge (VA) Artillery	
Salem (VA) Artillery	

Third Army Corps (Hill)

Anderson's Division

WILCOX'S BDE	MAHONE'S BDE	WRIGHT'S BDE (Wright, Gibson)	PERRY'S BDN (Lang)	POSEY'S BDE
8th AL	6th VA	3rd GA	2nd FL	12th MS
9th AL	12th VA	22nd FA	5th FL	16th MS
10th AL	16th VA	48th GA	8th FL	19th MS
11th AL	41st VA	2nd GA BN		48th MS
14th AL	61st VA			

ARTILLERY (Sumter BN) (Lane): Co. A; Co. B; Co. C

Heth's Division (Heth, Pettigrew)

1ST BDE (Pettigrew, Marshall)	2ND BDE (Brockenbrough)	3RD BDE (Archer, Shepard)	4TH BDE (Davis)
11th NC	40th VA	18th AL	2nd MS
26th NC	47th VA	5th AL BN	11th MS
47th NC	55th VA	1st TN (Provisional Army)	42nd MS
52nd NC	22nd VA BN	7th TN	55th NC
		14th TN	

ARTILLERY (Garnett): Donaldsonville (LA) Artillery; Huger (VA) Artillery; Lewis (VA) Artillery; Norfolk Light Artillery Blues

Pender's Division (Pender, Trimble, Lane)

1ST BDE (Perrin)	2ND BDE (Lane, Avery)	3RD BDE (Thomas)	4TH BDE (Scales, Gordon, Lowrance)
1st SC (Provisional Army)	7th NC	14th GA	13th NC
1st SC Rifles	18th NC	35th GA	16th NC
12th SC	28th NC	45th VA	22nd NC
13th SC	33rd NC	49th VA	34th NC
14th SC	37th NC		38th NC

ARTILLERY (Poague): Albemarle (VA) Artillery; Charlotte (NC); Madison (MS) Light Artillery; VA Battery (Brooke)

Artillery Reserve (Walker)

MCINTOSH'S BN	PEGRAM'S BN (Pegram, Brunson)
DANVILLE (VA) Artillery	CRENSHAW (VA) Battery
HARDAWAY (AL) Artillery	FREDERICKSBURG (VA) Artillery
2nd ROCKBRIDGE (VA) Artillery	LETCHER (VA) Artillery
VA Battery (Johnson)	PEE DEE (SC) Artillery
	PURCELL (VA) Artillery

Cavalry

Stuart's Division

HAMPTON'S BDE
(Hampton, Baker)

1st NC

1st SC

2nd SC

COBB'S (GA) Legion

JEFF DAVIS Legion

PHILLIPS (GA)
Legion

ROBERTSON'S BDE

4th NC

5th NC

FITZ LEE'S BDE

1st MD BN

1st VA

2nd VA

3rd VA

4th VA

5th VA

JENKINS'S BDE
(Jenkins,
Ferguson)

14th VA

16th VA

17th VA

34th VA BN

36th VA BN

JACKSON'S (VA)
Battery

JONES'S BDE

6th VA

7th VA

11th VA

W. H. F. LEE'S BDE
(Chambliss)

2nd NC

9th VA

10th VA

13th VA

STUART HORSE ARTILLERY (Beckham): Breathed's (VA) Battery; Chew's (VA) Battery; Griffin's (MD) Battery; Hart's (SC) Battery; McGregor's (VA) Battery; Moorman's (VA) Battery

IMBODEN'S COMMAND: 18th VA Cavalry; 62nd VA Infantry; VA Partisan Rangers; Virginia Battery

Confederates captured at Gettysburg. From a photograph. 3:433

Sources

Short titles given below are listed in full under works cited in the For Further Reading section.

Stop 1 (McPherson's Ridge): (a) Martin, *Gettysburg*, 43–48; (b) Coddington, *Gettysburg Campaign*, 264–67; Martin, *Gettysburg*, 59–88; Lt. Amasa Davis, 8th Illinois Cavalry, quoted in Michael Phipps and John S. Peterson, *"The Devil's to Pay": Gen. John Buford*, USA (Gettysburg: Farnsworth Military Impressions, 1995), 46–47; (c) Coddington, *Gettysburg Campaign*, 267–69; Martin, *Gettysburg*, 89–102, 140–49.

Buford's Defense Excursion: (A) Martin, *Gettysburg*, 59–69 (B) Martin, *Gettysburg*, 69–88.

Stop 2 (Herbst Woods): (a) Coddington, *Gettysburg Campaign*, 270–71; Martin, *Gettysburg*, 149–65; E. P. Halstead, "Incidents of the First Day at Gettysburg," in Clarence C. Buel and Robert U. Johnson, eds., *Battles and Leaders of the Civil War*, 4 vols. (New York: Century, 1887–88), 3:285; (b) Coddington, *Gettysburg Campaign*, 293; Martin, *Gettysburg*, 349–71 (c) Martin, *Gettysburg*, chap. 8.

Stop 3 (The Railroad Cut): (a) Coddington, *Gettysburg Campaign*, 268–70; Martin, *Gettysburg*, 102–10; (b) Coddington, *Gettysburg Campaign*, 270; Martin, *Gettysburg*, 110–19; William F. Fox, ed., *New York at Gettysburg* (1900), 992; (c) Coddington, *Gettysburg Campaign*, 271–72; Martin, *Gettysburg*, 119–40.

Stop 4 (Oak Hill) (a) Martin, *Gettysburg*, 205–10, 214–20.

Stop 5 (Oak Ridge): Robert K. Krick, "Three Confederate Disasters on Oak Ridge," in Gallagher, *First Day*, is essential reading; this account draws upon it freely. See also Coddington, *Gettysburg Campaign*, 289–90; Martin, *Gettysburg*, chap. 6.

Stop 6 (Barlow's Knoll): Martin, *Gettysburg*, chap. 8; Coddington, *Gettysburg Campaign*, 291–92, 295–96, 301–6; A. Wilson Greene, "From Chancellorsville to Cemetery Hill: O. O. Howard and Eleventh Corps Leadership," in Gallagher, ed., *First Day*, 57–91.

Stop 7 (Benner's Hill): (a) Coddington, *Gettysburg Campaign*, 317–21, 364–65; Martin, *Gettysburg*, 507–22, 552–67; Pfanz,

Culp's Hill, 76–87; (b) Coddington, *Gettysburg Campaign*, 360–63; Martin, *Gettysburg*, 505–6, 567–68; (c) Coddington, *Gettysburg Campaign*, 427–28; Pfanz, *Culp's Hill*, 178–89; Edward R. Geary to Mother, July 17, 1863, quoted in Pfanz, *Culp's Hill*, 184.

Stop 8 (Berdan's Loop): Pfanz, *Gettysburg*, 100–102.

Stop 9 (Pitzer's Woods): Pfanz, *Gettysburg*, chap. 6; Coddington, *Gettysburg Campaign*, chap. 14.

Stop 10 (Warfield Ridge): (a) Tucker, *Lee and Longstreet at Gettysburg*, 59–61

Stop 11 (Little Round Top): Pfanz, *Gettysburg*, chap. 10; Norton, *Attack and Defense of Little Round Top*; Desjardin, *Stand Firm Ye Boys from Maine*, esp. chap. 2.

Stop 12 (Houck's Ridge): (a) Pfanz, *Gettysburg*, 178–85; (b) Pfanz, *Gettysburg*, 185–90; (c) Pfanz, *Gettysburg*, 190–200.

Stop 13 (The Wheatfield): (a) Coddington, *Gettysburg Campaign*, 399–400; Pfanz, *Gettysburg*, 130, 241–53; Private John W. Haley, 17th Maine Infantry, diary entry for July 2, 1863, in Ruth L. Silliker, ed., *The Rebel Yell and the Yankee Hurrah: The Civil War Journal of a Maine Volunteer* (Camden ME: Down East Books, 1985), 101; (b) Coddington, *Gettysburg Campaign*, 401; Pfanz, *Gettysburg*, 253–66; (c) Coddington, *Gettysburg Campaign*, 401–8; Pfanz, *Gettysburg*, 266–302.

Wheatfield Excursion (A) Pfanz, *Gettysburg*, 128–29, 250, 262–64; (B) Pfanz, *Gettysburg*, 252–61; (C1) Pfanz, *Gettysburg*, 267–70; (C2) Pfanz, *Gettysburg*, 270–84; (D) Pfanz, *Gettysburg*, 284–88; (E) Pfanz, *Gettysburg*, 288–95; (F1) Pfanz, *Gettysburg*, 295–97; Dudley H. Chase, "Gettysburg," in Military Order of the Loyal Legion of the United States, Indiana Commandery, *War Papers* 1 (1898): 301–2; (F2) Pfanz, *Gettysburg*, 297–300; *War of the Rebellion: A Compilation of the Official Records of the Union and Confederate Armies*, 70 vols. in 128 parts (Washington DC: Government Printing office, 1880–1901), Ser. I, Vol. 27, pt. 1, p. 646; (F3) Pfanz, *Gettysburg*, 300–302; Robins quoted in Timothy J. Reese, *Sykes' Regular Infantry Division, 1861–1864* (Jefferson NC: McFarland, 1990), (F4) Pfanz, *Gettysburg*, 390–402.

Stop 14 (The Peach Orchard): (a) Pfanz, *Gettysburg*, 255–57, contains the rabbit story; (b) Pfanz, *Gettysburg*, chaps. 5, 6, 7, 11, 13; Coddington, *Gettysburg Campaign*, chap. 15.

Stop 15 (Trostle's Farm): Pfanz, *Gettysburg*, 82–83, 102–3, 124, 138–41, 336–46; vignette: Pfanz, *Gettysburg*, 142–44, 333–34; Freeman Cleaves, *Meade of Gettysburg* (Norman: University of Oklahoma Press, 1960), 147–49.

Stop 16 (South Cemetery Ridge): (a) Coddington, *Gettysburg Campaign*, 422–23; Pfanz, *Gettysburg*, 401–14; Richard Moe, *The Last Full Measure: The Life and Death of the First Minnesota Volunteers* (New York: Henry Holt, 1993); (b) Coddington, *Gettysburg Campaign*, 421–27; Pfanz, *Gettysburg*, 414–24.

Stop 17 (Culp's Hill): (a) Coddington, *Gettysburg Campaign*, 431; Pfanz, *Culp's Hill*, 111–15, 211; (b) Coddington, *Gettysburg Campaign*, 428–35; Pfanz, *Culp's Hill*, 205–34; (c) Coddington, *Gettysburg Campaign*, 465–76; Pfanz, *Culp's Hill*, 284–352; on Spangler's Spring, see Pfanz, *Culp's Hill*, 377–78.

Stop 18 (Culp's Hill Summit): Pfanz, *Culp's Hill*, 295–96.

Stop 19 (East Cemetery Hill): Coddington, *Gettysburg Campaign*, 435–40; Pfanz, *Culp's Hill*, 235–83; vignette: Pfanz, *Culp's Hill*, 259.

Stop 20 (High Water Mark): Coddington, *Gettysburg Campaign*, chap. 19; Tucker, *Lee and Longstreet at Gettysburg*, chaps. 6–9; Stewart, *Pickett's Charge*; (a) Stewart, *Pickett's Charge*, 141; (c) Stewart, *Pickett's Charge*, 186; (e) Robert Garth Scott, ed., *Fallen Leaves: The Civil War Letters of Major Henry Livermore Abbott* (Kent: Kent State University Press, 1991), 188; (f) Stewart, *Pickett's Charge*, 233.

Pickett's Charge Excursion: Coddington, *Gettysburg Campaign*, 493–517; Stewart, *Pickett's Charge*, 179–245; (a) Rawley Martin, quoted in Richard Rollins, ed., *Pickett's Charge: Eyewitness Accounts* (Redondo Beach CA: Rank and File, 1994), 150; (b) William Wood, quoted in Rollins, ed., *Pickett's Charge*, 167; (f) Henry Owen, quoted in Rollins, ed., *Pickett's Charge*, 162.

East Cavalry Excursion: Longacre, *Cavalry at Gettysburg*, chap. 13; Coddington, *Gettysburg Campaign*, 520–23; Stephen Z. Starr, *The Union Cavalry in the Civil War*, vol. 1: *From Fort Sumter to Gettysburg* (Baton Rouge: Louisiana State University Press, 1979), 432–38.

South Cavalry Excursion: (a) Coddington, *Gettysburg Campaign*, 523–24; Kathleen Georg Harrison, "Ridges of Grim

War [Gettysburg: The Third Day, July 3, 1863]," *Blue and Gray Magazine* 5 (July 1988): 30–32; (b) Coddington, *Gettysburg Campaign*, 524–25; Harrison, "Ridges of Grim War," 32–35; (c) Coddington, *Gettysburg Campaign*, 525; Harrison, "Ridges of Grim War," 35; H. C. Parsons, "Farnsworth's Charge and Death," in Buel and Johnson, eds., *Battles and Leaders of the Civil War*, 3:394.

In the Wake of Battle. 2:686

For Further Reading

The literature on the battle of Gettysburg and the entire campaign is immense. This bibliography lists the works of most use in preparing this guide as well as suggestions for additional reading.

Works Cited

Coddington, Edwin B. *The Gettysburg Campaign: A Study in Command.* New York: Scribners, 1968. The best single-volume study of the campaign.

Gallagher, Gary W., ed. *The First Day at Gettysburg: Essays on Confederate and Union Leadership.* Kent: Kent State University Press, 1992. Offers revisionist evaluations of commanders on both sides.

——. *The Second Day at Gettysburg: Essays on Confederate and Union Leadership.* Kent: Kent State University Press, 1993. More command studies.

Martin, David G. *Gettysburg July 1.* Rev. ed. Conshohocken PA: Combined, 1996. A thorough treatment of the first day.

Pfanz, Harry W. *Culp's Hill and Cemetery Hill.* Chapel Hill: University of North Carolina Press, 1993. A careful examination of the action in this area during the three days of battle.

——. *Gettysburg: The Second Day.* Chapel Hill: University of North Carolina Press, 1987. A detailed treatment of Longstreet's July 2 assault.

Other Titles

Desjardin, Thomas A. *Stand Firm Ye Boys from Maine: The 20th Maine and the Gettysburg Campaign.* Gettysburg: Thomas, 1996. A refreshing, no-nonsense look at the struggle on Vincent's Spur.

Frassanito, William A. *Early Photography at Gettysburg.* Gettysburg: Thomas, 1995. Fascinating photographs and insightful discussion of the battle.

——. *Gettysburg: A Journey in Time.* New York: Scribner's, 1975. A pioneering study of early post-battle photography.

Gallagher, Gary W., ed. *The Third Day at Gettysburg and Beyond.* Chapel Hill: University of North Carolina Press, 1994. Completes the trilogy of Gettysburg volumes.

Hassler, Warren W., Jr. *Crisis at the Crossroads: The First Day at Gettysburg.* 1970. Reprint. Gettysburg: Stan Clark Military Books, 1991. A concise narrative exploring the battle of July 1.

Longacre, Edward G. *The Cavalry at Gettysburg: A Tactical Study of Mounted Operations during the Civil War's Pivotal Campaign.* 1986. Reprint. Lincoln: University of Nebraska Press, 1993. A helpful overview of cavalry actions.

Norton, Oliver W. *The Attack and Defense of Little Round Top: Gettysburg, July 2, 1863.* New York: Neale, 1913. Packed with primary sources, concentrating on the Union defense of Little Round Top.

Stewart, George R. *Pickett's Charge: A Microhistory of the Final Attack at Gettysburg, July 3, 1863.* Boston: Houghton Mifflin, 1959. Remains the best study of this phase of the battle.

Tucker, Glenn. *Lee and Longstreet at Gettysburg.* 1968. Reprint. Dayton: Morningside House, 1982. Presents a detailed examination of the Lee-Longstreet controversy of July 2 and other disputes.

Farnsworth's Charge. 3:393

In This Hallowed Ground: Guides to the Civil War Battlefields series

Chickamauga: A Battlefield Guide
with a section on Chattanooga
Steven E. Woodworth

Gettysburg: A Battlefield Guide
Mark Grimsley and Brooks D. Simpson